WILL & CIRCUMSTANCE

WILL & CIRCUMSTANCE

Montesquieu, Rousseau and the French Revolution

By
Norman Hampson

University of Oklahoma Press : Norman

Library of Congress Cataloging in Publication Data

Hampson, Norman.
　Will & circumstance.

　Bibliography: p.
　1. France – History – Revolution, 1789-1799 – Causes.
2. Montesquieu, Charles de Secondat, baron de, 1689-
1755 – Political and social views.　3. Rousseau, Jean
Jacque, 1712-1778 – Political and social views.　I. Title.
II. Title: Will and circumstance.
DC138.H35　1983　　　　944.04　　　82-40455
ISBN 0-8061-1843-1

Original copyright © 1983 by Gerald Duckworth and Company,
Ltd., London, England. American edition, manufactured in the
United Kingdom, published by the University of Oklahoma
Press, Norman, Publishing Division of the University. First
edition, 1983.

Contents

To the York History Department

Preface

Various factors combined to make me want to write this book. I had been convinced for a long time that modern liberal and collectivist theories of government originated in the eighteenth century, in the writings of Montesquieu and Rousseau. Several years ago, when I wrote a short book on the Enlightenment, I was quite rightly reproached for treating these ideas, and the society in which they originated, in isolation from each other. I did not share my reviewer's belief that all that was needed to bring them together was to say that the Enlightenment was the ideology of the bourgeoisie, but I was ready enough to agree with him that political theories must bear some relation to the society in which they were born. At the time, I could not see what it was or how to set about discovering it. I gradually came to understand that any meaningful search for such a connection must involve the detailed examination of a short period. Any general enquiry over a long span of time would be only too likely to mean looking for evidence to support one's initial assumptions, and there is always so much evidence around that a more or less plausible case can be made out for almost anything. I was not so naïve as to imagine that tramping along a few narrow roads would somehow relieve me of the historian's version of original sin and allow the facts to speak for themselves, but I thought it might give them a better chance. My initial assumptions, whether conscious or not, were still likely to reappear as conclusions, but I would have a better prospect of making some unexpected acquaintances on the road than if I sped over great distances by motorway.

Quite apart from this, the writings of Robert Darnton and, in his more popular style, Claude Manceron, revealed to me the absurdity of treating the men of the French Revolution as though they had all been born in 1789. By that time the great majority of them had already reached their maturity, and although the revolutionary years were to impose their own imperatives and constraints, the men who reacted to them had been formed in a different period, and that formation was bound to influence their reactions. Any study of the ideology of the French Revolution had therefore to begin with the intellectual apprenticeship of the revolutionaries.

Somewhere at the back of my mind there must have been lying J.L.Talmon's *Origins of totalitarian democracy*, which I read many years ago. On the whole this got rather a frosty reception from historians of the French Revolution. This may have been partly because it told them things they were not keen to hear. Recent political controversies in England make it seem more relevant and perhaps more plausible.

Once I had decided on the field, the choice of political philosophers posed no problems. The most superficial glance at what was being written in the 1780s showed that everyone drew his inspiration from Montesquieu or Rousseau or, more often, from both. Voltaire may have done as much as either of them to determine the general character of the age, but his specifically political theories, and notably his inclination towards enlightened absolutism, had little appeal to the men who were going to make the French Revolution. Montesquieu and Rousseau, on the other hand, were quoted, paraphrased and misunderstood by everyone who wrote about politics. From my point of view, of course, the misunderstandings were more to the point than the findings of modern criticism.

The next step was less obvious. A possible line of approach would have been to look at political issues, especially those relating to the transformation of almost all French institutions between 1789 and 1791, to see on what basis, and in terms of what principles, these changes were discussed. This still tempts me. It might, however, have confused both author and reader in a maze of detail and it would have put the emphasis on theories rather than on people. As a historian, and not a political theorist, my concern is primarily with what some men thought and did, rather than with ideas themselves. This pointed towards a biographical approach but left me with the problem of choosing a team. Ideally, I wanted men who had written enough before

1789 for their attitudes to be identifiable, and then went on to take a leading part in the revolution. Necker, Condorcet and Babeuf were obvious candidates, but they have recently been the subject of excellent books, by Henri Grange, K.M.Baker and Barrie Rose, and there seemed no point in reploughing well-cultivated ground. In the end, after Billaud-Varenne, Carra and Gorsas proved disappointing, I opted for Brissot, Marat, Mercier, Robespierre and Saint-Just. In this distinguished company, Mercier is something of a political lightweight, but he was the only one of them who had actually seen Montesquieu and he claimed to have known Rousseau quite well. He also devoted two volumes to what he optimistically described as an investigation of Rousseau's contribution to the revolution. Saint-Just was too young to have published anything before 1789 but from 1791 onwards he was so active in both theory and practice that it seemed reasonable to make an exception in his favour. Granted Mercier's political nullity, this left me with three Montagnards to one Girondin (Brissot). This does not matter much in practice since I hope to have demonstrated that both sides shared the same basic principles and responded to the pressure of circumstances in similar ways.

The title of the book suggested itself at an early stage and I was encouraged to find later that the people about whom I was writing were themselves rather fond of talking about *la volonté* and *la force des choses*. The choice between volontarism and determinism was only one of many issues and it cannot be separated from the others. No one carried determinism to the point of fatalism and one of the constant concerns of the volontarists was to create by an effort of will the most desirable combination of conditioning forces (Saint-Just's 'republican institutions'). It is a way of looking at things that has its uses if one does not take it too far.

I shall have failed altogether if I give the impression of claiming to describe what the French Revolution was 'really' about. It was about so many other things as well. I am convinced that it is too complicated and too contradictory to be fitted into any book, however long. The same things have a particular significance when viewed from one perspective and a different one when viewed from another. They cannot have both at the same time, even though each may be 'true'. The most that one can hope to do at one time is to illuminate part of the evidence from one point of view. I do believe that if the men that I have described in this book could read what I have written about them, while they would not accept my criticism, they would understand what I was trying to say. This is not necessarily true of everything that has been written about the French Revolution.

It is a pleasure to have this opportunity of acknowledging some of my debts: to the generosity of the British Academy in helping to finance some of the early research; to Michel Fleury, President of the IVè Section of the Ecole Pratique des Hautes Etudes, for accomodation in the Hôtel Chalon-Luxembourg, which gives a special flavour to work in Paris; to Harry Fairhurst, the librarian of the University of York, for helping me to get hold of books; to Bill Doyle and Paul Ginsborg for making me think about what I thought I thought.

1983   N.H.

                    The inert
Were roused, and lively natures rapt away!
They who had fed their childhood on dreams,
The play-fellows of fancy, who had made
All powers of swiftness, subtilty, and strength
Their ministers, – who in lordly wise had stirred
Among the grandest objects of the sense,
And dealt with whatsoever they found there
As if they had within some lurking right
To wield it; – they, too, who of gentle mood
Had watched all gentle motions, and to these
Had fitted their own thoughts, schemers more mild,
And in the region of their peaceful selves; –
Now it was that *both* found, the meek and the lofty
Did both find helpers to their hearts' desire,
And stuff at hand, plastic as they could wish, –
Were called upon to exercise their skill,
Not in Utopia, – subterranean fields, –
Or some secreted island, Heaven knows where!
But in the very world, which is the world
Of all of us, – the place where, in the end,
We find our happiness, or not at all!

        Wordsworth, *The Prelude*, Book XI

PART 1

The Philosophes

Chapter 1

Montesquieu

Montesquieu's early years were not without their difficulties. In 1696, when he was only seven, his mother died.[1] At ten he was sent to the Oratorien school in Meaux, hundreds of miles away from his home in the south west of France. After returning to Bordeaux to study law, he was in Paris between 1709 and 1713, when the death of his father recalled him to take charge of the family estates. He was still only 24. There was enough here to have inflicted permanent damage on a man of a different calibre. If his subsequent life showed him to be someone who could temper Stoicism with a genial humanity, this was due as much to his own character as to the fact that things went easily for him after 1713. At 26 he married into a wealthy family. In the following year he inherited from an uncle a good deal of money, the barony of Montesquieu and the office of *président*, or judge, in the Bordeaux parlement, only two years after he had begun to practise there as a barrister. As he was to write in his notebook, 'My birth is so well suited to my fortune that I should be sorry if either were more distinguished.'[2] Almost at once he began to write the *Lettres Persanes*, which he published four years later, in 1721. The first major work of the French Enlightenment, the book had an immense success and established Montesquieu's reputation almost overnight. He sold his post in the parlement and henceforth divided his time between Paris and his château near Bordeaux. He received the ultimate accolade of election to the Academy when he was only 38 and spent most of the next four years travelling, mainly in Austria, Hungary and Italy, with

---

[1] For a biography of Montesquieu, see R.Shackleton, *Montesquieu*, London, 1961.

[2] *Cahiers*, I/2. (ed.B.Grasset), Paris, 1941. pp.252-3.

a long stay in England from 1729 to 1731. In 1734 he published his *Considérations sur les causes de la grandeur des Romains et de leur décadence* and began to accumulate the material for his greatest work, *De l'esprit des lois*, which was not published until 1748.

His career was so uniformly successful that he might perhaps have been expected to take the values of French society for granted. From his youth onwards, however, he was fascinated by all things foreign and exotic. There was a fair amount of English blood on his mother's side and his wife remained a Protestant all her life, at a time when religious persecution in France was only slowly losing its ferocity. When on his travels, he claimed to identify himself with each of the countries in which he stayed, and he remained all his life the most resolute of cosmopolitans. As always, when there were two camps, he had a foot planted firmly in each: 'When I act, I am a citizen; but when I write, I am a man and I regard all the peoples of Europe with as much impartiality as those of Madagascar.'[3]

Like most people with a touch of the Stoic in them, he could show a detachment from the vicissitudes of other people's lives that was faintly chilling. 'My constitution is so fortunately organised that things strike me sharply enough to give me pleasure, but not enough to give me pain.' 'I have always found study a sovereign remedy against the disagreeable things in life and never experienced any sorrow that an hour's reading would not dispel.'[4] At least he applied his philosophy to his own problems: 'Only two things remain for me to learn: to be ill and to die.'[5] There was, however, a less steely side to Montesquieu's character. As in the case of that other philosopher, cheerfulness kept breaking through. 'I awake in the morning with a secret joy; I see the light with a kind of rapture; I am happy for the rest of the day.'[6] His writing showed him to be a profoundly compassionate man, if not a sentimental one. The complex equilibrium of what he called his 'machine' was to be reflected in his distaste for the extreme, the monolithic and all straining after an artificial consistency that seemed to him a betrayal of life. As he put it, 'Let us try to accommodate ourselves to this life;

³ Ibid. II/137. Grasset p.256.   ⁴ Ibid. I/220. Grasset p.3.
⁵ Ibid. III/466. Grasset p.260.   ⁶ Ibid. I/220. Grasset p.3.

it is not up to this life to accommodate itself to us.'[7]

His early writings show him to have responded to the attraction of the classical mirage that fascinated so many eighteenth-century Frenchmen, even if one side of him dismissed it as, at best, inaccessible and at worst, an illusion. This consisted of a vision of a republican world, in ancient Greece and Rome, where a race of supermen, free from the petty egoism of the modern world, devoted themselves exclusively to the noblest aspirations of their city-states. As Montesquieu himself put it, 'The world has lost that smiling aspect that it had at the time of the Greeks and Romans. Religion was mild and always in harmony with nature. The greatest gaiety in worship went with complete freedom of dogma ... Nowadays Islam and Christianity, entirely devoted to the next life, completely destroy this one and while we are afflicted by religion, we are crushed by the universal spread of despotism.'[8]

The classical republics were 'the sanctuary of honour, reputation and virtue ... A crown of oak or laurel leaves, a statue, a eulogy, was an immense reward for a victory or the capture of a town.'[9] 'Love of country gives to Greek and Roman history a nobility lacking in our own ... When one considers our own petty motives, our ignoble means, the avarice with which we pursue base rewards, our ambition – so different from the love of glory – one is astounded by the contrast and it seems as though humanity has shrunk by an arm's length since the disappearance of those two peoples.'[10] These were also to be Rousseau's views – except that he cordially despised Athens – and like Rousseau, Montesquieu wondered if it might not be possible, by an effort of will, to restore these vanished glories. 'I am not one of those who regard Plato's Republic as wholly ideal and imaginary, something impossible to create in practice.'[11] Lycurgus, after all, had achieved something similar in Sparta.

Montesquieu, unlike Rousseau, put the classical dream reluctantly but firmly on one side. Perhaps it had been rather less attractive at the time than it appeared at a distance. One grim reason for the self-identification of the individual with his

[7] Ibid.
[8] Ibid. II/459. Grasset p.139.
[9] *Lettres Persanes* LXXXIX.
[10] *Cahiers*, I/243-4. Grasset pp.232-3.
[11] Ibid. II/93. Grasset p.114.

city-state was the fact that the losers in the incessant wars were either killed or enslaved.[12] Even if one overlooked such unpleasantness, perhaps the success of the Greeks owed more to circumstances than to their own genius. 'The Greeks had a great talent for self-advertisement. There was nothing very wonderful about their war against Xerxes.' It was, in fact, all done by sea-power, 'and all one can say is that it is virtually impossible to destroy sea-power except by superior sea-power'.[13] His English ancestors would have liked that. When he wrote his book on the rise and fall of Rome, the republic got fairly short shrift. Its temporary success was due to a more or less fortuitous balance of political forces. Success brought expansion and wealth and these in turn upset the balance and destroyed the republic. Man – even classical man – was always greedy for more power and never more than the product of his political environment. Caesar, Pompey and Augustus were merely the instruments of necessity.[14]

The classical myth had no place in the real world. Montesquieu nailed his colours to the mast in the first 'philosophical' passage of the *Lettres Persanes*.[15] This dealt with the Troglodytes, an imaginary people who passed from a condition of Hobbesian conflict to an anarchist utopia in which the virtues of the inhabitants dispensed with the need for laws. With some aspects of this utopia we shall become increasingly familiar: 'They instituted fêtes in honour of the gods. Flower-crowned girls and young men celebrated them with dances and with rustic music. These were followed by banquets where frugality (the banquets were *always* to be frugal) was no less evident than joy. It was in these assemblies that the voice of naïve nature made itself heard and it was there that lovers learned to give and receive their vows.' When envious neighbours invaded the territory of these pacific paragons, the entire Troglodyte nation rose up and overwhelmed them. This was very close to what was to be Rousseau's conception of an ideal future. For Montesquieu it was a transient stage in an imaginary past. Like the early Romans, the Troglodytes prospered and

---

[12] Ibid. I/488. Grasset p.159.   [13] Ibid. I/41-42. Grasset pp.160-1.
[14] *Considérations sur les causes de la grandeur des Romains et de leur décadence,* chs XI and XIII.
[15] *Lettres Persanes* XI-XIV.

multiplied. Eventually they invited their most venerable ancient to become their king – and received a somewhat dusty answer: 'I see very well how things stand, Troglodytes. Your *vertu* is becoming a burden to you. In your present state, without any leader, you have to be *vertueux* in spite of yourselves ... But this yoke seems too heavy and you would sooner be subject to a prince and obey his laws, less strict than your own customs.' The republican ideal, in other words, was too good to be true. At most, it was a fleeting passage in the evolution of primitive societies, of some anthropological interest but no contemporary relevance. Elsewhere, Montesquieu seems to have regarded the attempts of the British to create a republic, in the previous century, as somewhat similar to the activities of the Troglodytes.[16]

Implicit in this conception of republicanism were some fundamental problems of political theory. The identification of the citizen with his city-state applied to morals as well as to politics. The community was totally sovereign, it had its own religion and there were no absolute values, external to it, by which it might be judged. Most of us have had too much of this in the twentieth century to be very responsive to the delights of imagining social institutions that will turn men into what we think they ought to be. Anything of the kind was profoundly antipathetic to Montesquieu's temperament and it was only occasionally, and perhaps inadvertently, that his ideas could bear this construction. 'Whatever the laws may be, one must always obey them and regard them as the public conscience, to which that of individuals must always conform.'[17] 'Laws must begin by working to create worthy people.'[18] More of a deist than a Christian, he could not invoke religion as a source of transcendental values, since he regarded all religions as anthropomorphic, going so far as to say that if triangles invented a god they would give him three sides.[19]

More in keeping with his general attitude than such incautious comments was the statement in his notebooks that 'A thing is not just because it is legal; it must be legal because it is just'.[20] He put this in the most emphatic terms one could imagine, in the

[16] *Cahiers*, II/92. Grasset pp.155-6.
[18] *Cahiers*, III/115. Grasset p.222.
[20] *Cahiers*, I/393. Grasset p.119.

[17] *Lettres Persanes* CXXIX.
[19] *Lettres Persanes* LXI.

Lettres Persanes. 'Justice is a harmonious relationship which really exists between two things. This relationship never varies, whether it is viewed from the perspective of God, an angel, or of man … Even if God did not exist, we ought always to love justice … Justice is eternal and nowise dependent on human conventions.'[21] Liberty was a second absolute standard, by which all societies could be judged. The Germanic tribes who overthrew the Roman empire 'were not, properly speaking, barbarians, since they were free; they have since become barbarians since most of them, subject to absolute power, have lost the sweetness of liberty, so much in conformity with reason, humanity and nature'.[22] The harem scenes, which form the sub-plot in the *Lettres Persanes*, amount to a parable about liberty. The Persian traveller, Usbek, wise, tolerant and humane in his reactions to western society, is placed in the situation of a despot where his relationship to his wives is concerned. He deceives himself into thinking that they are content with their servitude in Persia and treats them with the consideration one would expect of such a man. As he becomes gradually aware that they reject their condition, the despotic situation in which he finds himself proves stronger than his character, his enlightenment and the ideas that he has come to appreciate in France. He can think of nothing but repression and ferocity and the book closes with the suicide of his favourite wife, Roxane, who writes to him that she has thwarted his tyranny by deceit. 'I may have lived in slavery but I have always been free. I have reformed your laws in accordance with those of nature.' Despotism, in other words, was as inherently unstable as the virtuous republic of the Troglodytes.

The issue of liberty raised the question of free-will, in its social sense: whether men could create the kind of social and political institutions that they were free to imagine, or whether their possible achievements, and perhaps also their conceptions of what they might or ought to try to achieve, were determined by the societies in which they had grown up. In the *Lettres Persanes* Montesquieu approached this problem from the religious angle: how to reconcile human freedom with the prescience of God. He asserted baldly that the human mind *was* free and sometimes

[21] *Lettres Persanes* LXXXIII.   [22] Ibid. CXXXVI.

acted from no other motive than the assertion of its own freedom, so that God himself was unable to predict the outcome of its deliberations.[23] He concluded an uncharacteristically cloudy and derivative discussion with the rather lame statement that God could foretell whatever he wished to know but that he chose not to know everything. When Montesquieu turned from theology to the more congenial subject of politics, he was less inhibited and showed himself more conscious of the social constraints on the exercise of the individual will. His essay on Rome attributed everything, or almost everything, to the force of circumstances. 'The mistakes that statesmen make are not always made freely: they are often the necessary consequence of situations; one disadvantage gives birth to another.' 'It is not chance that rules the world ... There are general causes, either moral or physical, which act in every kingdom, to raise it up, maintain it or cast it down. All accidents are subordinated to these causes and if a state is ruined by the chance issue of a battle, in other words, by a particular cause, there was a general cause which ensured that 'this state should perish as a result of the outcome of a single battle.'[24] In his notebook he attributed the decline of the spirit of glory and valour to the evolution of a complex of ideas and of social and military forces which had gradually transformed the nature of the societies in which the original spirit had grown up, and to which it was appropriate.[25] As he grew older he was to place more and more emphasis on physical conditioning factors and especially on climate.[26]

If one takes his early writings as a whole, what emerges, despite his occasional deflection by the siren songs of a real or imaginary classical past, is what one would expect from the man who wrote that we should accommodate ourselves to this life and not try to force it into patterns of our own devising. Man was largely the product of his environment and should learn to make the most of it. The best government was that which achieved its ends with the least fuss and ruled men in the way most suited to their own inclinations.[27] The men came first and the job of

---

[23] Ibid. LXIX.

[24] *Considérations* ... ch XVIII.

[25] *Cahiers*, I/499. Grasset p.50.

[26] See R.Shackleton, 'The evolution of Montesquieu's theory of climate', *Revue internationale de philosophie*, 1955.   [27] *Lettres Persanes* LXXX.

political institutions was to reflect their existing needs and wishes, rather than to provide them with different ones. This pointed towards a somewhat conservative attitude. 'It is sometimes necessary to change certain laws, but such occasions are rare and when they arise one should only touch the laws with a trembling hand.'[28] He developed this idea more subtly in his *Considérations*. 'When the form of a government has been established for a long time ... it is almost always prudent to leave things as they are, since the causes – often complicated and unknown – that have kept the situation in being, will continue to preserve it. When one changes the entire system, one can only counter such defects as one can envisage in theory and one overlooks those that can only be discovered by experience.'[29] This went with a belief in a kind of providential order – what Adam Smith was later to describe as the 'invisible hand' – which led Montesquieu into ironical praise of fops, whose tireless pursuit of fashion was one of the mainstays of French commerce.[30]

He was saved from mere acquiescence in the status quo by his belief that all political societies, ancient or modern, were to be judged by absolute standards of justice and liberty. Just as his complex mind could hold in balance the dangers of change and the obligation to pursue ideal goals, he conceived of political liberty, not as some static utopia, but as a kind of well-managed see-saw. It was not to be identified with republicanism (he maintained that the English, like the Dutch, would be less free if they did not have a king), but with moderate government. He defined liberty in terms of personal security rather than a share in political power – an opinion he was later to modify – and he was sceptical about over-indulgence in politics. 'I do not attach much value to the delights of furious disputation about affairs of state, to the endless repetition of *liberty* and the privilege of hating half of one's fellow-creatures.'[31] This somewhat modest conception of freedom was far from implying that he considered free states to be the rule. On the contrary, he thought despotism the normal consequence of human passions and moderate government was 'a masterpiece of legislation that chance

[28] Ibid. CXXIX.   [29] *Lettres Persanes* XVII.
[30] *Cahiers*, II/209. Grasset p.164.
[31] Ibid. I/459, I/35-37, II/6-7. Grasset pp. 156, 113, 97.

produces very rarely and men rarely allow prudence to create'.[32]
If there was much to fear from change there was also much that
needed changing.

He consistently refused to identify himself with the self-
interest of one particular society. 'If I knew of anything useful to
my own nation that would be ruinous to another, I should not
propose it to my prince, since I am a man before I am a
Frenchman, or rather, I am a man by necessity and a Frenchman
by chance.'[33] Well before the Physiocrats and Adam Smith, he
believed that international prosperity was indivisible. 'All
nations are connected and pass on their good or evil fortune to
each other. I am not making an oratorical statement, I am
merely telling the truth: the prosperity of the universe will
always be conducive to our own and, as Marcus Aurelius said,
"What is useless to the swarm is useless to the bee." '[34]

Finally, and perhaps most endearingly, coming from a
political philosopher: 'Great God, how can we possibly be always
right and the others always wrong?'[35]

With the temper of Montesquieu's mind and thought once
established, as it emerged in his earlier writings, it becomes
easier to find one's way through the profound, but complex and
sometimes contradictory insights of *De l'esprit des lois*. His life's
work – he liked to say that he spent twenty years over it – was
conceived, not so much as a study of the laws that regulate
political societies, as of the principles behind those laws. Book I,
which was presumably added at a relatively late date, tried to
sum up the argument. Montesquieu's definition of laws led him
straight into an argument about determinism. Laws were
'necessary relationships, derived from the nature of things'.[36]
This seemed to leave little room for free-will, but he was not the
man to put all his money on one horse, in a race of such
importance. Intelligent beings were subject to three kinds of law:
the universal laws of matter; equally universal moral laws,
anterior to society and independent of human volition;
regulations which they made for their own benefit. There was

[32] Ibid. II/10. Grasset pp.111-12. He used this sentence again in *De l'esprit
des lois* V/14.
[33] Ibid. I/344. Grasset p.9.
[34] Ibid. III/38. Grasset pp.216-7.
[35] Ibid. III/309. Grasset p.225.
[36] Ibid. I/2.

nothing they could do about the first of these. The second and third imposed obligations, in their own interest, which they had a duty to observe but also the freedom to violate. While it might be rational for such beings always to observe laws conducive to their own good, in practice they broke them all the time, either from ignorance or in order to assert their freedom. From the outset, therefore, he found himself confronted by necessity, universal moral obligations and the consequences of free social actions. The last of these posed further problems. The character of a people was shaped by a multiplicity of influences: physical geography, the nature of the economy, religion, wealth, population, trade, habits and manners. Peoples were therefore different from each other and individuals were born into a society in which they would be conditioned by a variety of social influences. Some of these, such as climate, were imposed by the physical environment. Many, however, were the product of the collective activity of previous generations. As the present helped to shape the future, the effects of social conditioning on this generation became the causes of the conditioning of the next, and cause and effect were two aspects of the same thing. Laws, moreover, could not be considered in isolation. The effect of any law (in the sense of a political enactment) would depend on its relationship to existing laws, to the traditions of a society, the intentions of the legislator and the particular sphere of activity (religion, politics, the family etc.) to which it applied. This was a splendid example of Montesquieu's simultaneous awareness of the complexity of life and the equally irresistible claims of a number of logically incompatible arguments. He probably found it very reassuring; if it made for ambiguity and a fair amount of self-contradiction, it kept both his feet on the ground. He had, after all, written in his notebook, 'Men have rarely been more grossly deceived than when they have tried to reduce human feelings to a system, and the least lifelike picture of man is unquestionably to be found in books, which are an accumulation of general propositions that are almost always wrong'.[37] As in the *Lettres Persanes*, his personal preference was for laws that respected the pre-existing nature of society rather than the reforming will of some legislator. 'The form of government most

---

[37] *Cahiers*, I/24-30. Grasset p.18.

in conformity with nature is that whose particular dispositions most accurately reflect the character of a people.'[38] This was to emerge in more detail as the argument of his book unfolded, but not for a considerable time.

Book II looks like the beginning of the original work. It was reassuringly straightforward: an essay in comparative government, without any normative implications. All states were divided into three types – republics, monarchies and despotisms – in accordance with three predominant types of political obligation. The republic rested on *vertu*, the total dedication of its citizens to the welfare of the community; monarchies were based on honour, the pursuit by the individual of distinctions that were awarded only in return for service to the ruler; despotism was maintained by fear. Montesquieu recognised that all three types of motivation existed in any society, but he claimed that one of them was the 'principle' that governed the operation of each particular regime.

He then went on to discuss the kind of institutions appropriate to each. As always, the republics he had primarily in mind were those of the classical world and once again he half-succumbed to the temptation to present them in utopian terms. Although he himself was to discard this view as his book unfolded, it was taken up by others – and most notably by Rousseau – and exercised so powerful an influence on eighteenth-century French thought that it deserves consideration in some detail. The characteristics of such a republic were the communal ownership of property, religion, isolation from corrupting foreign influences, the abolition of money and the conduct of trade by the state.[39] Since *vertu* was a matter of sentiment rather than instruction, it could be found equally at all levels of society and was likely to prove more resistant to corruption among the poor than among their social superiors. Love of country was conducive to *la bonté des moeurs* and virtuous habits in turn reinforced love of country.[40] Morals and politics, in other words, were inseparable. Republicanism also implied frugality although Montesquieu (who did not share Rousseau's contempt for Athens) was prepared to make an exception in the case of trading communities, on the ground that commerce, by its very nature,

---

[38] *De l'esprit des lois*, I/3.   [39] IV/6.
[40] V/2.

encouraged sobriety and moderation.[41] The republic was also characterised by the extreme subordination of the young to the old, of children to fathers and of citizens to magistrates. It did not, however, require the equal division of the land amongst all the inhabitants (the *loi agraire* that was to be something of a turnip-ghost during the French Revolution).[42]Everything was seen from the viewpoint of society rather than from that of the individual and Montesquieu commended what was alleged to have been the Samnite practice of allowing young men, in order of merit, to take their pick of the local girls, a custom, one would have thought, more inclined to promote *vertu* among the men than among the women.[43] Since republican government was only suitable for city-states, republics would need to join in federal leagues for their protection.[44]

As always, Montesquieu was not quite sure whether such a state of affairs had ever existed and, if it had, whether it had any relevance to the world of his time. He contrasted ancient peoples who 'performed the kind of deeds we no longer see, which astonish our puny souls', with contemporary statesmen who 'speak only of manufactures, trade, finance, wealth and luxury' and deplored the 'sediment and corruption of modern times'.[45] So far as the present was concerned, he had his doubts about the viability of a society that depended on the continual self-abnegation of its citizens – 'always a very painful thing' – and he did not see how any modern state could exist without money.[46] He believed that love of frugality could exist only where equality and frugality had first been created by political action, but he did not go into the question of how a legislator was to overturn the existing mores of a community and bring into being a society dedicated to the most unnatural pursuit of such uncomfortable virtues.

He devoted comparatively little time to despotism, which quickly came to appear as the negation of good government, rather than a viable system in its own right, and served mainly as a contrast to republics and monarchies. The latter had a good deal to attract him. As he saw it, in a monarchy the ruler was

---

[41] V/3-6.   [42] V/7.
[43] VII/16. Saint-Just was also to advocate this in his 'republican institutions'.
[44] XI/1.   [45] IV/4, III/3, IV/6.
[46] IV/5, 7.

restrained from his natural tendency towards despotism by the existence of a hereditary aristocracy, living by a code of honour that took precedence over human and divine law.[47] Such an aristocracy naturally aspired to distinctions which in eighteenth-century France could be obtained primarily, if not exclusively, from service to the king. The 'invisible hand' therefore led them towards the spontaneous service of the state, while they thought only of their own advantage, and monarchy was a superb instrument for obtaining the maximum output for the minimum expenditure of *vertu*.[48] Montesquieu was quite explicit that honour had no moral significance. 'Philosophically speaking, it is a false honour that directs all parts of the state, but this false honour is as useful to the public as true honour would be to individuals.'[49] If honour impelled men to serve the king in administration or to risk their lives for him in battle, in return for a title, a medal or some ceremonial privilege (Montesquieu was inclined to maintain a delicate silence about more material rewards), it also imposed limits on obedience, since the noble was expected, as a matter of course, to prefer death to anything considered dishonourable. His point was rather neatly made by de Gaulle, when Pétain corrected a sentence of his about the officer being sometimes obliged to sacrifice his career, his life and his honour. Pétain suggested that this would read better as 'his honour and his life'. 'I put them,' replied de Gaulle, 'in ascending order of importance.' There were plenty of Pétains in eighteenth-century France, and as a picture of how the French monarchy actually worked, Montesquieu's account was as idealised as his picture of Athens and Sparta. Nevertheless, when seen from the perspective of a more totalitarian age, the restraints – often self-imposed by rulers – observed by the nominally absolutist governments of central and western Europe, at least when dealing with their nobility, are very striking. To some extent the rest of society also benefited from the lengths to which governments chose not to go: religious toleration was greater in practice than in theory, as Montesquieu was personally aware, and the censorship of heterodox or seditious literature was mild

---

[47] On this subject, see N.Hampson, 'The French Revolution and the nationalization of honour' in M.R.D. Foot (ed.), *War and Society*, London, 1973.
[48] III/5.
[49] III/7.

by modern standards. Although it would be foolish to push the analogy too far, his conception of the difference between a monarchy, in which the amoral self-interest of personal ambition happened to further the well-being of society as a whole, and republican dedication to the austere pursuit of collective goals as a matter of principle, has points in common with some present-day attitudes to capitalism and socialism.

Montesquieu had originally aimed at a clinical analysis of his three types of government that would examine each of them with dispassionate impartiality. In practice, his belief in moral imperatives made this impossible. He could never entertain the completely relativist view that all societies got the governments they both deserved and wanted. Despotism had been a problem from the start, and as he progressed the three types of government came to bear a suspicious resemblance to heaven, earth and hell. The republic was perhaps too demanding for fallen man, as he existed in the eighteenth century, but Montesquieu found it difficult not to confuse *vertu* with virtue *tout court* and he tended to introduce into his discussion of monarchy moral criteria that were irrelevant to what he believed to be its essence. There were also some conclusions that he refused to draw, whatever their logic. An examination of forms of punishment appropriate to the three regimes brought him round to the question of torture. 'I was going to say that it might be appropriate to despotisms, where whatever inspires fear is a suitable means of government; I was going to say that Greek and Roman slaves ... But I hear the voice of nature crying out against me.'[50] He found slavery equally abhorrent and attacked it with the most bitter irony to be found anywhere in the book.[51] When he looked at the corruption of the different types of government, he found himself arguing that republics degenerated into monarchies and monarchies into despotisms, which left despotisms with nowhere to go. He concluded rather desperately that they were auto-corrupting. By the time he reached the end of Book X his initial project was shipping water on all sides. At this point he introduced political liberty as a universal good, to which all societies ought to aspire. This sank despotism at once, his original scheme lost most of whatever relevance it had managed to

[50] VI/17.   [51] XV/5,8.

retain, and he set off on an entirely new tack.

He began with an attempt to define political liberty – and quite typically produced two formulations that pointed in different directions: 'to be free to do what we ought to want' and 'the right to do whatever the law permits'.[52] The first definition raised the question of whether it was for the government, or the 'legislator' to decide, in what was alleged to be the people's own interest, what it 'ought to want'. Rousseau's answer to this was to take him a long way from what Montesquieu had in mind, but in a sense he was only building on the older man's foundations. Montesquieu himself, although he did not develop the point, was probably thinking in fairly conventional terms about universal moral obligations that were independent of any particular society. He went on, as he had not done in his earlier writings, to distinguish between civil liberty, an ad hoc state of affairs that could exist in a nominally absolute state, and political liberty, which implied a share in political power.

As soon as he began to write about political liberty he discarded his previous system of classification. It had nothing to do with either *vertu* or honour and could be achieved *only* by the balance of political forces. 'Democracy and aristocracy are not naturally free states. Political liberty is only to be found in moderate governments. It does not always exist in moderate states. It is only present when power is not abused; but all human experience shows that every man with power is led to abuse it. He presses on until he encounters some limit. Who would have thought it, *vertu* itself needs limits. If power is not to be abused, things must be so disposed that power checks power.'[53]

From this new vantage point he took a much more critical view of the classical republics. Sparta and Rome were rejected because of their dedication to war and expansion respectively. Only one state, said Montesquieu, had political liberty as the prime objective of its constitution, and in the famous chapter 6 of Book XI he provided an astonishing eulogy of the British constitution, as he understood it. Without going into detail, it is sufficient to say that he saw the essence of this constitution as consisting of the balance of power between three independent

---

[52] XI/3.   [53] XI/4.

sources: the royal executive, a legislature, itself divided between a hereditary Upper and an elected Lower House, and an independent judiciary, by which he meant *habeas corpus* and the right to trial by a jury free from government influence. 'These three powers ought to produce a state of inertia or inaction, but since, in the nature of things, they are obliged to act, they are forced to act in concert.' The political will of the state was therefore the result of the divergent wills of the different sections of the community.

This was something completely different from a monarchy based on honour. It was not merely different from the classical republics but superior to them. Representative government was not a *pis aller*, forced on a large population by the impossibility of collecting all the citizens in one place; it was better than direct democracy since it made possible the informed discussion of policy between a relatively small number of individuals, chosen for their merit. So far, Burke might have agreed, but unlike Burke, Montesquieu did not see politics as essentially designed to safeguard the economic status quo. His concern was with liberty as an objective in its own right, irrespective of the distribution of wealth, and he therefore insisted that the Lower House (which expressed what he called the 'general will' of the community) should be elected by all those not in a condition of dependence on others. This was a far cry from the British practice that he so much admired. In his own way, he was as much a democrat as Rousseau, and less given to making unflattering remarks about the political ineptitude of the masses. If his previous remarks on monarchy had anticipated some aspects of modern conservatism, his new analysis of the basis of moderate government can be considered the foundation deed of liberalism, and its central thesis is at least as relevant today as when it was first formulated.

Montesquieu's idealisation of the British constitution involved him in one or two awkward problems, such as how this happy state of affairs came into being. Ignoring the 1688 revolution and the Whig oligarchs, not even throwing a passing nod in the direction of Magna Carta, with a lack of realism truly staggering in a man so sensitive to history, he went right back to Tacitus and maintained that 'This fine system was found in the [German] forests'. Even there, it did not presumably grow on trees, but was a product of human wisdom rather than an automatic response to the pressures of the environment. The latter must have changed quite appreciably in the intervening 1700 years, so that the Germanic theory implied, even if Montesquieu did not realise it, that human will took precedence over circumstance – unless he imagined that a uniquely favourable succession of historical accidents had kept the 'Anglo-Saxons' on the right lines.

This raised the question of whether less fortunate peoples were merely called upon to admire, or whether they should also imitate. Montesquieu claimed that England was an example of 'extreme political liberty' and maintained that he had no intention of disparaging other governments. 'How could I say that, I who believe that any excess – even of reason – is not always desirable and that men are practically always more comfortable in the middle than at the extremities?' This was perhaps inserted in the hope of disarming the censors, for throughout the remainder of his book he was inclined to use England as a touchstone of political virtue.

He then turned to look at political liberty from the viewpoint of the citizen rather than the government. This was an altogether more subjective affair, reflecting habits, manners and precedents. Cosmopolitan as always, he insisted on the need to look outside one's society for guidance, especially in matters of criminal law. This was another indication that he had now opted for the modern world and rejected the intellectual autarchy of Greece and Rome. Forgetting all about republican frugality, he commended low taxation as a stimulus to economic activity, seeing the poverty of the nation as a cause, rather than a consequence, of the idleness of its citizens. Wealth was, however, to be redistributed, and he advocated the progressive taxation of personal income.[54] This was so radical that, even at the height of the Revolution, it was to be supported by only the more extreme republicans.

Having veered over in the direction of free-will, when he considered the British constitution, Montesquieu then tacked back again and devoted five Books to an examination of the extent to which systems of government were determined by

[54] XIII/7.

climate and terrain. Anticipating Marx, he wrote that 'Laws have a close relationship with the way in which different peoples procure their subsistence'.[55] Hunting, farming and trading societies would require different legal systems. He does not seem to have envisaged such societies succeeding each other in time and, unlike Marx, he did not believe that the economic structure of a society ultimately determined its other characteristics. Each factor had to be examined in its own right, without forgetting that all were mutually inter-related. Climate was relatively straightforward, in the sense that it was an obviously external force, but there were many who questioned the extent of the influence that Montesquieu attributed to it – over religious belief and the status of women, for example. Terrain raised more problems. He thought fertile soil conducive to monarchy and barren lands suitable for a republic, but he believed that the condition of agriculture was more dependent on freedom than on natural fertility.[56] Liberty and environment were once again at odds. Some environments, indeed, like that of the Netherlands, were actually the creation of human will. Republics encouraged fertility and fertility impelled them towards monarchy. As he was to write in his next Book, *Tout est extrêmement lié.*

It was perhaps a feeling that the argument was getting out of control that led him, before going on to examine socially determined conditioning factors, to insert a discussion on the relationship between laws and the specific characteristics of a particular society. Once more the emphasis was on a complex kind of determinism. Forgetting all about his moral absolutes for the moment, he began by claiming that all values were relative. 'Liberty itself appeared intolerable to peoples not used to enjoying it.'[57] Tyranny could be either 'real' or subjective – which confused the issue by bringing back absolutes. As usual, his undogmatic sensitivity to life had exposed more elements than he, or perhaps anyone else, could keep under control. The point he clung to was that, whatever the 'real' situation, the perceptions of a people imposed limits on what was acceptable to them. 'Men are governed by many things: climate, religion, the laws, the maxims of the government, the examples of the past, habits, matters. From these emerges a general spirit.'[58] This was

[55] XVIII/8.   [56] XVIII/3.
[57] XIX/2.   [58] XIX/4.

a re-statement of what he had already said (or was going to say) in his first Book, which presumably indicates the importance he attached to the relativist and deterministic element in politics. The *esprit général* then acquired a kind of life of its own, in which all aspects of a society were organically related. Each took its meaning, in part, from its relationship to the others. To alter one was to affect them all, and apparently similar innovations would have different effects in different societies. 'The habits of an enslaved people are part of its slavery; those of a free people are part of its liberty.' 'A free nation can have a liberator; a subject nation can only change oppressors.'[59]He followed this by a lengthy examination of how environmental pressures would lead a free nation ... to do everything that the British did.

Somewhat illogically – at least when he was wearing his determinist hat – he endowed societies with 'legislators' who had somehow or other escaped from the blinkers that circumstances imposed on everyone else. Rousseau was to give the legislator a much more significant rôle, but he was already a persistent presence in *De l'esprit des lois*. The problem therefore arose of what the legislator should do about the *esprit général*. In an earlier Book, Montesquieu had advised him to draft laws that would counteract the influence of an unfavourable climate.[60] There was, after all, not much point in a legislator who merely endorsed the thoughts of everyone else. This time, however, Montesquieu put the emphasis the other way. Chapter 6 of Book XVIII was called 'One should not correct everything'. In chapter 9 he reverted to his old argument that moral vices, such as vanity, might have their economic uses in stimulating demand. He had more confidence in the invisible hand than in meddling fingers. To legislate against the *esprit général*, however noble the legislator's motives, would be seen as tyrannous and the enforcement of such legislation would therefore really be tyrannous. Laws could be modified, but the only legitimate way to modify a nation's way of life was by example.

With the wind now blowing fairly strongly from a determinist quarter, Montesquieu next tackled the problem of environmental forces that were themselves the product of human decisions: commerce, demography and religion. He welcomed

[59] XVIII/27.   [60] XIV/5.

trade, as conducive to *moeurs douces*, if not to *moeurs pures*, opposed any ban on usury and thought that a balance between the supply of money and the availability of goods existed only where moderate governments could inspire confidence in their currencies. England was once again commended as outstandingly successful in religion, commerce and liberty. By now, Montesquieu's thoughts were centred on the modern world and he drew on classical examples merely by way of illustration. Unlike the Physiocrats, whose writings in the next twenty years or so were to shape the economic orthodoxy of the revolutionary generation, he was not obsessed with agriculture and he was no advocate of laisser-faire. He saw, more clearly than most of the revolutionaries were to do, that what mattered was employment rather than landownership. 'He who owns nothing but has a trade is no poorer than the man with a dozen acres.'[61] Montesquieu actually thought him better off, since he could teach his trade to each of his children whereas the smallholder was obliged to divide his plot into uneconomic parts. He regarded the economic activity of a community as only one aspect of its collective life, to be regulated in accordance with general social policy, and from this general principle he drew some radical conclusions. 'The obligations of the state are not discharged by a few alms given to the naked in the street. It owes to all its citizens assured subsistence, adequate clothing and a livelihood compatible with their health.'[62]

This would have horrified Burke. It was about as far as the most radical revolutionaries were to get in 1793-4 and, as late as 1922, it provoked the anonymous editor of the Garnier edition of *De l'esprit des lois*, generally very sympathetic to Montesquieu, into a sour footnote on the *erreur du socialisme*. It was, of course, a quite impractible programme for any eighteenth-century state, but, like justice and liberty, Montesquieu saw it as a moral aspiration, incumbent on any kind of society, and not as the attribute of a particular kind of government. He realised that adequate provision for the poor implied a thriving economy, which in turn depended on the development of commerce and industry. The prime objective was the provision of full employment, with a safety net for those thrown temporarily out of

[61] XXIII/29.   [62] Ibid.

work by economic change, rather than the organisation of public assistance as an end in itself. His writing on economic matters may have been over-simplified and over-optimistic, but it referred to the real world of the eighteenth century and not to the pastoral utopia that was to haunt the minds of some of the revolutionaries.

His views on religion were those of a very secular-minded deist. The object of religion was to make better citizens, and forms of belief were largely the products of the environment. In an earlier part of the work he had examined what he thought be the relationship between climate and religious beliefs. There could not be much argument there as to which was cause and which effect. Now, in contradiction to the theologians, he maintained that the religion of a society was determined by its government, and not vice versa. The independent peoples of the north therefore embraced Protestantism. Luther retained bishops since his dependence on princely support inclined him towards the idea of hierarchy. Calvin, with a more popular following, abolished them.[63] Although Montesquieu thought that all religions served to buttress morality, his preference went to Christianity, much as he regretted its destruction of the Stoics. Unlike Rousseau, he thought Christianity exceptionally favourable to the formation of good citizens, besides being conducive to moderate government. It was, however, unsuitable for export, especially to hot climates.

Montesquieu then concluded the general part of his book by looking at different areas of civil society, each governed by its appropriate laws: natural, divine, canon, international, political, civil and domestic. When he defined the spheres of each, it was notable that in every case where canon law was in competition with civil, his verdict went in favour of the latter. His final emphasis was on a pluralist conception of society. His postulate of the existence of an *esprit général* could have led him to stress the extent to which all aspects of society conformed to a common pattern. Instead, he chose to emphasise their autonomy which, in practice, meant resisting the encroachments of religion and the state. There were still five Books to go, but these consisted almost entirely of an attempt to apply his sociological

[63] XXIV/5.

methodology to an investigation of the origins of French feudalism, which was – and remains – a somewhat specialised interest.

As Voltaire commented, 'This defective book is full of admirable things'. It was partly Montesquieu's fault and partly to his credit that the final result was confusing, if not altogether contradictory. His initial attempt at clinical analysis had been something of a false start – which did not prevent it from being of considerable practical importance. Without Montesquieu, Frenchmen would still have idealised the classical world, but not in the same way. One could claim that he was the source of all the myths that were to shape French political thought for the rest of the century: classical republicanism, the veneration of an allegedly ancient constitution, Anglomania. His picture of the French monarchy as it was supposed to have existed before Richelieu and Louis XIV and might once more exist in the future, was to provide the parlements with a splendid justification for their attacks on 'ministerial despotism' that did as much as anything else to precipitate the Revolution.

When he changed his line of approach, Montesquieu put forward the basic thesis of liberalism, that liberty could only be secured, not by the sovereignty of the elect, the virtuous or the proletariat, but through a contrived equilibrium between the competing interests within a society. Throughout his long work he remained painfully conscious of the tension between will and circumstance and the interchangeability of cause and effect. This led him into many difficulties, but he was never prepared to sacrifice a particular insight for the sake of a consistent generalisation. Despite his waverings, his qualifications and his exceptions, he remained true to his basic beliefs: that government should be the instrument for what a society believes to be its needs, rather than the instrument for changing society itself; that institutions and attitudes are heavily conditioned, both by the material environment and by the legacy of the wise and foolish actions of past generations; that there nevertheless exist certain timeless and universal moral imperatives by which all men are bound. Chief amongst these are justice and liberty; one could perhaps add – although Montesquieu himself does not give it the same emphasis – a tolerable provision for those in need. It was probably beyond the wit of man to impose logical order and consistency on such conflicting postulates as these, but no one has tried harder than Montesquieu to keep them all simultaneously in focus. The result was not so much an ideology as a quarry, from which his successors took the materials for constructions of very different kinds.

Chapter 2

Rousseau

A surprising amount is known about Rousseau's early life, but since much of the information comes from his own *Confessions*, it has to be treated with some caution. Mercier, who claimed to have known him quite well in his later years, insisted on his paranoia and described his later writings – which included the *Confessions* – as those of a sick man rather than a philosophe.[1] He regarded the *Confessions* as a kind of novel, even suggesting that Rousseau's claim to have had several children, all of whom he placed in a foundling hospital, was fictitious.[2] The general outline of Rousseau's career, however, seems fairly well established.

He was born in Geneva in 1712, the son of a watchmaker, and his birth cost his mother her life. His father abandoned the family when Rousseau was ten. After a rudimentary education he was apprenticed to an engraver who, he claimed, treated him badly. At sixteen he ran away from the engraver and from Geneva, although he retained for the rest of his life the émigré's attachment to his native city-state and liked to style himself 'citizen of Geneva'. For the next dozen years he wandered about a good deal, earning his living as best he could, and spending long periods in Savoy with his protectress and lover, Madame de Warens, who helped him to perfect his education. He moved to Paris in about 1742 and established his reputation eight years later, when he won the prize offered by the Dijon Academy for an essay on whether or not the arts and sciences had been beneficial to humanity. Rousseau's vigorous assertion to the contrary set

[1] *De Jean-Jacques Rousseau considéré comme l'un des premiers auteurs de la Révolution*. Paris, 1791. 2v. I/247.
[2] Ibid. II/263-5.

him apart, as a writer and a moralist, out of tune with many of
the basic assumptions of the French Enlightenment.

Two years later his opera, *Le devin du village*, was performed
at Court. He claimed that it was very well received and that he
could have had a royal pension for the asking, but that he
preferred to disappear. Whatever the truth of that, it is clear
enough that his immense and diverse talents would have allowed
him to enjoy fame and comfort, if not affluence, had he chosen to
let them. Others might have been happy to go on being lionised
by the kind of society that they made their reputation by
denouncing. Rousseau broke with it and tried to support himself
by copying music and, at one time, making laces. If he was
nevertheless able to live in modest comfort with his humbly-born
mistress, Thérèse, this was mainly due to the protection of one or
two aristocratic ladies. One suspects that it was not merely on
intellectual grounds that he quarrelled with the first of these,
Madame d'Epinay, and with his friend Diderot. The passion
with which he pursued perfect communion, with people and
society, in his life and his writings, corresponded to his failure to
achieve it. There was, however, nothing pathological or
imaginary about the persecution that drove him to flee to
Switzerland in 1762. Four years later he accepted Hume's offer of
asylum in England, where he was granted a royal pension –
which he chose not to draw. After quarrelling with Hume he
returned to France in 1767 and died there in 1778.

As he was the first to proclaim, there has never been anyone
like him. In 1761-2 he published the *Nouvelle Héloise*, a novel
that had an immense success, *Emile* and *Du contrat social*,
which are still essential reading for the serious study of education
and politics. Most of what he wrote – and this is particularly true
of his novel – is a strange and often compelling amalgam of the
sublime and the absurd. In his personal life he found it
impossible to maintain any close relationship with his peers. It
was perhaps natural that he should have called Madame de
Warens 'Maman', but to address his mistress and housekeeper as
'Ma Tante' was rather peculiar. Sooner or later he quarrelled
with almost everyone, always insisting that he was offering
devoted and disinterested friendship to people who betrayed him
and became his bitterest enemies. Burke was to describe him as
'the mad Socrates of the National Assembly'. Many of his

insights about society presumably arose from his inability to live at peace within it – which does not necessarily invalidate them. It is easy enough to explain Rousseau away – and a singularly pointless exercise since he refuses to disappear. There are times when he must strike most people as seeing beyond the limited horizons of reasonable men. What matters in the present context is that what he said and the way in which he said it aroused the passionate enthusiasm of the generation that was to make the French Revolution.

In the present age of specialisation, Rousseau tends to be approached from particular angles: the French Department has the *Nouvelle Héloise*, Politics takes *Du contrat social* and Education *Emile*. This is understandable enough in a university context, but his eighteenth-century readers were not studying for degrees, and one must take his writings as a whole if one is to understand the effect they had at the time. It is probably true, as Mercier said, though not particularly important, that *Du contrat social* was the least read of his works before 1789.[3] Much of its argument had already been outlined in his *Discours sur l'économie politique*, which appeared in the *Encyclopédie* in 1755 and, in any case, contemporaries were more interested in the general bent of his thought than in speculation about what exactly he meant by the 'general will'.[4]

For Rousseau, the classical mirage that Montesquieu had found it so hard to resist, became a positive obsession: with the important qualification that it consisted only of Sparta and Rome and never included Athens. The Spartans were 'the most illustrious and respected people that ever existed on earth'.[5] He

---

[3] *De Jean-Jacques Rousseau* ... II/99n[1]. J.Macdonald (*Rousseau and the French Revolution, 1762-91*, London, 1965) goes much too far, however, in suggesting that *Du contrat social* was scarcely known. See the review of her book by J.Lough in the *Historical Journal*, 1961.

[4] What follows concerns Rousseau's writings, which were what affected the revolutionary generation. His private views on specific problems were often much more cautious and practical, but these were known only to his acquaintances. Strictly speaking, I should therefore have omitted from the following discussion any reference to his *Projet de constitution pour la Corse*, which was not published until 1861. It may, however, have circulated in manuscript or been known to acquaintances such as Mercier. Besides, it was too good to miss.

[5] *Fragments politiques*, p.512. Unless otherwise indicated, all references to the works of Rousseau are taken from vol.III of the Pléiade edition. In the case of *Du contrat social*, I have used book and chapter, for ease of reference.

considered Rome 'the seat of glory and *vertu* if ever they had one on earth'.[6] There followed the inevitable contrast with the decadent present: 'As for me, who loves to consider only what informs and honours humanity, seeing amongst my contemporaries only heartless masters and groaning subjects, wars of no interest to anyone ... I delight in contemplating those venerable pictures of antiquity where I see men raised up by sublime institutions to the highest peaks of greatness and *vertu* that human wisdom can attain.'[7] There were times when Rousseau, like Montesquieu, thought that the present could do no more than lament the vanished glories, gone beyond recall, when Rome became 'that continual miracle that the world can never hope to see again'.[8] As a moralist, however, he was convinced that, whatever the constraints of circumstance, 'in moral matters, the limits of the possible are less restrictive than we think; it is our own weakness, our vices, our prejudices that narrow them down'.[9] The fact that he regarded contemporary society, not with the indulgent irony of Montesquieu, who thought that there was some good in most things, but with the anger and contempt of a Savonarola, made it all the more urgent for him to believe that he could at least point the way towards redemption, even if his readers were too corrupted to be likely to take it.

It was therefore not enough for Rousseau to demonstrate that the classical republics had been based on *vertu*. He had the more daunting task of persuading the inhabitants of Vanity Fair to prefer the rigours of the New Jerusalem. Despite his passionate personal conviction of the existence of free-will he believed that men – other men perhaps – were very much the product of social institutions. The 'limits of the possible' for some included the social conditioning of others. To a quite remarkable extent, he believed that if the glories of the past were to be revived, it could only be by exactly copying classical institutions. If the Corsicans abolished all trade, even in food, they would become like the first Romans.[10] The Poles were even advised to model their armed

[6] *Emile* (Garnier ed. Paris, 1964), p.494.
[7] *Fragments politiques*, p.538.
[8] *Discours sur l'économie politique*, p.262.
[9] *Du contrat social*, III/12.
[10] *Corse*, p.925.

forces on those of the Spartans and the Parthians – which presumably implied the substitution of archery for artillery.[11]

The object of political institutions was not, as it had been for Montesquieu, to embody a pre-existing *esprit général*, but to transform human nature by means of society. In this sense, Rousseau was the more determinist of the two. 'Good institutions are those which most effectively denature man, depriving him of his absolute existence in return for a relative one and transferring his sense of identity to the community. In this way, each individual no longer believes himself to be single, but part of a [social] unity and is aware only of the whole. A Roman citizen was neither Caius nor Lucius: he was a Roman.'[12]

This evangelical determination to transform human nature, to make men positively *want* what one has decided that they are to have, to make them become what society has decided that they are to be, is central to the three great works of 1761-2. The boy Emile is given the impression that he is making free choices when all his decisions are, in fact, inspired by his tutor, who brings him to *desire* what the tutor thinks good for him. In the *Nouvelle Héloise*, Sophie's battle is not to persuade her former lover Saint-Preux to accept his new situation (given his rather feeble character, that would not have been very difficult), but to make him *prefer* it to what he originally thought that he wanted. This is also one of the central arguments of *Du contrat social*.

> The man who dares to provide a people with institutions must feel himself fit to change human nature, so to speak; to transform each individual, who is a complete and isolated unit in himself, into one part of a greater whole, from which that individual receives his being and his life, as it were; to reinforce the constitution of man; to substitute a partial and moral existence for the physical and independent existence that we received from nature ... The more our natural forces are destroyed and killed, the greater and more enduring our acquired characteristics, the more perfect and stable is the institution. If each citizen is nothing and can do nothing except through the others, and the force acquired by the whole is equal or superior to the sum of the natural forces of all the individuals, one can say that the laws have reached the highest possible degree of perfection.[13]

[11] *Considérations sur le gouvernement de la Pologne*, p.1019.
[12] *Emile*, p.9.   [13] *Du contrat social*, II/7.

He had put it rather more succinctly in 1755: 'If it is good to employ men as they are, it is still better to make them what one needs them to be.'[14]

How fallen man could be made to want his painful redemption – for he would not appreciate the worthlessness of what he had been induced to give up, until his redemption was complete – raised problems that Rousseau never quite managed to solve: in *Du contrat social* he was dealing with the theoretical basis of sovereignty rather than with practical problems of statecraft. Even if one assumed that the new social institutions would be entirely successful in moulding the character of future generations, there would still be the awkward matter of surviving a transitional period, when the young were becoming *vertueux* but those in control of things were still the vitiated products of a corrupt society. The latter would presumably have to be prevented from continuing to impose their own false values. It would therefore be impossible to introduce from the start the kind of free institutions that would be appropriate to the virtues of the rising generation. Transitional stages have a knack of proving remarkably permanent and states are not good at withering away. Inevitably, Rousseau was led to promote the 'legislator', who had made an occasional appearance in *De l'esprit des lois*, into a kind of political Moses who could guide – and when necessary bully – his recalcitrant charges towards a Promised Land of whose precise location only he was aware. It was a position for which there were to be quite a few candidates during the French Revolution.

Rousseau was certain that politics was about morals. This gave him a kind of compulsive persuasiveness that only sincere moralists can sometimes command. 'What placed Jean-Jacques Rousseau above all the writers of his century was the fact that his eloquence had a moral character, a real and necessary object of public utility.'[15] He was never entirely sure whether the problem was how to save the individual from society, or how a regenerated society was to save him from himself. Rousseau was to oscillate between these options as Montesquieu had wavered between freewill and determinism.

[14] *Discours sur l'économie politique*, p.251.
[15] Mercier, *De Jean-Jacques Rousseau ...* I/19.

One can state very briefly the essential basis of his political philosophy, as it appeared in 1755 and was developed until it reached its final form, seven years later, in *Du contrat social*. Political society involves the surrender by each of all his rights, in return for an equal share in the collective rights of the community as a whole. The latter acquire a new moral dimension, missing from the former, since individuals are now working for others as well as for themselves. If they are to remain as free within the community as they were outside it, they cannot be subjected to a mere majority decision, with which they may well disagree. Sovereignty within any community therefore resides, not in the will of a prince or senate, not even in a decision by the entire body of citizens, but in the *volonté générale*, which is what is best for all, and therefore for each. In this sense, 'The sovereign [i.e. the general will] by the mere fact of its existence, is always what it ought to be.'[16] Leaving aside the insoluble problem of how one can distinguish the general will from the majority, or even from the will of all (since an entire community might be misled as to the nature of its best interest), the man who has voted for something other than the general will must realise that he was mistaken as to his own interest, and change his mind. If he is reluctant to do so, he must be 'forced to be free' (i.e. to do what he 'really' wants, which is to serve his own long-term interests, which are those of the community, rather than defer to his selfishness, ignorance or prejudice).

There is a sense in which this is a remarkably acute perception of how free societies actually function. Unlike Montesquieu's assertion, however, that rulers should respect the *esprit général* – which was more a counsel of prudence than a moral imperative – Rousseau's theory, however ingenious its logic, raised some disturbing problems. Were there, as Montesquieu insisted, moral laws of a universal nature, or were there no obligations beyond the self-interest of a particular community – which might involve the enslavement or exploitation of its neighbours? In an early draft of *Du contrat social*, Rousseau had initially followed Montesquieu in asserting 'What is good and in conformity with order is so by the very nature of things and independently of any human agreements. All justice comes from

---

[16] *Du contrat social*, I/7.

God'. He had then immediately contradicted himself: 'Law precedes justice and not vice versa. If the law cannot be unjust, this is not because it is based on justice, which may not be the case, but because it is contrary to nature that one should wish to harm one's self.'[17] This is not very helpful.

An obvious way out of his dilemma would have been to treat the whole of humanity as a single community, in which case the well-being of the human race might well have been equated with universal moral law. Rousseau seemed to take this view in 1757, arguing that the duties of the man took precedence over those of the citizen and referring to the law of nations as 'the general will of the great city of the world'.[18] Already, however, he recognised that the feeling of human kinship weakened as the boundaries of the social unit were enlarged. Quite typically, he put it this way: 'Let us dare to confront Socrates himself with Cato. The former was more of a philosopher, the latter more of a citizen. Athens was already lost and Socrates had no country except the world at large, whereas Cato carried his country always in his heart.'[19] Rome one, Athens nil; the result was always the same.

His views hardened with age, persecution – both real and imaginary – and the malign influence of Sparta and Rome, neither renowned for its cosmopolitanism. By the time he wrote *Emile* the tone had become a good deal harsher:

> Every partial society, when it is small and united, cuts itself off from society as a whole. Every patriot is hard towards foreigners: they are only men, they are nothing in his eyes. This is an inevitable inconvenience, but a minor one. The essential thing is to be good to those amongst whom one lives. Abroad, the Spartan was ambitious, avaricious and unjust, but disinterestedness, equity and concord reigned within his walls. [Rousseau should have known that the Spartans had none!] Beware of those cosmopolitans who go looking afar in their books for the duties that they disdain to recognise around them.[20]

Rousseau was understandably uneasy about the consequences of his own logic and continued to affirm, in certain moods, that justice derived ultimately from God. Quite possibly he believed

[17] p.326.
[18] *Discours sur l'économie politique*, p.245.　　[19] Ibid. p.255.
[20] p.9.

that the general will was the voice of a collective conscience and that conscience itself was the voice of God. This would have squared quite a few circles, but he never actually said anything of the kind and his idealisation of the less attractive qualities of the Spartans suggests the opposite. Whatever he himself intended, the contemporary reader was likely to assume him to have said that there was no law superior to the self-interest of a nation, as expressed in its general will, and that the latter was not what the majority wanted, but what was good for everyone, the *actual* will only of those who, enlightened by their legislator, could see beyond their apparent self-interest, to discern what was best for the community as a whole. It was a point of view that has commended itself to a good many people since then.

The actual 'government' of a state was merely the executive organ of the general will. Its particular form (monarchy, republic, etc.) was a matter of convenience, to be determined by such factors as size and population. Rousseau's personal preference was for an elective aristocracy, without excessive social inequality, where, as a general rule, those elected to office were men of leisure.[21] This was rather how Burke saw the British constitution, but Rousseau was no Anglophil. Perhaps, like Montesquieu, he realised that one had to choose between Walpole and Lycurgus. Democracy he rejected, both because it confused the roles of sovereign and government and because it was suitable only for a people of gods.[22] The mass of the population – and here again he was to have Burke on his side – was not merely far from godlike, but destined to remain so, which seemed to limit the possible scope of future legislators. 'The social virtues of pure souls, which constitute the true cult that God desires from us, will never be those of the multitude. It will always believe in gods as senseless as itself.'[23] 'No government can make men live happily; the best is that which makes it possible if they are reasonable, and this happiness will always be beyond the multitude.'[24] 'It is difficult to find among the dregs of society a wife who can make a gentleman (*honnête homme*) happy.'[25] It is curious how radicals seem to need their

[21] *Du contrat social*, III/5.   [22] Ibid. III/4.
[23] Early draft of *Du contrat social*, p.285.   [24] *Fragments politiques*, p.513.
[25] *Emile*, p.516.

lumpenproletariat. What it probably amounted to is that Rousseau had some respect for peasants, especially those who lived in the mountains, like those idealised in the *Nouvelle Héloïse*, but a pretty fair contempt for the urban poor. Although he was a harsh critic of contemporary societies, with the exception of his native Geneva, he was no revolutionary. As Mercier put it – rather quaintly for a man writing in 1791 – 'Rousseau did not belong to the class of the turbulent and seditious writers who alarm the state and have to be proscribed. He respected persons and recent events.'[26] This was not a matter of principle, but of expediency: revolt against oppression was always legitimate, but not likely to do much good. 'Such changes are always dangerous and established governments should only be challenged when they become incompatible with the public good. Such caution is a question of politics and not of principle ... It is also true that in such cases one cannot be too careful to distinguish between regular and legitimate actions and seditious tumult, between the will of an entire people and the clamour of a faction.'[27] Almost everyone could have quoted *that*, at one time or another, during the Revolution.

Everything seemed to militate against the possibility of regenerating France by revolution: 'What man of sense would dare to undertake to abolish old customs, to change old maxims and to give to the state a form different from that to which 1,300 years of existence have brought it?'[28] There was, however, one possible exception to the general rule. 'Just as some illnesses turn men's heads and deprive them of memory, in the history of a state there are occasionally violent periods which have the same effect on an entire people that a medical crisis can have on an individual. At such times, revulsion against the past acts as a substitute for loss of memory and the state, blazing with civil war, is reborn from its ashes, so to speak, and resumes the vigour of youth as it escapes from the arms of death.'[29] This was not likely to make anyone aspire to become a revolutionary, but by 1792 when, if one can believe Mercier, everyone was reading *Du*

[26] *De Jean-Jacques Rousseau* ... I/246.
[27] *Du contrat social*, III/8.
[28] *Ecrits sur l'abbé de Saint-Pierre*, p.638.
[29] *Du contrat social*, II/8.

contrat social, it probably struck some people as not a bad account of what was happening in France.

Like Voltaire, Rousseau predicted a coming time of troubles. 'I believe it impossible for the great monarchies of Europe to last much longer. All have had their time of brilliance and whenever that happens to a state it is on the wane.'[30] The conclusion he drew from this was not that Emile should go into politics, but that he should learn a trade, so that he would always be able to earn his living. Rousseau thought that much might be done to improve society, but only in nations that were new or undeveloped, like Corsica and Poland. Nothing much was to be expected in France, though there was always the remote and dreadful possibility of regeneration through civil war. From this point of view, Rousseau was the man of 1793 rather than of 1789.

When he came to discuss practical questions of what governments should actually do, he often found himself in two minds. His awareness of the importance of environment inclined him towards the kind of accomodation to circumstances that Montesquieu had associated with moderate government. Rousseau, however, found it harder to resist the pull of the ideal. This was necessary for him, as it was not for Montesquieu, since he believed that a 'republic', in the sense of an ideal society, could actually be created, at least in certain circumstances, by the exercise of the legislator's will. This sometimes led him to treat questions in a conventional way: 'The best system for Corsica and for a republic is certainly not the best for a monarchy and for a large state.'[31] 'A country with poor soil and a surplus population should develop its trade.'[32] Rousseau's heart was not in this routine stuff. As the prophet of every kind of freedom, he was convinced that men *could* dictate terms to their environment, although they usually found it much more comfortable not to try. The choice was always there and it was always a choice between *vertu* and convenience. Poland, if it wished to trade *vertu* for power, could probably become a great conquering state.[33] 'In former days Switzerland, in its poverty,

[30] *Emile*, p.224.
[31] *Corse*, p.933.
[32] *Du contrat social*, II/11.
[33] *Pologne*, p.1003.

dictated terms to France; nowadays, in its wealth, it trembles if a French Minister raises an eyebrow.'[34]

Most of his writing on economic policy related to the measures that would be needed to transform the status quo into something that could serve as the foundations for the new Rome. To some extent he anticipated Marx in the extent to which he believed the economic infrastructure to be basic in any community. Where he differed, of course, was in seeing *vertu* as the ultimate objective. Economic policy should therefore satisfy the elemental needs of the individual and also secure his independence. He believed that what we would now call a consumer society had multiplied imaginary needs and thereby reinforced men's interdependence. He would not have disagreed with the economic analysis of Adam Smith: economic liberalism would indeed ensure a rich harvest of – poisonous – fruit. What Smith saw as progress was to Rousseau the road to perdition. What mattered most was independence and 'the only man who can have his own way is the man who does not need to add another man's arms to his own in order to do so'.[35]

Individual self-sufficiency obviously implied an agrarian society, but Rousseau was no physiocratic agronomist. On the contrary, his ideal was positively neolithic. 'I am so convinced that all trade is destructive of agriculture that I do not even except the food trade.' A little barter was, however, permissible. He cheerfully disposed of the objection that this might depopulate whole areas with the airy assurance that hard work would compensate for any deficiencies in the soil, and it was better to misuse land than men.[36] 'In every aspect of human activity, all machines should be strictly prohibited, likewise any invention that reduces labour, saves manpower and produces the same output with less effort.'[37]

This was so extravagant, even by Rousseau's rather elastic standards, that it calls for some explanation. In part it presumably reflects his admiration for mountain people and his conviction that the urban poor had been debased by their

---

[34] *Corse*, p.913.
[35] *Emile*, p.69.
[36] *Corse*, pp.920-5.
[37] *Fragments politiques*, p.525.

poverty. In part it stems from a hatred of social injustice, all the more passionate and personal from the fact that, unlike most of the philosophes, he himself could remember being at the receiving end. 'A wretch who, to get some bread, takes a crown from some hard-hearted man stuffed with gold, is a knave who is taken to the scaffold, while peaceful citizens suck the blood of the artisan and the peasant ... In this monstrous and forced inequality, the sensuality of the rich inevitably consumes in luxury the subsistence of the poor, scarcely selling them hard black bread as the price of their labour and servitude.'[38]

Populist economics of this kind had a long pedigree: the belief that riches for some must imply poverty for the rest and that this kind of poverty was the product of commerce and urbanisation. That had been the undoing of the classical republics. 'When these people began to degenerate, when vanity and love of pleasure took the place of patriotism and *vertu*, vice and laxity invaded on all sides and the only concern was luxury and the means to satisfy it. Individuals grew rich, commerce and the arts flourished and the state was not long before it perished.'[39] It has a modern ring, but it embodies an egalitarianism as old as the hills, that tends to surface in times of social crisis:

> When Adam delved and Eve span
> Who was then the gentleman?

Rousseau, however, was an egalitarian with a difference. His objective was poverty, rather than riches for all, not the employment of the productive resources of society so as to maximise consumption, but the kind of primitive self-sufficiency that he believed underpinned the ancient societies he so much admired. If he and Montesquieu shared a common concern for the livelihood of the poor, their ideas about how to assure it were diametrically opposed. Montesquieu was wildly over-optimistic in his view of what a developed eighteenth-century economy could achieve, but Rousseau had parted company with reality altogether. So far as France was concerned, the question was not self-sufficiency for all, but the survival of a population of twenty-

[38] Ibid. p.522.
[39] Ibid. p.517.

five million people, and the suppression of the grain trade would have destroyed every town in the country.

Even if no one took him literally, he made a powerful contribution to the myth of the independent – and *vertueux* – peasant. When the agronomists were preaching the unpopular, if ultimately accurate message that the only way to end dearth was by increasing productivity and the way to do that was by capitalist agriculture, Rousseau bequeathed to the revolutionary generation his own belief that what was needed was to give everyone his own bit of land. This raised the question of private property, which he found particularly difficult.

His sympathy for the poor, his acute awareness of the extent to which society tended to equate merit with money, and his conviction that will should prevail over what he called *la force des choses*, all pointed in one direction, traditional wisdom in another. He could be as categorical as Locke in making the defence of property rights the basis of the social contract. 'Public administration is established only to safeguard private property, which is anterior to it.'[40] 'It is certain that the right to property is the most sacred of all a citizen's rights and more important in certain respects than liberty itself.'[41] Burke himself could scarcely have gone further than that. 'Since all civil rights are founded on property rights, when these are abolished none of the others can survive.'[42] Even social mobility was to be deplored. 'Nothing is more fatal to *moeurs* and to the republic than for the citizens to be continually changing their fortune and station ... Those who are brought up for one thing find themselves destined for another; neither those on the way up nor those coming down can absorb the maxims and outlook appropriate to their new condition, much less fulfil their new duties.'[43] There had not been much of this sort of thing in Sparta and Rome.

These were, on the whole, the views advanced in his earlier writings and in this respect, as in others, his attitude tended to evolve. In the final version of *Du contrat social* he asserted that a fair measure of economic equality was the necessary basis for an acceptable society.

[40] *Discours sur l'économie politique*, p.242.
[41] Ibid. p.263.
[42] *Fragments politiques*, p.483.
[43] *Discours sur l'économie politique*, pp.263-4.

If one looks for what exactly constitutes the greatest good of all,
which should be the objective of every system of legislation, one
will find it reduced to two principal objects: liberty and equality
... equality because liberty cannot survive without it ... that no
citizen should be rich enough to buy another and none poor
enough to have to sell himself. This presupposes limited wealth
and influence on the part of the great and limited avarice and
covetousness on the part of the humble.[44]

The rich may have been called upon to surrender some of their
possessions and power, but Rousseau still saw them as better off
than the poor. Complete equality was a myth. 'Such equality is
not even hypothetically possible, since it is not in the nature of
things.'[45] To some extent therefore, will was the prisoner of
circumstance. The question remained of whether a satisfactory
state could only be constructed where rough economic equality
happened to exist, of whether the 'legislator' was entitled to use
political means to bring it into being. This time he suggested a
positive answer. 'Each individual's right to his own property is
always subordinate to the community's rights over everyone.' 'It
is precisely because circumstances are always trying to destroy
equality that the force of the laws should always try to maintain
it.'[46]

Rousseau's advice to the Corsicans and the Poles revealed
what this meant in practice. He told the former that the state
was not entitled to confiscate private property. On the other
hand, 'Far from wanting the state to be poor, I should like it to
have everything, so that each citizen received only a share in the
common wealth, proportionate to his services ... In a word, I
should like the property of the state to be as great and strong and
that of the citizens to be as limited and weak as possible.'[47] The
state was therefore to appropriate the property of the unmarried
on their death and no one was allowed to own land outside the
area where he lived. Some of the land thus acquired would be
redistributed in the form of dowries. Rousseau was rather vague
about the details and he made no attempt to find out whether
the area required for the subsistence of the population on a

[44] *Du contrat social*, II/11.
[45] *Fragments politiques*, p.522.
[46] I/294, II/11.
[47] *Corse*, pp.936, 931.
[48] *Pologne*, p.954.

purely agrarian basis would not exceed the total cultivable land in the island.

He had a particularly soft spot for Poland, saying that he had not the honour to be Polish. Like the Poles themselves, he identified the 'nation' with the nobility and had little to say about the rest of the population. Poland 'demonstrates all the fire of youth ... I seem to see Rome besieged, calmly ruling the lands where its enemies have just pitched their camp.'[48] This was praise indeed. Although Polish society was in fact one of the most backward and oppressive in Europe – so much so that people like Voltaire welcomed its partition by more enlightened neighbours – Rousseau claimed to see in it so much *vertu* that he advised extreme caution before making any changes. He did recommend the emancipation of the serfs – when they had been prepared for freedom – but one finds in his writing on Poland none of that fierce sense of outrage at the humiliations of the poor that punctuates his other works. He tended to push the serfs to one side and turn with relief to counselling their masters. He regretted the gulf between the magnates and the squires but explicitly rejected any idea of economic levelling, even within the nobility. Money could not be absolutely abolished, but he claimed to be following the example of Lycurgus in trying to circumscribe its use as much as possible. As in Corsica, all taxation should be paid in kind, since this had been the practice in early Rome. 'It was not surprising that there was more *vertu* among the Romans than anywhere else.'[49]

The economic prescription for Poland was therefore different from that for Corsica. It would scarcely be an exaggeration to say that he recommended the former to revert to the Middle Ages and the latter to go right back to classical antiquity. This was to pay some attention to the *force des choses*, but not much. The objective was always to use the legislative will to drive a people as far as it would go along the road to a fixed pattern of perfection that existed only in his own mind. Rousseau without an independent peasantry had something in common with Lenin without much of a proletariat. It was for the legislator to create the kind of economic relationships that should, in theory, have created him. Rousseau's contemporaries could not read his

[49] *Corse*, p.930.

advice to the Corsicans, which was not published until much
later, and they do not seem to have paid much attention to what
he told the Poles, which was perhaps just as well for his
reputation during the Revolution. What they did learn from him
was that property rights were, in the last resort, social rather
than personal, that wealth implied corruption and the
enrichment of some involved the impoverishment of the rest, and
that the ideal society was one of independent peasant
proprietors. His aim was a static society that would be Spartan
in more ways than one. It was not likely to make much appeal to
those wealthy enough to be able to buy his works, although his
conviction that a more egalitarian society could be created, if one
wanted it badly enough, aroused the disinterested enthusiasm of
the young, and the general proposition that the rich should be
forced to make sacrifices for the benefit of the poor was to
command a wider audience, the rich being, almost by definition,
other people.

It seems absurd at first sight to discuss Rousseau's views on
education without a careful examination of *Emile*. From his
point of view, however, this treatise on private education was a
pis aller: 'The public institution does not exist any more and
cannot exist since, where there is no longer a *patrie* there can be
no more citizens.'[50] Public education was concerned, not with
guiding the development of the individual personality, but with
the process by which society inculcated *vertu* into the body of the
citizens. To be effective, it must therefore be universal and
compulsory. Even in Poland, where he recognised that he would
not persuade the nobility to give up the private education of
their children, all should be made to participate in some public
exercises. Homeric games and medieval tournaments would
allow young noblemen to impress the masses by their natural
superiority. The latter should be allowed to participate too,
'provided that subordination was always maintained and that
[the people] did not mingle [with the nobles]'.[51] 'If you train up
citizens you will have everything ... It is all the more important
not to abandon the education of children to the ideas and
prejudices of their fathers, since it is of even more concern to the

---

[50] *Emile*, p.10.
[51] *Pologne*, p.964.

state than to the fathers.'[52]

Education had nothing to do with culture. Like other
moralists, Rousseau loved to denounce his readers. In the preface
to the *Nouvelle Héloïse* he warned all chaste girls that they were
lost if they read a single page ... of what he considered to be a
highly moral work! There was much more to this than ingenious
self-advertisement. It corresponded to some profound need to be
always the outsider, the prophet calling sinners to repent.
Culture was an Athenian sort of thing, whereas the Spartans,
'always made to conquer, smash their enemies in every kind of
war and the babbling Athenians feared their words as much as
their blows'.[53] There are times when Rousseau reminds one of
Goering's apocryphal remark about reaching for his revolver.
'Taste for letters is born of idleness and feeds on idleness, so that
culture in a people both announces the onset of corruption and
promptly finishes it off. Apart from idleness, the liberal arts also
announce inequality of wealth, love of small things and the
introduction of luxury, three springs from which vice pours in
streams throughout society.'[54] This was the central theme of his
Lettre à d'Alembert, denouncing the latter's suggestion that the
building of a theatre would help to civilise the Genevans.

Education was not concerned with the development of talent.
As Rousseau advised the Corsicans, 'See that the people take
pleasure in public matters, look for *vertus* and leave your great
talents alone; they would do more harm than good ... Common
sense is enough to direct a well-constituted state, and that comes
as much from the heart as from the head.'[55]Not merely was
talent unnecessary, its promotion among the poor was bad for
social stability. He made much of this in his description of the
patriarchal society of the Wolmars in the *Nouvelle Héloïse.* As
Julie explained,

> 'I can scarcely believe that so many diverse talents all need to be
> developed. If that were the case, the supply of talented people
> would have to be exactly proportioned to the needs of society. If
> agriculture was practised only by those with a talent for it and one
> took away all those more suited to something else, there would not

[52] *Discours sur l'économie politique*, p.260.
[53] *Emile*, p.120.   [54] *Fragments politiques*, p.556.
[55] *Corse*, p.940.

be enough farm workers left to cultivate the land and assure our livelihood ... Simple and good people do not need so much talent; their own simplicity serves them better than the others are served by their skill.'[56]

Rousseau had a particularly strong dislike of educated women, whom he blamed for most of the ills of contemporary society, a fairly obvious example of his tendency to express his personal problems as social criticism. The *Lettre à d'Alembert* is one long anti-feminist diatribe. 'Women in general have neither love for nor knowledge of any sort of art, and no genius at all.' 'Women can never have good *moeurs* unless they lead a retiring and domesticated life.'[57] That was Sparta all over again. He willingly conceded that, deprived of feminine society, men were somewhat inclined to the bottle, but he treated this proof of masculinity so indulgently that one is not surprised to hear from Mercier that it was rather a weakness of his own.[58] He also seemed, in the *Lettre*, to derive some kind of titillation from the contemplation of feminine frailty. One wonders what on earth the noble ladies who protected and maintained him while he was writing this sort of thing, thought about his views of their sex.

Public festivals were an important part of the educational process. In aristocratic Poland, the people were to be mere spectators, applauding their betters, and it was not without condescension that Rousseau wrote 'One can scarcely believe how much the hearts of the people follow their eyes and what an impression the majesty of ceremonial makes on them'.[59] That lesson was not to be lost on later 'friends of the people'. In a republican state like Geneva, everyone should participate and the people constituted their own spectacle, which should involve 'a certain martial spirit, becoming to free men'.[60] That was to be remembered too. Women should play an important, but separate part, with the most virtuous young lady being crowned queen of the fête. The justification for all this was the same as ever: 'That was how Sparta – which I never cite too often as an example – called its citizens together by modest feasts and unpretentious

[56] *Nouvelle Héloïse* (Pléiade ed.), p.538.   [57] *Lettre à d'Alembert.*
[58] *De Jean-Jacques Rousseau ...* I/254.
[59] *Pologne*, p.964.
[60] *Lettre à d'Alembert*

games.'[61] Reluctantly, he conceded that even the Genevans were not yet pure enough for naked games.

Rousseau's views on public education were unusually consistent. It was all about character-formation and toughening the body by military exercises. Even so, he went to rather unnecessary lengths to advertise his dislike of both culture and meritocracy. When one thinks of the man himself, with his self-confessed indiscipline and his self-indulgence, one can sense yet again that what he sought to impose on society was what he lacked himself. No European state had the resources to provide schooling for all its children, but public festivals were relatively cheap. Whether a fête was to be the symbol by which a community spontaneously expressed its collective identity – like the *banquets fraternels* in the streets, which greeted the return of some ex-servicemen in 1945 – or whether it was the means by which Authority tried to indoctrinate a community with an ideology that it might come to accept but would not have invented for itself, was another matter. When Montesquieu wrote of the religion of his Troglodytes and of ancient Greece, he inclined towards the former. Rousseau was committed to the latter, since the object of political action was not to give people what they wanted, but to make them want what they were given.

His conception of the full scope of the educational process went a very long way. Men obtained their moral liberty by exchanging an individual for a social existence, 'for the impulsion of appetite alone is slavery and obedience to the law one has prescribed for one's self is liberty'.[62] This was a secular version of what Christian theologians had been saying for a very long time: that men achieved freedom from the flesh by total self-surrender to the will of God. Rousseau substituted the community for God, which created a new problem. In a society of angels the general will (the highest interest of the collectivity) would be synonymous with the will of all. In the actual world this was not so. Rousseau thought it could only become so if people were provided with institutions that would bring them to want what they ought to have. They might eventually come to welcome their moral regeneration but they were obviously in no

[61] Ibid.
[62] *Du contrat social*, 1/8.

position to initiate it. Someone – and that could only mean government – had to do it for them. It therefore followed that 'So long as the government acts only for the public good, it cannot possibly infringe liberty'.[63] Since the people were, by definition, as yet incapable of understanding what *was* the public good, they would have to take the government's word for it.

Rousseau's proposals for Corsica and Poland show how far he was prepared to go in practice to force recalcitrant human nature on to the Procrustean bed of republican principle. The property rights of the Corsican were to be restricted, as we have seen. If he moved to another part of the island, he lost his civic rights for three years and had to pay to get them back. If he had not married by the time he was 40 he lost them for good, as he did if he married below the age of 20, or above 30, or chose a bride under 15, or more than 20 years younger than himself.[64] The population was to be divided into three classes: *aspirants, patriotes* and citizens. Everyone began as an *aspirant*, became a *patriote* when he married an appropriate partner, provided that he owned some land, and a citizen when he had fathered two children, owned a house and enough land for self-sufficiency.

In the case of Poland, he concerned himself only with the nobility, who were also divided into three classes, along somewhat different lines: lawyers, judges and tax inspectors; teachers and senators; patricians. Promotion from one class to another was by *vertu* alone, which might have posed some problems for boards of examiners. Rousseau then lost himself in a fantasy world, playing toy soldiers with his troops of *cives electi, custodes legum* and so on. As a game it was harmless enough, but he was in deadly earnest and men with the power to destroy people's lives were to take him seriously. One wonders if those who have contrasted the abstraction of *Du contrat social* with the sense of reality he is supposed to have shown when advising the Corsicans and the Poles, have actually read what he wrote.

When he came to deal with religion, the conflict between Rousseau and Jean-Jacques became positively schizoid, since his most passionately held opinions came into head-on collision. He

[63] *Fragments politiques*, p.484.
[64] *Corse*, pp.941, 945.

was a man of deep and profound religious convictions. The *profession de foi du vicaire savoyard* in *Emile* is a moving and clearly sincere statement of deeply held religious belief. Rousseau's contemporaries saw him as the evangelist of a new kind of emotional deism and many who had lost their belief in Christianity recovered a kind of religious faith as a result of his influence. When he dealt with political subjects, however, he judged religion merely by its contribution to civic virtue. He rejected, not merely the warring Christian churches, but Christianity itself, because he thought it less effective than paganism as a reinforcement to patriotism. 'The Christian law, at bottom, does more harm than good to the strong constitution of a state. I know of nothing more opposed to the social spirit.'[65] 'Since the Gospel does not establish a national religion, a holy war is impossible for Christians.' This revealed a curious ignorance of European history. He wrote with obvious relish than an army of classical pagans would have routed a Christian force any day, and although he was no advocate of wars of conquest, he took it for granted that there was something badly wrong with a society that did not know how to fight.

Rousseau's rejection of Christianity applied equally to any transcendental system of values. Montesquieu had not been much preoccupied with God either, but he never lost sight of certain moral absolutes. For Rousseau nothing took precedence over the interests of the state, and religion had only a subordinate part to play. 'It is very important to the state that each citizen should have a religion that makes him love his duty.' This created an impossible problem for him. Christianity was rejected because of its other-worldliness and international character. Paganism was ideal from a social point of view, but 'founded on error and lies, it deceives men and makes them credulous and superstitious'. There was a limit to what even Rousseau was prepared to borrow from Sparta and he drew the line at importing the Olympian gods.

His well-known solution was 'a purely civil profession of faith, whose articles should be fixed by the sovereign, not specifically as religious dogmas, but as social sentiments, without which one

---

[65] All references to Rousseau's religious views come from *Du contrat social,* IV/8.

cannot be either a good citizen or a faithful subject'. This credo involved belief in the existence of God, in an afterlife of rewards and punishments, in the sanctity of the social contract and of the law. On the negative side, it implied the rejection of sectarian intolerance. As a solution to his problem, it was virtually useless. Since it was designed to be acceptable to all the religious beliefs that stemmed from Judaism, it was no good as the fighting creed of a specific society. Since Christians would be allowed to continue their worship, they would presumably continue to believe that salvation was even more important than *vertu*. The very fact that Rousseau's religion corresponded to the feelings of a great many eighteenth-century Europeans prevented it from serving as a state religion. To achieve *that* purpose he would have had to nationalise God. There was no middle way.

To dissect his ideas in this way is, however, to be blind to the way in which they appeared to his contemporaries. A generation weary of the battles between Jansenists and Jesuits, increasingly uneasy about the persecution of Protestants, whose spiritual needs demanded something more than the mathematical deism of the philosophes, saw Rousseau as the agent of its spiritual redemption. In enchanted prose, he freed it from the trammels of theology and gave a kind of religious sanction to the awakening interest in nature and the belief that feeling held the key to doors that reason could never unlock. For eighteenth-century Frenchmen, as for Milton, Christianity and classical paganism could coexist without too many questions being asked. There were fêtes that already had a good many pagan attributes – to the classically educated, there were no other symbols – even if they culminated in a Te Deum. The people of Dijon celebrated the return from exile of their parlement in 1788 with such a fête in which a young girl, said to represent the *patrie*, and described as a *jeune divinité*, presented the senior judge with a laurel crown. The *société des patriotes* had built a triumphal chariot on which sat more *petites divinités*, representing France, Liberty, Minerva, Religion, Justice, Peace, Abundance, *la Patrie* (France's sister, one hopes), the Muses and the Fine Arts.[66] In this sort of context, Rousseau's civic religion looks more at home.

[66] *Recueil de pièces intéressantes pour servir à l'histoire de la Révolution en France.* n.p., n.d. (John Rylands Library, Manchester), v.IX.

When he dealt with the relations between nation-states, Rousseau's tendency to occupy both horns of a dilemma took on a particular form. His various commentaries on the writings of the abbé de Saint-Pierre were entirely different from all his other political works. Sparta and Rome were not mentioned at all and if he wanted a historical example, he took it from France. His outlook was consistently international and it was precisely in the exclusive pursuit of their own self-interest by sovereign states that he saw the threat to any kind of international order.[67] The man who elsewhere applauded the victories of the Spartans here denounced the horrors of war; the enemy of luxury said that disarmament would allow more to be spent on commerce and the arts, as well as on agriculture.[68] His own prescription for peace – an anticipation of the Holy Alliance of 1814 – was a league of nineteen European states with an international court that would guarantee rulers, not only against foreign attack but also against domestic revolt. In this mood, circumstances triumphed over will: 'If governments have degenerated, it is by the force of time and circumstances, and there is nothing that human wisdom can do about it.'[69] These writings were not the product of a momentary whim; he produced half a dozen different commentaries, over a period of two or three years, and the same attitude pervades them all.

Everything else that he wrote on the subject is equally consistent – in the opposite sense. He was always ready to denounce cosmopolitanism. When he quoted Cicero to the effect that the Latin word for foreigner had once been 'enemy' (*hostis enim apud maiores nostros dicebatur quem nunc peregrinum dicimus*), Rousseau clearly thought that even in republican Rome, things had been better in the good old days.[70] He did oppose wars of conquest, which he thought often a pretext for the introduction of despotism at home. His ideal was a state that did not seek war but lived in a condition of constant preparedness for it and welcomed it when it came. As Montesquieu had seen, this scarcely fitted Rome, but at a pinch it might do for Sparta. Rousseau told the Poles that 'Every citizen should be a soldier as a duty, and none as a profession. That was the military system of

---

[67] *Ecrits sur l'abbé de Saint-Pierre*, p.590.   [68] Ibid. p.583.
[69] Ibid. p.638.   [70] Early draft of *Du contrat social*, p.287.

the Romans.'[71] As always, when Rome and Sparta took over, *la force des choses*, which in this case meant the existence throughout Europe of large, highly trained professional armies, was disregarded; all choices were open and successful national defence was merely a question of will.

At the time, Rousseau's attitude was in sharp contrast to the cosmopolitanism of the rest of the Enlightenment. His persistent criticism of England – perhaps because Montesquieu had presented it as the alternative to the classical twins – conflicted with the prevailing Anglomania. It would nevertheless be rash to detect his influence in every subsequent manifestation of xenophobia; any demonstration of *patriotisme* in the eighteenth-century sense was liable to slip over into jingoism. What Rousseau did do was to provide anyone who disliked foreigners with an easy conscience.

By no feat of even the most tractable imagination can Rousseau's ideas be considered to have anything at all to do with the interests of a supposedly 'rising middle class'. If middle-class people idolised him – as many did – it was not because they were middle class. However one defines that elusive will o' the wisp, Rousseau had nothing to offer it, except perhaps a feeling of guilt. He regarded industry and commerce as parasitic and corrupting. Bordeaux merchants were scarcely likely to warm to the proposition that shipwrecks were *vrais avantages*.[72] He was equally hostile to the agrarian capitalism of the physiocrats. Where Montesquieu, after some hesitation, had rejected antiquity in favour of the modern world, Rousseau remained wedded to a literal re-creation of Sparta. If he could not have that, his second best was the patriarchal world of the Wolmars, in the *Nouvelle Héloïse*, based on a primitive self-sufficient economy and strict social subordination, with enlightened nobles protecting an innocent but gullible peasantry from the temptations of change. There *were* writers in eighteenth-century France whose ideas might be considered relevant to a future capitalist society – Turgot, for example and, up to a point, Necker – but they had nothing in common with Rousseau and they were soon to be discarded by the revolutionaries.

Rousseau was talking about Jerusalem – even if he called it

[71] *Pologne*, p.1014.
[72] *Fragments politiques*, p.525.

Sparta. His intentions were moral, and politics was merely the vehicle for social regeneration. Even though his specific kind of utopia had little to commend it to anyone, he was to become the spokesman for a new kind of radicalism. His message: that man is *not* the prisoner of his environment, that 'the limits of the possible, in moral matters, are less restrictive than we think', is a healthy corrective to the justification of the status quo in the name of necessity. His rejection of technology and his demand for a closed society where the remodelling of all by the enlightened can proceed unhindered by pressures from an unregenerate world, has never ceased to commend itself to some people. His belief that men were made free by being given, not what they wanted, but what they would eventually come to recognise that they ought to have wanted, was the necessary justification for a minority to act in the name of the general will. Like Montesquieu, he was the first to formulate a political philosophy that, for better or worse – in his case mainly for worse – has survived to the present day.

PART 2

The Writers

Chapter 3

Montesquieu, Rousseau and the Revolutionary Generation

Montesquieu won over his readers by his arguments; Rousseau swept them off their feet by the power of his exhortation and the excitement of his prose. Tastes have changed and we no longer respond to sensibility as they did in the eighteenth century. Rousseau himself admitted that he had rather overdone things in the first two books of the *Nouvelle Héloïse*. Even so, one can only feel sorry for the modern reader who is totally insensible to the spell of Jean-Jacques. This is naturally more pronounced in books like *Emile*, the *Confessions* and, above all, in the *Nouvelle Héloïse* – the works by which everyone knew him – than in his political writings. In this respect as in others, he was unlucky in his disciples. During the generation after his death, *sensibilité* became the excuse for every kind of hyperbole, windy bombast, emotional gush and exhibitionist beating of the breast. If the linguistic hyper-inflation probably owed something to his influence, it also reinforced it, and Montesquieu's quiet reasonableness came to seem increasingly out of place in the land of superlatives.

As Burke realised, Rousseau was either a moralist or he was nothing. He led the revolt against a fashionable tendency to see the upright man as no more than the winner in a genetic lottery. He reasserted the claims of nature and conscience against the anodyne of determinism and the exquisite formalism of polite society. His writing coincided with a mood and fulfilled a need. As Chamfort said, 'True feelings are so rare that I sometimes stop in the street to watch a dog gnaw a bone'. Amateurs of *sentiments vrais* could find plenty to excite them in the works of the man they liked to call 'Jean-Jacques'. He did not persuade people so much as convert them: not to his rather peculiar political ideas, but to his intense emotional deism and his view of man as a responsible moral agent, entangled in the heartless conventions of an artificial society.

The example of Madame Roland, who was to become the Egeria of the Girondins during the Revolution, illustrates very well how Rousseau struck the young with the force of revelation. She was well-prepared for his message before she read him, unless, when she was writing her memoirs, she adjusted her account of her life before her conversion. Describing a visit to Versailles as a young girl, she said, 'I sighed for Athens, where I could also have admired the works of art, without being deadened by the spectacle of despotism; in my imagination I was in Greece, watching the Olympic Games, and I was irritated to find myself French.'[1] Of course, she chose the wrong city-state, and Rousseau would have been uneasy about the works of art, but she was on the right lines. A formidable blue-stocking, while still in her teens her reading of the philosophes had destroyed her religious faith and left an emotional vacuum in its place. Eventually she came to Rousseau. 'I read him very late, which was just as well, for he would have driven me mad and I should have wanted to read no one else.'[2] Soon after her mother's death, at the age of 21, she encountered the *Nouvelle Héloïse*. '[Rousseau] seemed to be just the nourishment I needed, the interpreter of feelings that I had experienced but that only he could put into words.' Describing his works, she wrote to a friend, 'I feel that I owe to them all that is best in me. His genius has warmed and ennobled my heart.'[3] If his devotees usually expressed their debt to him in language that the present generation is likely to find embarrassing, the fault may not be altogether theirs.

What made people feel that Rousseau had transformed their lives was not his speculation about the nature of the general will. Free-will was much more to the point. The first principle of the *vicaire savoyard* was 'To find the first cause, we must always go back to some will ... there is no real action without will', and his third, 'The principle of all action rests in the will of a free being; one cannot get any further back. It is not freedom that is a

[1] *Mémoires* (ed. M.P. Faugère) Paris, 1864. 2v. II/100.
[2] Ibid. II/135.
[3] Ibid. II/176.

meaningless word, but necessity. Man is therefore free to act and as a free being he is animated by something spiritual.'[4] Man was 'born free', both politically and morally. If he was 'everywhere in chains', rivetted on him by rulers or by his own false values, he had the power to cast them off. Freedom implied conscience and conscience meant emotional communion with a Supreme Being who was not specifically Christian but who seemed nearer and more accessible than the logical First Cause of the rationalists. Rousseau, like a good many evangelists, invited his readers to become new people. He was more successful in converting them to his form of deism than in turning them into Spartans.

Where politics was concerned, the ideas of Rousseau and Montesquieu were basically antithetical because of their conflicting concepts of freedom. For Montesquieu, freedom was in the first place freedom from ... It implied the recognition of the right of the individual to order his life in accordance with the rules of the different circles to which he belonged by necessity or choice: family, religion and state. It meant that governments respected the autonomy of these circles and ruled in accordance with an *esprit général* that was the spontaneous expression of what people actually wanted. In this sense, civil liberty was theoretically compatible with absolute government, if the ruler was wise, but it was most effectively secured when associated with political liberty. The latter consisted of the division of power and the representation in government of the main sections of society and their necessarily divergent attitudes and interests. For Rousseau, political freedom meant freedom from political sin. It was a matter, not merely of liberating citizens from external constraints, but of enabling them to fulfil their own highest aspirations (which were identified with the well-being of the community) by liberating them from the ignorance and evil within themselves. Since everything was judged from the perspective of the communal interest, a free people should ideally be a unanimous one. All intermediate bodies – so dear to Montesquieu – that might interpose their collective wills between the individual and the state, must be abolished. To devise the machinery for the manifestation of the general will, and the institutions that would gradually lead the citizens to

[4] *Emile* (Garnier edition) Paris, 1964. pp.330, 340.

make it their own, required a legislator whose object was to 'denature' man and to transform the way of life of the society over which he presided.

The irreconcilability of the two theories did not stop virtually all the political writers of the 1780s from borrowing from both at once. The implications of Rousseau's theory of the general will were not fully understood and it was generally assumed to mean little more than that governments should be responsible to public opinion. Taken in that sense, Montesquieu would have been the first to agree. In fact, he had already agreed. On the issue of free-will and determinism, although the two men differed substantially, it was all a question of emphasis. Montesquieu never suggested that men could do no more than try to find out what was bound to happen anyway, and Rousseau did not actually believe that, given sufficient *vertu* on the part of the local population, Barnsley could defy the universe. Montesquieu's belief in certain transcendental moral values to which all societies should aspire kept his awareness of environmental pressures within bounds. So did his belief that most of the pressures were social rather than purely physical. Rousseau maintained that, although the general will must always be sovereign, the nature of the actual government should be relative to local circumstances.

Both writers thought that the objectives of political action were ultimately moral. Although Montesquieu appeared to be urging governments to leave their peoples to their own devices – which would be likely to include quite a few vices *tout court* – he did in fact impose on them the obligation to pursue freedom and justice. The moral basis of Rousseau's system was more obvious but more suspect, in the sense that it could never transcend the self-interest of the nation-state. With this rather important reservation, he was even more concerned than Montesquieu with regeneration – which was to become one of the most abused words of 1789. Both were concerned, in their very different ways, to succour the poor, and the full extent of Rousseau's 'Spartan' economics was revealed mainly in works that very few had read. In a rough and ready sort of way, a general disapproval of 'luxury' and a vague egalitarianism did not seem incompatible with the development of the economy.

Such niceties, however, miss the main point. In the 1780s,

although French absolutism was breaking down, Louis XVI was still 'By the Grace of God, King of France and of Navarre'. He had been anointed at his coronation, as God's lieutenant and charged with the extirpation of heresy. Practice had already moved some way from theory and those who wanted to oppose the king were rarely inhibited from doing so, even if they pretended to be only concerned with his wicked Ministers. Nevertheless they needed theorists to repudiate Divine Right, to legitimise resistance to royal authority and, on occasion, to clothe self-interest in the becoming robes of universal principle. Montesquieu and Rousseau were almost the only men they had got, the only major philosophes to have devoted much of their attention to specifically political issues. Both had written about a 'general will' and challenged the traditional assumptions about the legitimacy of royal authority. In their different ways, each had argued that government was no private matter but was only entitled to claim obedience when it pursued national ends and fulfilled national needs. Montesquieu could be quoted either as the defender of an allegedly 'traditional' constitution or as the advocate of a new kind of representative constitutional monarchy. Rousseau had said that any government was merely the agent of the general will. As writers plucked up their courage to challenge the existing political order – and courage was still required – they needed authorities to invoke, and two were better than one. When everything was still to be won, there was no great difficulty about inscribing both names on the banner of reform, the one as the herald of national regeneration, the other as the expert on constitutions. The parting of the ways would come later.

This raises the problem of how one is to distinguish the influence of each upon writers – often not very good ones – whose works consisted of a rather muddy mixture of the two. One can, of course, look for specific references and borrowings, but this does not get us very far. The language itself is an unreliable guide since a kind of debased Rousseauism had become common currency and the ideas of Montesquieu were sometimes served up in the kind of booming hyperbole that would have made their author wince. A general respect for Greece and republican Rome is equally inconclusive. A classically educated generation knew more of either than of French history and took its analogies and its inspiration where it found them. Montesquieu himself had done the same and enthused over the vanished glories as enthusiastically as the next man. More revealing was the attitude to England, as the symbol of 'realistic' politics, based on a balance of interests, in contrast to the idealisation of the classical world. More generally, the choice between cosmopolitanism and an assertion of the superiority of a regenerated France was a fairly reliable indicator, although mainly from 1789 onwards, since the main object of pre-revolutionary writing was to stress how bad things were. To a surprising extent, the publicists of the 1780s had seized on the issue of will and circumstance, although this may exaggerate the apparent influence of Rousseau, since the argument from circumstance could be seen as merely a justification for the status quo.

The second part of this book will examine in some detail the influence of Montesquieu and Rousseau on a few particular writers, who went on to play an active part in the Revolution. These were not isolated and untypical men, remarkable mainly for their singularity, but the spokesmen for their generation. No one who has even glanced at the enormous mass of pamphlet literature produced in 1788 in support of the parlements' challenge to the Crown, can fail to be impressed by the use the lawyers made of Montesquieu.[5] *De l'esprit des lois* was quoted all the time. Much of the rhetoric was traditional stuff and the objectives backward-looking, but one catches occasional signs of Rousseau's influence, and there are one or two references to *Du contrat social*. 'Can a king coexist with good government? Yes, but if they had more *vertu* men would have no need for one ... The state of monarchy is only useful for corrupted nations.' Of course, that could take us back to our old friends the Troglodytes, rather than to Rousseau. Another pamphlet is less equivocal. 'The source of all political power resides in the nation ... The power of the prince is therefore only secondary and derivative since its moral force comes from the general will.'

---

[5] *Recueil de pièces intéressantes pour servir à l'histoire de la Révolution en France*. 18v. in the John Rylands Library in Manchester, contains hundreds of these and there are many more in the British Library. (The 'revolution' in question was the judicial coup d'état of 8 May 1788).

What is most striking is the eclecticism of so many of the writers. 'Man is born free, laws are acts of the general will, government is an agent of the general will and not a party to the social contract' – this clearly reflects the influence of Rousseau, but its author promptly goes back to the Germanic tribes to justify the claim of the French to be a free nation. 'O holy entity! Ray of the divinity itself. You whom the beneficient hand of the Supreme Being engraved in indelible characters on the heart of man ... ' certainly suggests a devotee of Jean-Jacques, but comes from a conservative. The noble officer from the French Guards who wrote that *'We are all born citizens*, we are all *enfants de la patrie* before being subjects of the king ... *the king is only the first subject of his kingdom*' quoted two authorities: Montesquieu and Locke! It is very rare to find any awareness that Montesquieu and Rousseau might have been saying different things, but there is one case, from Dauphiné (where the political debate had attained an unusual degree of refinement) of a man rejecting the argument that the law derived from the general will and all legislative power belonged to the nation alone, on the ground that there was no historical precedent for this, either in England or France. What all shared was a common vocabulary. The subjects of the kingdom had been replaced by the citizens of the nation. Those of whom the writers approved were the *enfants de la patrie* and their opponents agents of 'ministerial despotism'. This was a victory for Rousseau, in the sense that it was republican language, even when it served as the vehicle for moderate ideas.

If one turns to the actual elections to the Estates General in the spring of 1789, the language was much the same. The nobility of Artois claimed to be ready for 'the greatest sacrifices, in order to regenerate the *patrie* in the face of an astonished universe ... We shall see the freest of nations, freely deliberating about the clauses of its political association, removing from its social contract the errors, vices and abuses that centuries of ignorance, superstition and seduction have almost reduced to principles.'[6] 'Thirty years ago, people did not have such clear ideas of the rights of man, considered both as man and as citizen ... Are we Frenchmen? ... What is the use of being noble if we are

[6] Archives Nationales, C12.

no longer citizens?'[7] What this splendid stuff meant in practice was that most of the nobles of the province were excluded from the meetings of the provincial Estates and were proclaiming the equality, not of man, but of members of the nobility. When they won control of the meeting that then chose the deputies who were to go to Versailles, they devoted fourteen articles of their *cahier*, or list of grievances, to the defence of the exclusive privileges of the nobility.

Ideas borrowed from Montesquieu or Rousseau could be pressed into the service of many causes. In the same sort of way, men's political attitudes in the 1780s gave little indication of how they were to behave during the Revolution. Robespierre wrote an essay on the law of bastardy, intending to submit it for the prize offered by the Academy of Metz in 1786. The gold medal was actually awarded to a rather more radical essay, written by a military engineer who subsequently fought against the revolutionaries and was killed in 1807, defending Dantzig against Napoleon. Carra, who worked in the royal library before the Revolution and was to become a Girondin, published an extraordinarily violent *Système de la raison* in 1782, all about the overthrow of tyrants ('scourges of the human race') and priests ('fearful spectres defiled with blood and armed with daggers'), the advent of 'distributive equity' and foretelling 'more serene days, virtues more constant, more energetic and more just' that would unite 'the great family of man'. He expressed his somewhat condescending approval of Rousseau and included a long quotation from *Du contrat social* in support of popular sovereignty.[8] This did not prevent him from arguing that everything in the universe was 'subject to the laws of necessity', that liberty was relative and that it consisted in the right to do anything that did not infringe the liberty of others.[9]

Billaud-Varenne, who was one of the members of the Committee of Public Safety when Carra was executed, and saw himself as an ideologist of the Terror, on a par with Robespierre, published three works in 1789. He too professed his admiration for the 'fine thoughts of Rousseau, who describes so well the power of the Supreme Being'.[10] His *Despotisme des ministres de*

[7] Archives Nationales, B$_a$15.
[8] *Système de la raison*. London, 1782. pp.29, 177-9.   [9] Ibid. pp.20, 179.
[10] *Le dernier coup porté aux préjugés et à la superstition*, London, 1789, pp.348-9.

France contained some very Rousseauist patriotic sentiments. 'Superior, by our knowledge, our industry and our force, to every nation in the universe, when we could be *second Romans, betrayed by our generals, strangled by our ministers*, every day we risk being subjugated to foreign domination or becoming wholly *enslaved to our own*.'[11] The object of his three-volume work, however, was to support the campaign of the parlements to 'restore once more to France its ancient constitution'. He quoted 'the famous Montesquieu' when arguing the need for diversity within France's different provinces, admired England and insisted that only minor changes were needed in his own country. 'Great agitation within a state should always be avoided as much as possible.'[12] In another book attacking the Church, he wrote, 'however attractive the revolution that people would like to be able to prepare might seem to be, we should renounce it for ever if it could be effected only by constraint ... Consciences should be subdued only by persuasive means.'[13] The revolutionaries were to be rather fond of turning each other's past opinions into offensive weapons. It was a dangerous game since, like politicians in every age, most of them lived in glass houses.

It is clear from this brief but quite wide-ranging sample that Frenchmen in the 1780s turned above all to Montesquieu and Rousseau when they were looking for distinguished names with which to belabour their government. Their understanding of the texts they cited, and especially their grasp of the problems that Rousseau posed, may often have left something to be desired, but they generally knew enough to associate a particular point of view with its appropriate author – even if this did not deter them from combining the two in rather odd ways. It would therefore be fruitless to try to establish any close connection between a man's ideological preferences during this period and his political behaviour during the Revolution. Options changed with bewildering speed and one's initial choice might be largely a matter of chance. Mistakes could sometimes be discreetly rectified without anyone noticing, but there were other times when they helped to create a self-perpetuating division between men who had previously regarded themselves as enlisted in a

---

[11] *Despotisme des ministres de France*, Amsterdam, 1789. 3v. II/209.
[12] Ibid. III/223, I/93, III/243.
[13] *Le dernier coup porté aux préjugés* ... p.363.

common cause. I have been able to distinguish no criteria of age, temperament or class that would impose any sort of pattern on the whole chaotic business.

Chapter 4

Mercier

Sebastian Mercier was the oldest of the revolutionaries to appear in this book. He was also the only one of them to come from Paris, where he was born in 1740, the son of a swordsmith of some means.[1] After a good education at the Collège des Quatre Nations, he taught for a year or two in Bordeaux and was back in Paris by 1765 where he tried, with a pertinacity that made up for his lack of outstanding talent, to win a reputation as a man of letters. Looking back on his earlier years, when he was already 41, he said that he was swept off his feet by Rousseau's writings but eventually came to reject them in the name of common sense and more conventional values. 'At eighteen when I was full of strength, health and courage, I developed a great taste for the system of Jean-Jacques Rousseau ... But when this impetuous temperamental phase was over, when, at 27, I had become familiar with sickness, with men, and above all with books, I experienced various kinds of ideas, pleasures and pains. When I had learned to know privations and joys, with a less active imagination that had been enriched and softened by the arts, I was less delighted with Rousseau's system and I realised that it was more convenient to buy my bread with a small coin than to hunt over hundreds of leagues in order to catch game.'[2] There is a hint of regret behind the irony; something had faded into the light of common day, since Mercier's latter-day wisdom was in part the product of a weakened imagination and resignation to the world as it was.

It seems to have been the *Nouvelle Héloïse* that first fired his enthusiasm. 'Suddenly it caught my attention; I became

[1] For a good account of Mercier's life up to 1789, see L. Béclard, *Sebastien Mercier, sa vie, son oeuvre, son temps*, Paris, 1903.

[2] *Tableau de Paris*, 1782 ed., Amsterdam, I/27.

animated, heated, on fire ... I read the book straight through and when I discovered that there were six volumes, my heart throbbed with pleasure and joy.'[3] Appropriately enough, the first of his works to have survived seems to have been a 'lost letter from Julie', which he wrote when he was 24, although he did not publish it until much later.[4] People who describe their spiritual pilgrimages are not always the best guides and Rousseau was less easily discarded than Mercier believed. Up to a point, however, what he wrote during his twenties did evolve along the lines that he suggested.

He opened his assault on the world of letters with a salvo of essays submitted for the essay prizes awarded by the Academy, none of which had any success. His choice of subject was dictated for him and he began with eulogies of Descartes and Charles V. *Des malheurs de la guerre et des avantages de la paix*, the topic chosen for 1766, gave him rather more scope. Mercier's essay was conventional enough, with its invocation of the abbé de Saint-Pierre, its appeal to Christian morality ('Kings of the earth ... remember that, as the earthly representatives of God, you must rule, like him, through justice and mercy'), and its implausible tribute to Louis XV: 'I can praise my king without flattery; sparing of human blood, he knows its price; embellished with the light of humanity, his crown inspires a mixture of veneration and love.' There were hints, however, of sterner stuff. 'What could persuade men who were born free to give themselves masters?' Heads of state were not arbitrary masters but defenders of the liberty and property of their peoples. His pessimistic view of the degeneracy of his own times echoed Rousseau. 'The citizen no longer defends his walls; he has become a kind of slave bound to the soil, which is sold, surrendered or retained without anyone consulting him. Thrones and towns are bartered for money, states have their price and gold, which has corrupted everything, more powerful than saltpetre, gives the world its rulers.'[5] Unlike Rousseau, he had not much use for Rome. 'Do not speak to me of that conquering people, bellicose on principle, which is said to have possessed all

---

[3] *Mon bonnet de nuit*, Neuchâtel, 1784-5, IV/212, 227.
[4] In vol.I of *Mon bonnet de nuit*, in 1784.
[5] *Des malheurs de la guerre*, n.p. 1767, p.26.

the heroic qualities and never knew human virtues.'[6] This was not an opinion dictated to him by his subject, but remained his fixed conviction. Mercier proclaimed himself a cosmopolitan: 'Of all forms of patriotism, the most noble, the most just, the most true, is love of humanity.' The sentiments were worthy enough, but one can understand why the jury remained unimpressed.

When he published this unsuccessful effort in 1767, he had already brought out an essay on a subject dear to his heart, *Le Bonheur des gens de lettres*, in the previous year. Despite its naïve optimism, this expressed views that he was to hold until the Revolution. He declared himself to be living in a 'philosophical century, when it was merit that made a man, when talent was distinguished from power, when rank was accorded formal respect but true veneration was reserved for genius'. For Mercier, the rôle of the philosophes was primarily political. They had already put an end to religious fanaticism and when they raised their voice, 'kings, wars and tyrants will disappear'. Some of the things he wrote were surprisingly blunt for 1766. 'Let us not be surprised if genius is the particular friend of liberty and abhors despotism ... that is why it prospered under the clear Greek skies and fled from those states where one man is all.'[7] A disarming footnote explained that he was thinking of Orientals, but he was still taking a risk. What distinguished the philosophe was depth of feeling rather than of thought; ordinary people 'exist without being moved'. For him, as for Rousseau, Nature was the guide, 'whose sacred hand engraved on men's hearts the primitive sense of justice' and it was a source of moral sentiments rather than a demonstration of order. Men's crimes were due, not to their nature, but to government, to tyranny, 'which forces them to be evil by making them unhappy'. Not having Rousseau's unique literary qualities, Mercier's more emotional passages already showed the kind of strident hyperbole that was to become so wearisome during the Revolution. 'It is impossible for the virtuous man to keep silent when the plaintive cries of the victims of oppression ring in his ears and strike his feeling heart, while the laws of eternal Justice are violated to satisfy a few avid monsters, while a whole people

---

[6] Ibid. p.23.
[7] *Le bonheur des gens de lettres*, London, 1766, p.14.

lives in tears and has even forfeited its pathetic right to raise a sigh.' A list of modern writers of whom he approved included both Montesquieu and Rousseau, but Voltaire was conspicuously absent.

Mercier never bothered overmuch about consistency and in the same year he published a Voltairean conte, *Izerben,* in which he praised both Voltaire and Rousseau. He claimed, much later, that Rousseau was so pleased with this tribute that he made a copy of it. The year 1767 also brought *L'Homme sauvage,* an account of the education of a young savage, which was presumably inspired by Voltaire's *Ingénu,* and developed into a defence of civilised values. In *Les Songes philosophiques* in 1768, Voltaire had become his favourite author. This is more or less consistent with his own account of his recovery from Rousseauitis. Temperamentally, however, he remained much closer to the passionate *homme sensible* from Geneva than to the great rationaliser. In 1768 he published a few *Contes moraux* of the most cloying sentimentality. To quote the conclusion of one of them: 'They all lived happily on account of their virtue and their virtue was for each of them the source of their happiness.' One has to remember, of course, that he was writing for his living and had to think of his market. Incredible as it may seem today, the *Contes moraux* brought him a modest reputation and they may have reflected nothing more reprehensible than a determination to mine the profitable vein of sensibility, on the part of a facile and prolific writer.

In 1770 Mercier met Rousseau and also published his first major work, *L'An 2440.* If we can accept his own account, written much later, the meeting did not exactly bowl him over. 'When I found myself face to face with the author of *Emile,* I saw that the famous writer was mentally ill ... Jean-Jacques Rousseau was the victim, in his private life, of a mania that was all the more impossible to cure since his outward appearance was always tranquil and calm.'[8] Even in 1791, when Rousseau had become the patron saint of Mercier and of the Revolution, he still insisted that towards the end of his life (i.e. when Mercier got to know him) Jean-Jacques had become paranoid. Although Mercier claims to have spent a good deal of time with him, he

---

[8] *Tableau de Paris,* Amsterdam/Paris, 1779-89. 12v. VIII/131-2.

nowhere suggests that he found the experience particularly inspiring. This, together with the fact that *L'An 2440* had been on the stocks since 1768, suggests that its many similarities to Rousseau's ways of thinking owed more to literary influences than to personal contact.

The new book was a utopia, a dream of Paris as it was to become, 600 years after Mercier's birth. In actual fact, he did not have to wait so long. To a quite remarkable extent, the book anticipated the kind of society that the more radical revolutionaries were to try to create in 1793-4 although, for Mercier, the dream had become a nightmare and he himself was to spend much of that time in gaol. The book opens with an invocation of the year 2440 when 'the names of the friends and defenders of humanity will shine out in pure and radiant glory, but the vile populace of kings who tormented the human race will be dead and forgotten'. If this seemed to echo Mercier's earlier views about the political rôle of *gens de lettres*, he had become much more pessimistic about his own times. 'The spirit of my century surrounds me and presses down upon me; stupor reigns and the calm of my *patrie* is that of the tomb. Around me I see only painted corpses who walk and talk without ever having given birth to the least spark of life. Already the voice of Philosophy itself, weary and discouraged, has lost its power. It cries out amongst men as though in the depth of the wilderness.'[9] He kept up the same lamentation in his preface. An old Englishman had told him that Paris was the centre of extremes of wealth and poverty and of an eternal war between the two. Rousseau was right: man was corrupted by society and a tolerable life was only possible in some country retreat. In fact, Mercier remained as optimistic as ever, but he had transferred his hopes to the distant future.

His book took the form of a description of the glories of Paris in 2440, punctuated by numerous footnotes in which he pointed the moral and commented on his own times. One is immediately struck by the fact that the changes of which he dreamed were all moral and political rather than technological. With the apparent exception of the swivel chair, there had been no inventions. The 'discoveries' of the intervening 600 years were *all* the products of

---

[9] *L'an 2440*, London, 1772,p.v.

a successful search for the lost secrets of antiquity, such as the composition of Tyrian purple. Mercier was quite indifferent to the economic basis of his utopian society and seemed to take it for granted that people would be earning their livings in much the same way as they had done in his own days. This implied that the creation of his utopia depended only on an effort of human will and not on the gradual development of resources that were not available to his contemporaries. The whole work was backward-looking. Although Mercier's regenerated Paris was a long way from Rousseau's dream of Sparta, the inspiration for change came from the past, both French and classical. In essence, it was a matter of returning to a more 'natural' society, which implied one based more on feeling than on knowledge.

France still had a king – one rather suggestive of Louis-Philippe, a citizen-ruler who went everywhere on foot and lived in Paris, since Versailles was in ruins. The Bastille, incidentally, had been demolished. The principle of the government was republican: princes and dukes survived, but honour was attached only to personal merit. In an endearing flight of imagination, Mercier had the king reward deserving citizens by authorising them to wear hats with their names on – a very nineteenth-century conception of armorial bearings. Although dukes remained, the aristocracy had gone: 'that class of men who, under the name of nobility (which, to carry ridicule to extremes, they could purchase), rushed to crawl around the throne, wanted to live only as soldiers or courtiers, spent its time in idleness and glutted its pride on old parchments, presenting the deplorable spectacle of vanity equalled only by its wretchedness.'[10] The king reigned rather than ruled. Executive power was in the hands of a senate, which was responsible to him, but both monarch and senate were in turn responsible to a legislative assembly, elected every two years. This corresponded roughly to the democrats' interpretation of the constitution of 1791.

When he described how this happy state of affairs was brought into being, Mercier made the best of both worlds. There had been some sort of a revolution. A man of 2440 told him, 'It only needed a powerful voice to rouse the multitude from its torpid

---

[10] Ibid. p.311.

sleep! If oppression thundered over your heads [i.e. in 1770] all
that you had to blame was your own weakness. Liberty and
happiness belong to those who dare to seize them. All is
revolution in this world.'[11] To this Mercier added some vigorous
exhortation for the benefit of his contemporaries. 'In certain
states a period becomes necessary, terrible, bloody, but the
signal of liberty. I am talking about civil war.' 'Man! Choose to
be either happy or wretched, if you are still capable of choice.
Fear tyranny, hate slavery; arm yourself; die or live free.'[12] Some
of his many readers may have remembered that in later years.
On the other hand, the revolution in France had taken place
'without effort, as a result of the heroism of a great man. A
philosopher-king, worthy of the throne, since he disdained it ...
offered to restore to the Estates their ancient prerogatives.'
People may have remembered that too.

Although the government had none of the pomp of the
eighteenth-century monarchy, as the voice of public opinion, it
was more absolute than the Bourbons had ever aspired to be. As
with Rousseau, *on ne badinait pas avec la république.* ' "One
must respect popular prejudices." That is the language of the
narrow-minded and weak-willed, for whom a law has only to
exist for it to seem sacred. The virtuous man, who is the only one
with the right to love and hate, knows no such criminal
moderation. He takes upon himself the rôle of public prosecutor,
his rights are founded on his own genius, and the justice of his
cause on the gratitude of posterity.'[13] Robespierre was eventually
to come to pretty much the same conclusions. So, although there
was no censorship in 2440, authors of books that public opinion
regarded as morally corrupting were made to wear masks. All
theatres were state-controlled and used as 'a public school of
morals and taste'. During Mercier's visit, they were showing
improving plays about Calas, Henry IV and Cromwell (he was
one of the very few Frenchmen to regard Cromwell as a patriot
rather than a military usurper). Men of letters had naturally
come into their own as a new elite, but the productions of their
predecessors got short shrift. Most books had been burned and

[11] Ibid. p.300.
[12] Ibid. pp.300n_a, 301n_b.
[13] Ibid. p.297n_a.

most of the remainder preserved only in digests: there were moments when 2440 looked rather like 1984, but Mercier, unlike Orwell, thought it was all for the best. Despite the fact that Voltaire's works enshrined 'the first, the most noble and the greatest of virtues: love of humanity', most of his books had gone, perhaps because he had attacked Rousseau, whose writings were preserved *in toto*. Mercier singled out for special praise *Emile*, the *Nouvelle Héloïse* and the *Lettres écrites de la montagne*; he did not mention *Du contrat social*. *De l'esprit des lois* was also among the chosen few – perhaps a sign of Mercier's growing interest in Montesquieu. Since he thought that history was only a chronicle of facts, it was confined to a few chronologies, whose significance it was left to the painters to illustrate.

All the arts were harnessed to the service of morality. 'Just as they were dangerous in my time, because they favoured luxury, display, cupidity and debauchery, so they had now become useful since they were employed only to inspire lessons of virtue.' Every picture told an appropriate story and was 'the equivalent of a moral and instructive book'. The men of 2440, like their predecessors of the year II, were great ones for allegory and Mercier especially commended a royal throne surrounded by representations of force, temperance, justice and clemency.

In this astringent world, as in those of Rousseau and the Jacobins, women were put in their place, which was the home. 'They concerned themselves only with the functions assigned to them by their Creator: those of bearing children and consoling those around them for the troubles of life.' Dowries had been abolished, 'in order that nothing should remove them from that legitimate rule that is always less terrible than the yoke they impose upon themselves by their fatal freedom'. Divorce was permitted – as another means of making women more attentive and submissive to their husbands.[14] Even Rousseau, who might have agreed with much of this, would have used less punitive language.

Religion was a matter of private feeling rather than of theology and public worship. 'We speak of the Supreme Being only to adore him in silence ... It is the soul that feels God, it needs no

---

[14] Ibid. pp. 23, 328-9, 333n$_a$.

outside help to soar to his presence ... The man of feeling is moved by the spectacle of nature and has no difficulty in recognising a beneficent God who reserves for him other blessings' [i.e. in an after-life]. There were priests, but no theology; civil, but not religious festivals; pure morals, but no extravagant dogma. 'Proselytising atheists were banished, although only after they had failed to respond to a compulsory course of experimental physics. In one of his footnotes, Mercier explained that 'Morality is the only religion man needs; he becomes religious as soon as he becomes reasonable. He is virtuous as soon as he makes himself useful.'

As with Rousseau, morality was grounded on sentiment rather than on reason. 'We work out the finest theories in the world; we calculate, we write, we intoxicate ourselves with our political ideas – and we have never made so many blunders. There can be no doubt that feelings would guide us with a surer light. We have become sceptical barbarians, pretending to hold balances in our hands. Let us become men again. It is the heart not the intelligence that produces great and generous works.'[15] Logically enough, therefore, education was designed to cultivate virtue rather than to develop talent. Formal teaching was deliberately neglected and education, *toute en sentiments*, was adjusted to what each individual would need to fulfil the social rôle that awaited him.

In such a static society the function of the economy was to reconcile people to their lot rather than to improve it. Although Mercier shared the general belief in free trade and outlawed guilds in his utopia, he saw economic policy in terms of people rather than of commodities. He therefore advocated price controls, public granaries as a protection against bad harvests, and a ban on the export of food, under the impression that these measures would guarantee a plentiful supply of bread to the labouring poor; those who refused to work would be deported. Like Rousseau, he disliked the idea of foreign trade and even banned the importation of tea, coffee and tobacco, on the familiar ground that trade encouraged luxury, that luxury was the cause, rather than the consequence of inequality, and that the wealth of some automatically impoverished others.

[15] Ibid. p.153n$_a$.

On the whole it was a fairly consistent performance. To suggest that it was roughly in line with what his contemporaries believed Rousseau to be advocating is not to imply that Mercier systematically, or even consciously, took his ideas from Jean-Jacques. He did not hesitate to disagree with him on occasion, still detested Rome and had a soft spot for the English, 'still the first people in Europe' in 2440. What matters is that the two men shared a great many assumptions about the nature of the good society, that Mercier acknowledged his general debt to Rousseau ('I admit that I am not worth more than Rousseau; would to God I were worth as much') and that through his book – which had a wide readership – a Rousseauist point of view was gaining wider currency.

It would not have been like Mercier to keep up the consistency to the end. When he had almost finished he introduced out of the blue an extravagant eulogy of Catherine II of Russia who had broken the fetters of the Russian farmers, liberated the Poles (Rousseau would not have liked *that*) and given back to the peasant his property and his goods, whatever that meant. Perhaps he was hoping for a pension, or at least an invitation to St. Petersburg. This should at least serve as a reminder to us that eighteenth-century social critics were often very much less radical than they sounded; their hyperbole concealed a readiness to settle for a good deal less than they had seemed to be demanding.

The next decade was relatively unproductive. In 1773 Mercier published an essay on the theatre, in which he showed himself to be a passionate admirer of Shakespeare and a severe critic of the French classical tradition. This lost him much of the popularity that he had won with *L'An 2440*. Sensibility was all very well, but sacred cows remained sacred cows. Six years later he began publishing a somewhat ambitious *Histoire des hommes ou histoire nouvelle de tous les peuples du monde*, which eventually ran to six volumes. A somewhat cursory inspection of this dreary work suggests that it confirms the view of history that he had expressed in *L'An 2440*. In 1779 he found a much more appropriate vehicle for his real, if limited talents, and reconquered his public with his *Tableau de Paris*, of which he completed twelve volumes by 1789. This might be described as 'philosophical' journalism, a collection of short sketches of

Parisian sights, customs and institutions, with such comments as they happened to prompt in him. It was a genre that suited his observant but discursive pen, always better at the vignette than at the construction of a disciplined argument. The mood of the first two volumes reflected the pessimism of *L'An 2440*. 'The people are soft, pale, diminutive, wizened; at the first glance one can see that these are no republicans.' 'The Parisians seemed to have realised instinctively that it was not worth sustained effort and thought to win a small amount of liberty.' 'If a Spartan were to return to earth, what would he think when he saw a *Parisiensis*, all pale, clutching with his trembling hand the lottery ticket that sends him off to the war?' In such a world, the best thing was not to be too ambitious. 'It is bad politics, instead of sticking to the present day, to throw one's self into a time that does not yet exist, since even the greatest genius cannot foretell the future ... Palliatives are the only cures for a state infected with ancient vices and in no condition to undertake a total cure.'[16] By now, *De l'esprit des lois* had joined *Emile* in his list of chef d'oeuvres.

When the *Tableau de Paris* first appeared, Mercier thought it wise to withdraw to Neuchâtel, presumably because of the unkind things he had said about lawyers, since his political comments were comparatively tame when compared with what he had already published. He claimed that he spent some time reading Rousseau's early contributions to various Swiss newspapers.[17] Memories of Rousseau, who had lived near Neuchâtel for three years, must have been all about him. In 1784, a year before he returned to Paris, he published the first two volumes of *Mon bonnet de nuit*, an extraordinary collection of bits and pieces he claimed to have written each night before going to bed. It certainly reads like it. His first subjects were: the ocean, the last judgment, fire, sleep, the economy, Horace, conscience, a hymn to spring, whales and sailors. This was carrying discursiveness a little far. Essays of this kind allowed him to indulge his inclination to take both the cake and the halfpenny: to berate his contemporaries for not even trying to climb summits that ought to have been within their reach, and

[16] *Tableau de Paris*, 1782 ed., Amsterdam, pp.I/55, I/72-3, II/17, II/68-70.
[17] *De Jean-Jacques Rousseau, considéré comme l'un des premiers auteurs de la Révolution*, Paris, 1791, I/236.

at the same time to preach worldly wisdom to those who were unlikely to listen to anything more demanding. Thus foreign trade, if only it were not a cause of war, would be a universal blessing, since it helped to satisfy cravings of the heart, the imagination and the soul. 'Man is not made for privation, which makes him hard and fierce. He is more tender, more human and more cheerful when his life is more pleasant.' On the other hand, he ought not to be. 'The philosopher, aware of the human cost of satisfying these brief delights, regards such riches as poisonous fruit.' He extolled the modern virtues of the printing press, 'scarcely born when everything took on a general tendency towards perfection'. Classical armies, however, had achieved feats far beyond the scope of modern ones 'since they have not got the burning patriotism that alone works miracles ... Why do we still bother with battles when there are no more revolutions?'[18] He was going to live to see the answer to that one. Granted his tendency to settle for the reasonable when the heroic seemed beyond the will, if not the means, of his generation, granted too that he was 45 when he returned to Paris, it was not surprising if his old radicalism seemed to have burned itself out.

This would be confirmed by *L'Observateur de Paris et du royaume*, ostensibly by 'the author of the *Tableau de Paris, Mon bonnet de nuit* etc.' if Mercier actually wrote it. It seems, however, to be the production of a lawyer who was borrowing his identity in order to put some special pleading on behalf of the legal profession.

What Mercier did publish, in 1787, was a couple of volumes with the optimistic title of *Notions claires sur les gouvernements*. Béclard claimed that this was actually written in 1784, but the preface carries the date 8 June 1787 and there is a reference in the body of the text to the meeting of the Notables, which took place during the first half of 1787. The date is of more than merely academic interest, since there were few signs of an impending political crisis in 1784, whereas the convocation of the Notables was the first clear indication that major political changes might be in the wind. As the crisis actually broke, other writers, such as Brissot and Marat, were to sound a new note of optimism and, at the same time, to retreat in the direction of

[18] *Mon bonnet de nuit*, I/378, I/121, I/357-8.

cautious pragmatism, and it is tempting to put Mercier in the same category.

The preface to the *Notions claires* was Rousseauist enough, apart from Mercier's habitual invocation of England as an example to France. Rousseau would probably have agreed that it was better to proceed 'in a slow and imperceptible fashion, more certain than a sudden transformation'. Even though the means should be gradual, however, the end was nothing less than 'the noble transformation of the human race'. With *Du contrat social* fairly obviously in mind, Mercier stressed the need for a providential legislator and rather ingenuously seemed to be offering his services. 'Everything announces the possibility of such a genius and if so many men had not diverted their talents in pursuit of the deceptive charms of the *beaux arts*, we should have discovered that union of the laws of morals and politics; everything would have been predicted, at least in theory. In default of such a genius (a rôle that I can glimpse and would have been ambitious to undertake), I have merely done as much as lay within my powers.' Will was certainly taking precedence over circumstance: 'When legislation cannot be the product of political circumstances, does it not come to the same thing if it is the product of enlightenment and of the systems of men of genius?' Montesquieu had been at some pains to show that it did not come to the same thing at all.

Mercier's preface was followed by an *avant-propos* in the same vein. The eighteenth century had erred because of its lack of confidence in human virtue. Governments had been too preoccupied with material considerations, they had relied too much on reason instead of feeling. 'It is *vertu* that divines with the speed of instinct what will be conducive to the general advantage ... Reason, with its insidious language, can paint the most equivocal enterprises in the most captivating colours, but the virtuous heart will never forget the interests of the humblest citizen ... Let us therefore place the virtuous statesman before the clever politician.'

After all this it comes as a distinct shock to find that a good deal of the book itself is devoted to a systematic attack on most of Rousseau's principles. This is far too comprehensive not to have been intentional. To argue that man was better off in a pre-social state was to juggle with superficialities for the pleasure of showing off one's eloquence. It was ridiculous for modern authors to put forward ancient constitutions as models for the present. 'What is there in common with Lacedaemon [he even refused to call it Sparta] and Paris?' Natural man must never be destroyed in order to create civil man. Rome, Athens and Sparta were no more republican than St. Domingue, since in all of them most of the population were slaves. The problem was not to legislate for a new country with a poor rural population, but for an old one, with its inherent vices, wealth and prejudices. 'Everything shows that it is not a matter of creating it but of preserving it and maintaining it with all its imperfections, since we can do no more than attenuate them.' Enthusiasm for political liberty was just as bad as religious fanaticism. In theory no doubt, some forms of luxury were undesirable, but 'It is not for moral theories to oppose everyday practices with which everyone seems to be quite satisfied'. Luxury made wealth circulate and distributed it more easily. 'It is not your moral precepts that will make men happy, but furniture, clothing etc. etc.' Inequality was so necessary to the welfare of society that if it did not exist it would be politically necessary to create it. Mercier even threw in some contemptuous references to the Swiss and the Genevan revolt of 1782 with its 'metaphysico-political arguments'.[19]

This was quite a remarkable performance that demolished, not merely a substantial part of Rousseau, but much of what Mercier himself had written in previous years. What makes it all the odder is that the man whose writing took on a sharper polemical edge whenever it approached subjects dear to Rousseau's heart, was to help in bringing out an edition of Jean-Jacques's works in 1788. In the *Notions claires*, at any rate, the place of the fallen idol had been taken by Montesquieu, 'the best thinker we ever had', who had changed the ideas of his century.[20] A good many of his arguments paraphrased *De l'esprit des lois* in letter or in spirit. 'A policy that tyrannises contemporaries to build a more prosperous future is demonstrably wrong.' Change must be slow, to avoid upsetting small property-owners and the middle-aged. People, in other words, must be taken for what

---

[19] *Notions claires sur les gouvernements*, 1788 ed., Amsterdam, 2v, I/32, I/42, I/66, I/185-7, I/225, II/37, II/193-5, II/283.
[20] Ibid. I/5.

they are and not changed into what they ought to be. He believed, as usual, that England was the least imperfect of existing states, and that democracy was incompatible with social and economic inequality. When he argued that peoples got the government most suited to their natures, he confused the issue by talking of the *volonté générale* when what he meant was the *esprit général*: not the moral will that *ought* to give a nation a common purpose, but the actual resultant of all the forces that made it what it was. For him, as for Montesquieu, this national character determined what was possible. His own preference, like that of Montesquieu, was for a moderate monarchy, and he repeated the argument of *De l'esprit des lois* that the people were good at electing the best men, but not at exercising power themselves. 'One can expect nothing sensible from absolute power in the hands of the people. Fanaticism has too much scope and zealots, obsessed with their own power, take it to extremes.' He went appreciably further, in a conservative direction, when he argued that people of humble birth were generally more violent and difficult to control than those born into a higher social station. Montesquieu might have agreed as to the fact, but he would have ascribed it to the influence of education and environment.[21]

Mercier was more concerned with the reality of how power was exercised than with the abstract classification of different kinds of constitutions. Indeed, he hoist Montesquieu with his own petard when he accused him of being too preoccupied with labels and failing to perceive that the character of governments changed, without affecting their formal constitution. The king of France, for example, although nominally absolute, was the prisoner of circumstances and had to take account of public opinion and rule with moderation. In this vein, Mercier naturally agreed with Montesquieu about the desirability of dividing power between intermediate bodies. He quoted Montesquieu's defence of trade, although rather against the grain: Montesquieu had been very much aware of his links with the most prosperous port in France and Mercier was a very self-conscious man of letters. He conceded that overseas trade had its uses, but not if essential commodities were exchanged for luxuries, which

---

[21] Ibid. I/71, I/67, I/111, I/128, I/297, I/335, II/38, I/338.

somewhat contradicted his earlier defence of luxury. Besides, industry constricted the soul, whereas farming was more conducive to *vertu*. Some of Montesquieu's seeds were not germinating very well. Mercier's conclusion, however, showed how well he had understood the essential message: 'Where is sovereignty located in such a state? I don't know ... it is disseminated. I see forces in equilibrium and that is what is needed ... the more states are simplified, the more dangerous they become, because then they become military. Governments must be complicated; human liberty finds its defences amongst these opposing forces. Nothing is more fatal than to take political questions to extremes: that means invoking the unjust right of force.'[22] If he remembered writing that, when he was in gaol in 1793, he could at least have said, 'I told you so'.

Part of the charm of Mercier arises from the fact that he was not a more systematic thinker. The way he felt was never concealed for very long by the tyranny of a logical argument. One can, so to speak, see the wheels going round. The purpose of his book seems to have been to refute Rousseau with the arguments of Montesquieu, but just as he had failed in former days to liberate himself from the spell of Jean-Jacques, despite his protestations to the contrary, so now, a good many of his feelings were at variance with the political option that claimed his intellectual allegiance. His preface and introduction showed that he still saw politics as the vehicle for the moral transformation of society by the exercise of human will, enlightened by a 'legislator' who was free from the prejudices of social and political conditioning. The same attitude kept cropping up in his book, interspersed between his attacks on Rousseau and his invocation of Montesquieu.

True to his belief in the vocation of the man of letters, he distinguished from the start between 'the party that governs' and 'the party that instructs' and believed it was the latter – in other words, the philosophes – that was responsible for political change. 'The book called *Common Sense*, if it did not cause, at least determined and accelerated the famous declaration of American independence.' Despite his concluding defence of pluralism, he argued that particular wills are always suspect but

[22] Ibid. I/128, II/115-6, II/333, II/410-11.

the *volonté générale* is infallible. If one couples this with his claim that legislative power resides in the nation alone, one has the basis for a Rousseauist system. Any political creed that is founded on moral regeneration is bound to emphasise will rather than circumstance and Mercier contradicted his own argument about the need to respect long-established prejudices when he asserted that all moral ideas were 'implanted' by governments, which could 'give birth to courage and *vertu* in any latitude'. National character evolves and such changes are largely the work of government: perhaps uneasily aware that he had more or less said the opposite, he added that the process took centuries. In contradiction to his earlier cosmopolitanism, he now maintained that love of one's *patrie* took precedence over love of humanity.[23]

He was still trying to have it both ways, as he had done in *Mon bonnet de nuit*. An inner voice told us that all men were equal and equally entitled to the world's goods. Rulers should bear this in mind, even though its realisation was impracticable since there was not enough to go round. Governments must therefore control the grain trade, since the lot of the majority of citizens was very hard at the best of times and they had to be protected against bad harvests and the caprice of the rich. They must not expose the lives of their citizens to the hazard of illusory systems. This was his constant criticism of the physiocrats. Free trade was no doubt excellent in theory but it should not be carried to a point where people's lives were endangered. 'We must never neglect the danger of alarming the people's imagination by the unlimited export of corn. If it sometimes flares up gratuitously, I ask myself if it is mistaken ... Subsistence is dearer to men than liberty.' It was an abuse of the idea of property to extend it to the means of existence. 'Is the citizen a proprietor when sacrifices are needed from all? ... Is the state not a single community and should bread not be reserved for the labouring men who do most of society's work?' This was to be exactly Robespierre's position in 1792, an indication of the extent to which the revolutionaries lived off the intellectual capital accumulated before 1789. Such qualified economic liberalism may have been short on logic, if all men ought to have been equal, but it made excellent practical sense. Mercier took up a similar position on politics. The original

[23] Ibid. I/1-4, I/19, I/28, I/59, I/313, I/241.

sovereignty of the nation was incontrovertible in theory but nul in practice. 'The people are, as it were, bound to those whom they have charged with the execution of their own sovereignty, even though the nation is entitled to resume the powers it has delegated. The exercise of this right is so difficult and rare that history offers few examples of it.'[24]

Mercier may well offer a better guide to the state of French public opinion, just before the Revolution, than more profound, consistent or systematic writers. *Sensibilité* was everywhere and on the point of most people's pens. The slowly maturing political crisis that came to a head in 1789 brought the expectation of better things to come. Reform meant essentially moral regeneration. It was taken for granted that this would also mean making life easier for the poor, whose sufferings were real enough, and whose *vertu* was generally assumed to be proportionate to their misfortune. Up to a point, such feelings may have owed something to Rousseau or predisposed people in his favour, but one could go into raptures over the *Nouvelle Héloïse* or *Emile* without knowing anything about the political arrangements that Rousseau suggested in some of his other works. Where politics was concerned, Montesquieu was the almost unchallenged expert, the idol of the parlements and respected by virtually everyone else. Provided one kept everything vague – which is usually not difficult in political argument – one could dream both of moral regeneration and of political liberty secured by the fragmentation of power. It was not immediately obvious that the *esprit général* and the *volonté générale* were in fact opposites. Moreover, the age was one of hyperbole, when a handful of troops, sent to arrest a couple of members of the Paris parlement became 'an unbridled soldiery, their axes raised against the portals of the temple of the laws'. This sort of language is always dangerous since people eventually come to take it at its face value. Mercier himself was rather addicted to it. If one were to take the writings of the 1780s too literally, one might get the impression that France was on the verge of civil war, but no one thought so at the time. Radical, even revolutionary language generally concealed the expectation of quite modest improvements. In the *Notions claires*, despite his

[24] Ibid. II/138-9, II/167, II/285, II/407.

fiery theoretical passages, Mercier even argued that French interests would be better protected by the parlements – 'those popular national tribunals are both a curb on tyranny and one of the strongest ramparts of public liberty' – than by a meeting of the Estates General. It was not the writers who made the crisis. They had been denouncing tyrants and glorifying republican principles for over a decade, and some of them tended to shorten sail when the storm cones went up. It was the crisis itself, and the sudden realisation that the impossible had started to happen, that gave a misleading impression of prophecy to what had often been more like whistling in the dark.

Chapter 5

Brissot

Jean-Pierre Brissot, like Mercier, came from quite well-off bourgeois stock.[1] His father was a prosperous hotelier in Chartres, who left 150-200,000 livres when he died in 1779. Brissot himself was born in 1754, into a large family, conspicuous for its religion. His father, an active churchman, took his opinions from the local clergy; his mother, towards the end of her life, suffered from delusions of demonic persecution; one of his brothers became a priest, and emigrated during the Revolution. In such a pious and parochial household, it was not surprising that Brissot received a conventional and somewhat rudimentary education, completed by the age of 15, when he was apprenticed to a local solicitor. According to Brissot himself, his first adolescent revolt took a religious form. 'I went to bed a materialist and got up a deist. I spent several years in this state of doubt and error until at last, enlightened by the works of Jean-Jacques Rousseau, after a deep examination of the witness of my inner sense, I opted for belief in God.' 'The profession of faith of the *vicaire savoyard* was the first work that took the blinkers from my eyes.'[2] This Rousseauist deism was not enough for his father, who more or less disowned him and left him to make his own way in the world.

[1] See E.Ellery, *Brissot de Warville*, Boston and New York, 1915, and J.François-Primo, *La jeunesse de Brissot*, Paris, 1932. Most of the evidence for Brissot's career before 1789 comes from the memoirs that he wrote in gaol in 1793. These were 'edited' by Montrol in a four-volume edition published in Paris in 1830-32, a process that consisted of padding out the original manuscript with extensive quotations from Brissot's published works. C.Perroud, in a three-volume edition of Brissot's memoirs and correspondence (Paris, n.d.) eliminated as many of these borrowings as he could detect, although one or two escaped him. References to the memoirs here refer to the Perroud edition.

[2] *Mémoires* I/60-1,I38.

This was to create problems, not merely for Brissot, but also for his biographers. Before the Revolution established him as a successful journalist, he had to wage a daily struggle to make some sort of a living, with nothing to sell but his pen. He was rarely in a position to write what he wanted – quite apart from the question of the official censorship – and many of his attitudes were dictated to him by those who hired him. There is no reason to doubt his dedication to what he saw as his mission to help in the emancipation of the human race, but one can never be quite sure what he was up to at any given time. It was not his fault if he had to rub shoulders with some rather unsavoury characters, but one need not believe that his trusting and open nature meant that he was invariably their dupe.*Libertin* in French had always carried the double meaning of free thought and libertinage and there was often, in the 1780s, a very tenuous distinction between political opposition and pornographic scandal-mongering. If one is to believe Brissot, he stuck to the former and left the latter to his associates. This could be more or less true without his having been quite so unaware as he suggested of what was going on. All one can do is to stick to what he published at the time and to treat his subsequent explanation of what he was doing with a certain amount of caution.

In 1774, at the age of 20, he moved to Paris, working in a lawyer's office and spending his spare time learning languages and writing an account of the political theories of St. Paul and an essay on the fashionable Rousseauist theme that property did not exist in a state of nature. It was writing of a different kind that first landed him in trouble: a scandalous pamphlet against a lady ·who had enough political influence to secure a *lettre de cachet* against him. Given advance warning by the policeman sent to arrest him – a man who made a second income out of selling the forbidden literature that he confiscated in his official capacity – Brissot fled back to Chartres where his pious father, unimpressed by the parable of the prodigal son, soon packed him off back to Paris. This was in 1777, when France was about to enter the war between England and her American colonies. Living, as he admitted, on credit and by means of *expédients peu délicats*, Brissot tried to ingratiate himself with the French Foreign Office by a pamphlet called *Testament politique de l'Angleterre*. This began, inevitably, with a prophecy of

England's impending bankruptcy and political eclipse, but it worked its way round to a warning to France to avoid wars of conquest. A final survey of the state of Europe cautioned Switzerland against trade and luxury. 'She must remain poor if she wants to be free. Sparta only fell because she went beyond that limit.'[3]

This was standard Rousseauist stuff. It failed to impress Vergennes, the French Foreign Minister, but it brought Brissot an offer from Swinton, the English publisher of the *Courrier de l'Europe*, whose digest of the British press was a useful source of information to the French intelligence service. Unable to ban the publication – a useful lesson to Brissot on the virtues of freedom of the press – the British Government vetoed its export to the Continent, as merchandise. Swinton had therefore secured Vergennes's permission to reprint it in Boulogne. He invited Brissot to supervise this edition, allowing him to add a column of his own, called *Variétés*. This arrangement lasted for a year or so, until Vergennes banned Brissot's column, Swinton sacked him and Jean-Pierre returned to Chartres, where his father refused to have him back unless he returned to God. It was not a promising start.

In the meantime, with the self-educated man's conviction of his ability to put everyone else right, he was writing all the time, preparing a *Théorie des lois criminelles* and winning prizes from the academy of Châlons-sur-Marne for two essays on the reform of French law. These attracted some favourable reviews but did nothing to provide him with an income. His father died in 1779, leaving him as little as the law, and rather less than decency permitted. His inheritance of 5,000 livres was not much but, together with what he got from the *Théorie des lois criminelles*, it would keep him for a couple of years in Paris and allow him a fresh start. In the hope of a regular occupation that would allow him to marry, he bought a law degree from Reims, only to find that the Paris bar refused to accept him because of his youthful scrapes and his subversive views. *Un indépendant à l'ordre des avocats sur la décadence du barreau en France* probably relieved his feelings but marked the end of another false start.

It was at this time that he produced *De la vérité*, which was to

---

[3] *Testament politique de l'Angleterre*, n.p., 1680 (sic), p.103.

be published at Neuchâtel in 1782. This was intended to be nothing less than a new *Discours de la méthode*, an infallible means of distinguishing truth from error that would rectify the mistakes of Descartes, Mallebranche, Bacon, Locke, Helvétius, Leibniz and Spinoza and serve as the curtain-raiser to a subsequent work that would contain an account of all that was certain in the whole field of human knowledge. What it amounted to in practice was a general defence of induction and some random comments on life. Its contribution to the intellectual history of the Enlightenment was minimal, but it said a good deal about how the world appeared to Brissot at the age of 28.

Despite his approval of Montesquieu – 'above all political writers' (since he based his conclusions on induction) – Brissot's whole work was dominated by Rousseau, 'a great man, whose works I shall never tire of citing'.[4] That was to be a true prophecy: in the memoirs that he wrote when awaiting his trial and execution, he claimed to be reading Rousseau's *Confessions* for the sixth time.[5] Despite its title, Brissot's work was really about moral regeneration. 'When I emerged from schools where reason is stifled by scholastic prejudices ... My only ambition was to distinguish myself and to excel in everything. I wanted to learn everything, to know everything ... Vanity was my first motive, desire for fortune the second ... Now I no longer believe in glory and I am not interested in riches. I am looking to the good of my fellow-beings, not that I have much faith in *that*, but enough to support me in my labours. The good of humanity, that is the only thing that must distinguish true knowledge from false; that is the character of the sublime writer.'[6]

The rest of the book was in the same vein. The philosophe was a man whose ideas were determined by truth and whose actions by *vertu*. As with Rousseau, *vertu* was a political rather than a personal quality. Whenever Brissot thought about the abuses of despotism, 'I form a thousand wishes, senseless because they are impracticable, for the destruction of the wicked and the restoration of order'.[7] He shared a fair number of Rousseau's prejudices, such as his contempt for blue-stockings and his belief

---

[4] *De la vérité, pp. 70, 359.*   [5] *Mémoires* I/18.
[6] *De la vérité*, pp.5-8.   [7] Ibid. p.19.

that the poor needed to be taught moral principles, rather than how to think. He quoted Rousseau to the effect that children were made to read too much. 'People have argued about whether the discovery of printing was useful or harmful to the human race. Rousseau pronounced against it and wise men will believe that he was right.'[8] All knowledge should begin with self-knowledge and the way to truth was by meditation, preferably at dusk and in solitude. He turned on Rousseau's critics who 'dared to assert that the philosopher who lived alone ended up by keeping bad company – a witticism that came no doubt from those ... who crawl about the antechambers of important people'.[9] All this, of course, pointed to *Emile*. 'Do you want to know the man best equipped to search for truth? Look at Emile ... Happy, a hundred times happy, the man who received Emile's education.'[10]

The whole framework was underpinned, for Brissot as for Rousseau, by an emotional deism. 'Reason shows me nothing but darkness, whereas the moral sense enlightens and directs me ... I am happy when I feel myself under the eye of a Supreme Being, when I think I see him smile at my feeble efforts and encourage them. I am happy when I invoke him, when I pray to him, and I pray only when carried away by irresistible need, by pleasure; he is my master, I report to him, we converse, and I draw renewed force, greater energy, from that conversation and from the hope that he gives me.'[11]

Time and again Brissot quoted Rousseau, not merely the famous works like *Emile*, that everyone had read, but *Du contrat social* and obscure passages from Rousseau's published letters. The first part of the *Confessions* had appeared in 1781 and many people had been shocked by their revelation of Rousseau's – and other people's – frailties. Brissot would have none of this. 'I know men have described him as a knave, a slanderer, a hypocrite, a villain. The most moderate said that he was mad. I have the misfortune to love, to adore that madman, and I share this misfortune with a whole host of sensitive and virtuous souls, not for his style, but for his *vertu* ... I will believe in my own inner feeling. If the whole universe were to testify against him, I would

[8] Ibid. p.132.   [9] Ibid. p.95.
[10] Ibid. pp.196-7.   [11] Ibid. p.212.

rather think it peopled by false witnesses than believe Jean-Jacques a criminal. I am sorry for those whom his *Emile*, whom Julie and Saint-Preux have not enchanted and set on fire; I am even sorrier for those who can see only horrible, petty or ridiculous things in the *Confessions*. Who can ever judge you, O great man! ... If all the libraries perished in a fire or from the decay of ages, our descendants would have nothing to complain about if they still had the good Rousseau. With him they would raise up degraded humanity once again.'[12]

This was to out-Mercier Mercier but, like his older contemporary, Brissot drew the line at Rousseau's conception of exclusive patriotism. Philosophy drew a man away from attachment to any particular country. 'It destroys patriotism – but is that such a bad thing?' Perhaps with his own misfortunes in mind, he thought that philosophes needed a free country, such as Greece, Rome or England, in which to operate but, in sharp contrast to Rousseau, he thought one could have too much of politics, and republics were often troubled by faction. 'Politics is the first, the exclusive science there; patriotism is the exclusive virtue.' He believed this to be the case in both London and Geneva – he had only spent a fortnight in London.[13] Like Mercier in his sunnier moments, Brissot took a cheerful view of the future: 'We have reached the point where public opinion shares power with kings ... Awakened by the cries [of the philosophes], rulers will gradually correct all abuses. Torture is now abolished; tomorrow criminal proceedings will be made public ... the reign of conquerors is over; this is the age of the benefactors of humanity, of the great legislators.'[14]

Before he reached this comforting conclusion, a rather jaundiced section on the state of French journalism and the intrigue that dominated the academies had given him the opportunity to include an enthusiastic tribute to his friend, Marat, who had suffered at the hands of the *Académie des Sciences*.[15] 'You whom nature has endowed with the genius of observation and tireless zeal in the search for truth, who, trusting only to experiment and neither to reputations nor received wisdom, have bravely overthrown the idol of the

[12] Ibid. pp.109-12. [13] Ibid. pp.227, 251-7.
[14] Ibid. p.300. [15] See below, pp

academic cult and substituted for Newton's mistakes about light
a coherent system of well-authenticated facts ... This is the story
of the celebrated physicist, M. Marat, to whose philosophy and
research it is a pleasure to render justice.'[16]

Reading *De la vérite*, one can understand why Brissot decided
to concentrate on journalism rather than on *les livres
profondément pensés et purement écrits*. 'Such was the
reasoning that led me, like all the most distinguished writers of
that time, to take to periodicals and newspapers. Like them, I
worked to influence the readers of my time and not for my
reputation in the coming century.'[17] He was now absorbed in a
new scheme, to create a 'lycée' in London, that would serve as an
international centre of enlightened thought and diffuse the
gospel throughout Europe by means of a journal with the modest
title of *Correspondance universelle sur tout ce qui intéresse le
bonheur de l'homme et de la société*. He was by now well enough
known to be able to approach possible sponsors in Paris. With his
invariable optimism, he under-estimated the money that would
be needed and assumed that his financial backers were more
effectively committed than proved to be the case. Part of the
plan was to arrange for the publication in Neuchâtel of
translations of works that had first appeared in England, with a
view to smuggling them into France and disseminating them
across Europe. Brissot therefore set off for Switzerland in 1782 to
make the necessary arrangements. He arrived in Geneva just
before that rebel city capitulated to a French army. Brissot
published the lessons he drew from the Genevan revolt a year
later, in *Le Philadelphien à Genève, ou lettres d'un Américain
sur la dernière révolution de Genève*. Rousseau would have
appreciated both Brissot's homage to his birthplace – 'Here I saw
man in all his strength and dignity, just as nature, no doubt,
wanted to make him' – and Brissot's outlook in general. The
conflict at Geneva had been basically moral. The Senate,
composed of *aristocrats* (he was already using the term in a
political, rather than a social sense), 'brought the taste for luxury
to Geneva, the surest way to corrupt the people and destroy its
republican virtues'.[18] It had naturally persecuted Rousseau.

---

[16] *De la vérité*, pp.173-4.   [17] *Mémoires* I/308.
[18] *Le Philadelphien à Genève*, Dublin, 1783, p.22.

Eventually the democrats revolted, claiming that 'since the magistrates had broken all their promises, their sovereign was entitled to dispossess them ... but they spoke a language that was incomprehensible in monarchies and aristocracies'.[19] It was, of course, the pure language of *Du contrat social* and he was well aware of it. He twice quoted the book, once correctly ('Those who wield the executive power are not the masters of the people') and once when he wrongly ascribed to 'chapter 12' the statement that 'Every people where property is not respected by the sovereign, where individuals are oppressed, has the right, first of all to complain, and then to break the social pact and become free again'.[20] This seems to have been his own invention and it suggests that he had a rather shaky understanding of Rousseau's location of sovereignty in the general will. Rather inconsistently, in view of this defence of property, he went on to say, 'The greatest criminal of lèze-majesty in a republic is the man with 2-300,000 livres of interest', and to advocate banishing the rich.[21] Despite a couple of approving references to Montesquieu's definitions of despotism and aristocracy, the whole emphasis of the work was solidly Rousseauist.

While he remained in Switzerland, Brissot met Mercier. More importantly, he established a lifelong friendship with Clavière, a banker who escaped from Geneva with much of his fortune intact. If anyone had predicted that within ten years the down-at-heel journalist would be helping to make the refugee banker France's Minister of Finance, he would have seemed mad indeed. Together, Brissot and Clavière went on a pilgrimage to some of the more famous Rousseauist sites. From du Peyroux, Rousseau's friend, Brissot no doubt got plenty of information about his hero's domestic life.

It was about this time that Brissot may have written – the attribution is uncertain – *Lettres sur la liberté politique*. Much of this consisted of a sharp criticism of British institutions, written from a radical Whig point of view and showing a considerable knowledge of current controversies across the Channel. Most of the letters began with an appropriate quotation from Montesquieu, although the author criticised him for flattering the British constitution because he did not know it

[19] Ibid. p.44.   [20] Ibid. p.67.   [21] Ibid. p.148.

very well. Brissot – if it was he – commented accurately enough that what was represented in Parliament was property rather than people. He saw with unusual clarity that legislature and executive were not separate powers, as Montesquieu had imagined. He believed that members of parliament betrayed the interests of their constituents but, like Montesquieu, he thought that a mass assembly of the people would be capricious, violent and despotic. His own solution to this problem was to divide the electorate into tens, hundreds and thousands, with each 'constituency' mandating a delegate to the next above it. This smacks more of Rousseau than of Montesquieu, who preferred representatives to delegates. It would not have been like Brissot to write a substantial pamphlet without once invoking Rousseau, so the question of authorship must remain uncertain. If it is his work, it shows once again that the most ardent Rousseauists still turned to Montesquieu for guidance when dealing with the actual working of political institutions.

Brissot returned to France in 1782 with contracts for the diffusion of his journal and the publication of his translations. This time he seemed to be on the slipway at least, if not actually launched. In Paris he married Félicité Dupont, who was working as an assistant to the formidable Mme de Genlis, ex-mistress of the Duke of Orleans and governess of his children, both hers and those of his wife. When he reached London he was a very different man from the unknown hack who had paid a brief visit there three years before. He met Bentham, David Williams, Catherine Macaulay and Priestley. He also met Swinton and his associate, the sinister adventurer and pornographer, Théveneau de Morande. London, at that time, served as a haven for a somewhat scruffy bunch of French exiles who lived on their wits, alternately writing lampoons against the ladies of the French Court, in the hope of being paid for not publishing them, and denouncing others engaged in the same unpleasant trade. How far Brissot was involved with these people it is impossible to say. He took over, for a time, the literary editorship of the *Courrier de l'Europe* but claimed to have rejected Swinton's offer to put him in charge, with Théveneau as nominal editor, and said that he broke with Swinton. He certainly knew rather a lot about the activities of some unsavoury people.

As with most of Brissot's schemes, everything went wrong with the London venture. He complained that his backers failed to produce all the money he needed. Vergennes, his old enemy, for a time excluded the *Correspondance* from France. Brissot had arranged for a German edition to be printed in Hamburg, but the printer went bankrupt. A glance at the journal suggests that Brissot was soon scraping the barrel to find material to print. What he seems to have had in mind was the kind of universal encyclopaedia that he had announced in *De la vérité* (which he commended to his correspondents as a kind of text book), partly a vehicle for the dissemination of news and 'philosophical' comment, and partly the creation of a kind of club whose members would be scattered all over Europe. How far he intended a subversive political message to be read between the lines, it is hard to say. The overt doctrine he preached was the familiar brand of dilute millenarianism: 'Thanks to the immortal works of Locke, Montesquieu, Rousseau etc., the empire of routine is falling into ruin.' This amounted to a 'revolution', but the agents of revolution whom he acclaimed were not the philosophes but Catherine II, Joseph II (who would soon be more famous than Caesar or Alexander – who were models of a somewhat military kind) and Frederick II ('If ever a prince ought to make despotism pardonable, it is without doubt Frederick II'). One can see why Vergennes thought this unsuitable for French consumption, but it was scarcely 'revolutionary' in the political sense and it was what a good many people had been saying for rather a long time.

Brissot tried to boost the flagging sales of the *Correspondance* by the free distribution to his subscribers of serialised parts of his *Tableau de la situation des Anglais dans l'Inde*, an attack on British imperialism which showed that the freedom of the press in England was rather more substantial than in those continental countries whose rulers he found it politic to praise. Out of the blue, he suddenly found himself arrested for debt, as a result of a warrant taken out by his printer. He himself ascribed this to the enmity of Swinton and Théveneau, and since he used the same printer as the powerful *Courrier de l'Europe*, this could have been the case. If Swinton actually was trying to dispose of a possible rival, he certainly succeeded. Brissot was soon released, when his mother-in-law paid his debts, but when he hastened to Paris to raise more money for his lycée, he was promptly sent to the Bastille. This seems to have been a put-up job. He was accused of writing a political libel, *Le diable dans un bénitier* and also of circulating scurrilous attacks on Marie Antoinette. He claims to have had little difficulty in convincing Lenoir, the *lieutenant de police*, that these were false charges, invented by his enemies in London, but he *had* agreed to send substantial numbers of the offending pamphlet into France, under the cover of his own *Correspondance*. Like other 'revolutionaries', Brissot tried to have it both ways. If, as he later maintained, he was trying to subvert royal absolutism in France, he could scarcely pretend that it was somehow unfair of the king's ministers to stop him. If their action was arbitrary, his must have been inoffensive. It was his own acquaintances who had landed him in trouble and he owed his quick deliverance to the workings of the system that he claimed to be attacking, to the intercession of the influential Mme de Genlis.

In a very interesting, but rather hostile article, Robert Darnton has suggested that Brissot's London venture had been something of a confidence trick: the lycée had never had any tangible existence and when Brissot's sponsor discovered what was going on, he not unnaturally asked for his money back.[22] Towards the end of 1784 he certainly owed over 12,000 livres to the *Société Typographique* of Neuchâtel, which had printed a good many of his works at his own expense. A condition of his release from the Bastille was that he should liquidate his London ventures, which left him with further debts and perhaps deprived him of the means of honouring them. It may well be that he was so desperate and disgusted by the behaviour of his 'radical' acquaintances in London that he decided to follow the example of Beaumarchais and some of his less distinguished compatriots in England, and turn from poaching to gamekeeping. He seems to have made some kind of a deal with the French police. Lenoir, writing his memoirs at a time when he was an opponent of a revolution that Brissot was supporting, said that he volunteered his services. 'I refused them, but for about a year he had *des relations d'espionnage* with one of the departmental secretaries, who presented his reports to me, for which he was paid. Just

[22] See R.Darnton, 'The Grub Street style of revolution: J.-P. Brissot, police spy', *Journal of Modern History*, 1968.

before my retirement [in August 1785] Brissot *resta* [this is presumably a misreading for *cessa*] to be employed as a police spy.'[23] Brissot's political opponents during the Revolution had got wind of this and used it as ammunition against him. Marat claimed that Brissot remained in police employment until threatened with exposure in 1789, but nothing that Marat said can be accepted without corroboration. Brissot's admirers have suggested that any payment was by way of compensation for the enforced liquidation of his enterprises in London. If it was, it was not enough, and he had to borrow 20,000 livres from Clavière to settle his English debts. The question remains obscure, but Darnton's suggestion that the experience may have turned the idealistic Brissot into the embittered opponent of an Establishment that had forced him to sell himself, seems rather too neat. He had been involved in scandal-mongering well before 1784 and his political attitude did not become more revolutionary.

Whatever the truth about his relations with the police, another enterprise had collapsed. Brissot was now a family man – his wife had born him a son just before his arrest in England – and even his optimism must have been rather discouraged. In this predicament he was in no position to resist an invitation – or summons – from Clavière to work for him in Paris, towards the end of 1784. This introduced him to an environment scarcely more edifying than the one he had left in London. Most of Clavière's money was in shares and he lived by speculation. This brought him into contact with the government, for the finance minister, Calonne, was trying to engineer a boom by stimulating public confidence. His colleague and rival, Breteuil, was trying to do the opposite and each needed pamphleteers. Calonne employed Clavière who, in turn, hired a team of writers to make appropriate noises when instructed. The chief of these was Mirabeau, who relied on lesser men to produce most of the publications that appeared under his name. Brissot found himself on the bottom rung of this not very philosophical ladder. It taught him a few more things about the press and it kept the wolf from the door.

There is not much ideological content in his pamphlets against

---

[23] Darnton, art. cit., p.318.

the Perrier Company's attempt to float a new fire insurance company, even if he did manage to preface one of them with an ingenious quotation from the beloved Rousseau: *On commence par mettre le feu à la maison pour faire jouer les pompes.* Like all his fellow-hacks, Brissot professed to be scandalised by speculation, when practiced by the other side, but he cannot have been enjoying himself very much and he possibly thought of emigrating to America. In 1786 he wrote to Calonne announcing his intention of going to the United States and asking, without success, to be made the official historian of the French navy. It was a form of semi-blackmail from which Mirabeau did rather well, but Brissot was too unimportant to be worth buying off.

Like other journalists he tried to combine earning a living with writing what he wanted and 1785 saw the appearance of *Un défenseur du peuple à l'empereur Joseph II.* This was rather different from the encomium that he had printed in the *Correspondance.* He began by criticising Joseph for his paternalism: 'A good country is one where the government does little and the people do much. I know this maxim overthrows all our political contrivancies: all the better, since they are bad.'[24] This was followed by an invocation of the people. 'I have been terrified by the slavery in which you have languished for so long ... I feel myself to be a kind of visionary when I read your titles and see you so great in nature, so degraded in the social state ... Almost everywhere you are wretched and despised. Everywhere they make it a sacred law for you to keep your chains, they make it a crime for you to break them.'[25] He continued with the familiar argument that men were born free and equal, that ancient precedents had no authority if they were wrong, and that property was a social institution, with the state entitled to claim a share of it in return for the protection it afforded. His conclusion was somewhat less revolutionary, and less Rousseauist. Classical patriotism was *l'inhumanité même* and the modern version an ignoble absurdity. True patriotism consisted of 'love of one's self, of one's wellbeing, of the laws that protect it and the citizens who share it, the liberty that honours it and the reflection that extends it. In this sense, the *patrie* is

---

[24] *Un défenseur du peuple à l'empereur, Joseph II,* Dublin, 1785, p.3.
[25] Ibid. p.4.

the universe.' After rejecting the xenophobic patriotism of the classical republics, he continued with the somewhat equivocal argument that everything had changed, if not for the better, at least for good. 'If one considers the present state of nations, I see that they have all arrived at more or less the same stage, that political and moral corruption is roughly universal. They have therefore nothing to fear from foreign contagion. I see that if improved communications have been bad for *moeurs* (and that question has not been finally solved), politics have profited and governments have improved with the improvement in communications. Ignorance has disappeared and taken ferocity with it. The shock has been given and it is too late to prevent its effects. The universe is tending towards enlightenment; everywhere the light is attaining the same level.' All this amounted to a revolution, but not one of the 1789 variety. 'It will come at last when cosmopolitanism replaces ridiculous patriotism or national honour, words invented by despots to bind their slaves to their chariots.' The whole process was irresistible and every state was moving in the same direction. 'The prince thinks he is commanding when he merely follows.'[26] This was visionary enough – and singularly bad prophecy – but it was very far from the assertion of moral will with which Rousseau was associated. It put the emphasis entirely on circumstances, it repudiated the classical example and it implied a willingness to trade *vertu* for civilisation.

With his remarkable knack for backing losers, Brissot then took up Mesmerism and became an active member of Bergasse's *Société d'Harmonie Universelle*.[27] He maintained in his memoirs that the society was a cover for the dissemination of political propaganda and that it was responsible for most of the anti-ministerial pamphlets produced in 1787 and 1788. This is certainly exaggerated, but there may be an element of truth in it. Brissot's political creed was such a cloudy business that it is hard to distinguish it from the equally nebulous dreams of the Mesmerists. What is clear is that membership of the society brought him into contact with men who were to be of some

[26] Ibid. pp.48-50.
[27] On this subject, see R.Darnton, *Mesmerism and the end of the Enlightenment in France*, Harvard, 1968.

political importance during the coming years: Bergasse himself, Lafayette, d'Eprémesnil, Sabatier, Carra and Gorsas. Their political views were, however, so opposed that it is difficult to see them as the nucleus of any kind of party, even if they were agreed in their dislike of 'ministerial despotism' as practised by Calonne and Brienne.

A more promising opportunity seemed to present itself with the death of Orleans in November 1785. The new duke was not averse to playing a political rôle, provided that it did not interfere too much with his pleasures. Still under the influence of Mme de Genlis, he made her brother, the marquis du Crest, his chancellor, and du Crest took Brissot as his secretary at a salary of 3,000 livres a year. Brissot seems to have helped to organise 'philanthropic bureaux' in Orlean's vast appanage, which were no doubt intended to promote his political interests at the same time. Brissot now found himself on the fringe of Court politics and he may have taken a rather less lofty view of the dilettantism and immorality of the Orleans circle than he was to pretend in 1793 when Philippe Egalité, as the duke then called himself, had become a political embarrassment. Du Crest was hoping to force himself on the king as prime minister and it may have been as his agent, as well as Clavière's, that Brissot was sent to Holland in 1786 to investigate the possibility of a loan to a future French government. Amsterdam, like Geneva in 1782, was in a state of revolution. This one was suppressed by the Prussians. Brissot was becoming quite an expert on what some recent historians have seen as an international democratic revolution. In his advice to du Crest, he suggested that if the ministerial plan failed, du Crest and Orleans should form an opposition party, after the English model, with the slogan of 'no taxation without representation', backed by the parlements in the first instance and eventually by the Estates General.[28] As usual, he saw this as part of a 'torrent' that was carrying all nations towards liberty. In other words, the 'revolution' that he was fond of predicting was probably a much less dramatic affair in his own mind than it turned out to be in practice.

To support du Crest's political campaign, and perhaps to serve Clavière's financial interests at the same time, Brissot wrote

[28]*Mémoires* III/150-60.

Point de banqueroute où lettre d'un créancier de l'état. This may
have been intended to discourage Brienne, the Finance Minister,
from a partial repudiation of the Debt, or to discredit him by
implying that he had inclinations in that direction. After a few
pages on this theme Brissot, as usual, broadened the subject, in
words reminiscent of his letter to Joseph II. 'Nowadays people no
longer greet political crises with epigrams and songs; they talk,
they reason (women have no part to play ... In times of trouble,
women should only be the secret consolation of their husbands)
and public spirit shows itself almost everywhere.'[29] The
American revolution had opened the eyes of peoples, and of
kings, who had learned that despotism impoverished and liberty
enriched them. All this was inevitable: even a reborn Richelieu
would have had to behave very differently. Nevertheless, it
would not do to force the pace. 'Public spirit ... is not yet equally
spread throughout all classes of society. It is unknown among the
people ... it is almost unknown amongst the class of townspeople,
so divorced from public affairs as to have lost, if not all interest,
at least all enlightenment about public matters.' Even the better
educated were only beginning to be politically conscious and the
upper ranks of society were concerned only with pleasure and
ambition.[30] The king, for his part, should help matters forward
by demolishing the Bastille, abolishing *lettres de cachet* and
granting freedom to the press.

He concluded his pamphlet with a rather hasty sketch of the
state of Europe. His general theme was that France should avoid
getting involved in the Dutch revolt or the Russo-Turkish war.
She had nothing to fear from Prussia, a paper tiger since the
death of Frederick II, or from Russia. If Russia became free she
would cease to be warlike and if not, she could never be
dangerous. At the same time he wondered why France 'which
had given liberty to America', had not saved the Dutch, and his
assertion that the only legitimate wars were wars of liberation
begged all the usual questions. One does not have to know what
was going to happen in 1792 to find this dangerously superficial.
Whenever Brissot wrote about foreign affairs he did so with a
cheerful insouciance that took it for granted that what was

[29] *Point de banqueroute, ou lettre à un créancier de l'état*, London, 1787, p.17.
[30] Ibid. pp.33-4.

ideologically convenient was what was most likely to happen. Foreign policy, in other words, was merely a question of deciding what one wanted.

During the same year – 1787 – appeared *Observations d'un républicain sur les différents systèmes d'administrations provinciales*, Brissot's most violent and radical pamphlet. He equated the monarchy in France with 'the actual despotic order' and denounced seigneurs and courtiers. He demanded the right to vote for all adult consumers (since they all paid indirect taxes) and came out with what was, for him, an unusual attack on social inequality. 'Without property there is no *patrie* ... Society cries [to the poor man] "Respect the goods of your rich neighbour." He could reply to society, "Have you respected my primitive right to property?" Can the man who owns nothing bring up his children? Can he be pious, can he love the Being who seems to him to decree his wretchedness? ... If one wants to restore their rights to the people one must smash the machine altogether; if one preserves it, one must continue to despoil the people.'[31] Much of the pamphlet was devoted to a savage attack on Necker, perhaps in the hope of discrediting him as a possible rival to du Crest. After criticising his *style d'un courtisan timide*, Brissot damned him for arguing that reform must be slow and gradual. 'I maintain that if a revolution is to be total, it must come suddenly.' Necker had argued that men must not indulge in ideas of abstract perfection: 'Another ministerial expression; the words of a man who lacks either the talent or the courage to aspire to perfection.'[32] This is so different from the cautious tone of *Point de banqueroute* as to suggest that Brissot was getting desperate.

In fact, his latest house of cards collapsed like all the previous ones. Du Crest's French equivalent of an English attempt to 'storm the closet' failed, Orleans was banished to his estates for his opposition to the king and Brissot thought it wise to withdraw to England for a time. Fortunately he still had Clavière.

That gentleman was now turning his attention to the United

---

[31] *Observations d'un républicain sur les différents systèmes d'administrations provinciales*, Lausanne, 1787, pp.145-6.
[32] Ibid. pp.117, 119, 138.

States, with a view to taking over the American debt to the French government and also buying land for retail to prospective French settlers. In 1787 he and Brissot published *De la France et des Etats-Unis*, to draw attention to the advantages France might hope to gain from developing economic links with the United States. Whenever the two men collaborated in this way it is impossible to distinguish Brissot's propaganda for the coming 'revolution' from his activities as Clavière's publicity agent. Probably he saw no conflict between the two. Clavière directed Brissot's attention in the direction that suited his business interests and Brissot turned Clavière's concerns into grist for his own political mill. The result was a curious amalgam of special pleading and political principle.

Brissot began his introduction to the book by warning his fellow-countryman that England, after losing the American war, looked like winning the peace because of France's failure to exploit the possibilities of trade with the new nation. This led him on to more general considerations about commerce, as practised and understood in England and France. In his own country, 'The science of commerce is almost unknown since its practice is debased by the prejudice that prevents the nobility from participating in it ... since the nobility is mistakenly regarded as a necessary part of the monarchical constitution'. He hoped that 'philosophy' would eventually substitute for such erroneous notions the idea of meritocracy, 'without which there are only aristocrats, in other words, men incapable of entertaining any lofty idea, debased men incapable of producing anything'.[33] Brissot's preface was a mixture of principle and party politics. He attacked the reconstitution of the French East India Company (to the advantage of one of Clavière's rivals, the abbé d'Espagnac), praised Mirabeau's financial pamphlets (some of which he had helped to write) and argued that the Marriage of Figaro should have been banned (Beaumarchais was the enemy of one of the leading members of the Mesmerist circle). This sat rather uneasily alongside 'The physical and moral regeneration of man that must be the inevitable consequence of the [American] constitutions'. The American war had raised many important political issues: 'The discussion of

[33]*De la France et des Etats-Unis*, London, 1787, pp.xiv-xv.

the social contract, of civil liberty, of what constitutes the independence of a people, of the circumstances that legitimise its insurrection.' As always, what he had in mind was a revolution that would be far-reaching, but the inevitable – and peaceful – product of social and economic forces. Inspired by the American example, 'The governments of Europe will be driven gradually to correct their abuses.' He had shifted his ground since his letter to Joseph II and now saw trade as a positive encouragement to *vertu*. Rulers would come to recognise that their power rested on an economic basis, which implied sound public credit and 'consequently *des vertus publiques*'. A footnote explained that this *renaissance des vertus publiques* would gradually reduce the violence of tyranny.[34]

Three times Brissot invoked the irresistible power of the *force des choses*, 'the political law that controls everything in the political, as in the physical world. It is this *force des choses* that overthrew the Roman empire.'[35] His political vision retained its nebulous and messianic character, a vague compound of free trade, civil rights, cosmopolitanism and moral regeneration, but he was moving away from the tendency to reject existing social values that he seemed to advocate in the *Observations d'un républicain*. He now identified the good with a type of society that already existed in America and, to a lesser degree, in England, and he saw its advent on the continent as the inevitable consequence of economic determinism. This marked some sort of a move in the direction of Montesquieu. Like a good many of his contemporaries, however, Brissot wanted both the cake and the halfpenny. Although free trade was the motor of prosperity, 'inequality is the source of evil'. Farmers were superior to artisans since they were self-employed, and the slow progress of industrialisation in America would delay *la décadence des moeurs et de l'esprit public*.[36] His invitation the Americans to concentrate on agriculture and the good life, leaving the corrupting effects of luxury to French merchants, showed how tenaciously the old feelings lingered, even if Brissot was off on a new tack.

The book closed with the prospectus for a Gallo-American

---

[34] Ibid. pp.xxviii-xxxii.   [35] Ibid. pp.xxxiv, 10, 65.
[36] Ibid. pp.57n[1], 61.

Society, which was created in 1787. This pressure group no doubt suited Clavière's financial interests. It was also a new version of the idea behind Brissot's London lycée: to create a centre for the dissemination of 'advanced' ideas that would gradually modify the character of the French monarchy. During his retreat to England, towards the end of 1787, Brissot had made contact with the movement to promote the abolition of the slave trade. As soon as he returned to France, in February 1788, he set up a similar society, the *Amis des Noirs*. Its founder-members included, besides Lafayette, Bergasse and Carra from the Societé d'Harmonie Universelle, Mirabeau, Condorcet, Volney and Valady, who signed a letter to Brissot, 'G. d'Izarn, called marquis de Valady in accordance with vain usage'.[37] Brissot was now in contact with Clavière, Carra, Gorsas, Condorcet, Mercier, Volney and Valady; Pétion was an old school-friend from Chartres, and he had also begun to correspond with the Rolands. This constituted a substantial proportion of the leadership of the future Girondin group during the Revolution. Rather curiously, at a time when everyone's ideas were in a state of flux and no one could foresee future party divisions, Brissot's associates do not appear to have included any future Montagnards, with the exception of Marat. Brissot emphasised in his memoirs that Hérault de Séchelles refused to join the *Amis des Noirs*.

In the summer of 1788, Clavière and his syndicate sent Brissot to America. With 10,000 livres for his expenses and the prospect of commission, it must have been as comfortable a trip as eighteenth-century travel permitted. A letter of introduction from Lafayette enabled him to meet Washington, who was somewhat equivocal on the subject of the slave trade. Brissot seems to have had a favourable reception from everyone except the French ambassador, who regarded him as a dangerous radical. He may still have been thinking of emigration, for he made enquiries about the kind of things that colonists should bring from Europe. If this was the case, the news from France that the Estates General were to meet in the spring of 1789 made him change his mind and brought him back in a hurry.

According to the editor of his memoirs, he tried to get himself elected in Chartres, where his failure is not surprising, since he

[37] *Mémoires* III/174-5.

can scarcely have been known there. He chaired a meeting in his
Paris District, but was not selected as one of the electors who
were to choose the deputies to the Estates General. It was
unusual for chairmen to be passed over, but since his District –
which corresponded to the City – was to become renowned as the
most conservative in Paris, it may have preferred more
substantial citizens.

As usual he was left with nothing but his pen, and he joined
the crowd of pamphleters who took advantage of the virtual
abolition of press censorship to give their compatriots the benefit
of their advice. It was perhaps the first time that he had been
quite free to say what he liked. His *Plan de conduite pour les
députés du peuple aux Etats-Géneraux de 1789*, published in
April 1789, began, understandably enough, on a note of
exaltation. He contrasted the France he had left to go to America
with that which he found on his return. 'You were languishing in
slavery and you are free; you were thought to be enervated and
you have shown the greatest energy; you were thought to be
ignorant and you have shown profound political sense.'[38] To his
long-standing conviction that men in a state of nature were free
and equal he now added the dangerous corollary that popular
debasement and ignorance were merely the accidental products
of bad government. Aristocrats would argue that national
regeneration was impossible, but they were wrong. With some
prescience, he saw that the Estates General would not merely
provide France with a constitution, but would undertake a
profound transformation of all French institutions, something
that could not be completed in a few months, in one, or even two
years. He believed that absolutism was now a thing of the past
and the only future danger came from aristocracy. This was not
some sort of a 'middle class' attack on the nobility, for he defined
the enemy as the *haute noblesse, le haut clergé, la haute
magistrature, le haut tiers*. The king would surely see that the
monarchy must now become popular and the government, with
Necker as its chief minister, was on the right side. In his 1787
diatribe against Necker's insistence on gradual reform, Brissot
had insisted on the need for radical measures to overthrow the

---

[38] *Plan de conduite pour les députés du peuple aux Etats-généraux de 1789*,
n.p., 1789, p.i.

old order but he had also said that, in a republic, he would have argued in favour of gradual reform. He now retracted his previous criticism of Necker, which implied his belief that 'republican' criteria now applied in France.

When he came down to details, Brissot combined radical objectives with quite a shrewd sense of political realities, born of his considerable knowledge of the working of parliamentary institutions in Britain and the United States. Legislative power resided theoretically in the people, but they would need training before they could exercise it responsibly, and it could provisionally be shared with the king. The Estates General had no mandate to assume such power or to draft a constitution. No doubt influenced by what he knew of England, Brissot was apprehensive about the annexation of sovereignty by a coalition of king and parliament. He mistrusted the popular cry of 'all power to the representatives' since 'men and corporations tend only to increase their own powers'. On the same grounds, he specifically excluded any appeal to a providential legislator. 'Even if a Solon or a Lycurgus existed it would be unwise blindly to entrust him with the right to constitute the nation.'[39] The men who drafted the constitution must be a cross-section of the existing interests of the nation – in other words, they must reflect the *esprit général* rather than any *volonté générale*. His belief in popular sovereignty led him to suspect the corporate self-interest of any parliament and to insist that the Estates General should meet in Paris rather than at Versailles, and should vote publicly, so that it could be kept under the people's eye. He was equally aware of the danger of large unicameral assemblies being swept away by enthusiasm. 'If one reads the history of Athens and Rome, it is full of iniquities perpetrated by tumultuous assemblies.'[40] His own plan was therefore – since he rejected separate voting by the three Orders – that the Estates General should be split into two halves, whose agreement would be necessary for all legislation. Its only function was to determine the conditions for the election of a constituent convention – an obvious borrowing from America. This convention would then draft a constitution which would be sent to the provinces for their comments and an amended version would then be

[39] Ibid. p.233.   [40] Ibid. p.30.

submitted to a national referendum. In the immediate future, if the clergy and nobility should refuse to co-operate with the third estate, it should declare them to be *des corporations peculiers* (sic: this reads as though he was thinking in English) *étrangères au Peuple Français*, and proceed without them to draft a Declaration of Rights. Although they were entitled to do this on their own, it would be polite to communicate it to the king. He took it for granted that they would have the support of the government – in other words, of Necker.

To search this programme for specific borrowings from Montesquieu and Rousseau would be an exercise in pedantry – his insistence on the election of a convention may have been partly designed to give him a second chance of election and he was thinking in terms of the tactical moves appropriate to a particular crisis. Any discussion of constitutional machinery was bound to have more in common with *De l'esprit des lois* than with *Du contrat social*. Had Rousseau been alive in 1789 he too would probably have stressed the need for caution. Even if one thinks in terms of the general attitudes of Montesquieu and Rousseau, Brissot borrowed from each, He was concerned with national regeneration, a transformation of the political character of the French people rather than a modification of its political institutions to conform to some pre-existing *esprit général*. On the whole, however, he put the emphasis on fallibility rather than perfectibility. He drew his examples from Britain and America rather than from the classical world, and quoted Greece and Rome as warnings rather than as examples. He rejected the appeal to a lawgiver who would transform the people into what it ought to be, in favour of the representation of the divergent interests that made it what it was. He specifically claimed to have tried to adjust Anglo-American parliamentary procedure to allow for the weaknesses of the French temperament – notably loquacity. If one bears in mind all his past disappointments, his elation at the fulfilment of his revolutionary prophecies, his hopes for the future of his country and, no doubt, himself, one cannot help being struck by the sobriety of his *Plan*. It was a bold political programme which tried to encompass the possible resistance of opponents and the probable temptations of power, rather than a blue-print for the millennium. At bottom, he was thinking of freedom rather than of *vertu*.

Chapter 6

Marat

Jean-Paul Marat, or Mara, was born near Neuchâtel, in what was then Prussian territory, in 1743.[1] He was therefore three years younger than Mercier and eleven years older than Brissot. His mother was Swiss but his father was an Italian who had left Sardinia when he became a Protestant. According to Marat himself, 'From my earliest days I was consumed by the love of glory, a passion that often changed its goal during the various periods of my life, but never left me for an instant. At five I wanted to be a teacher, at ten a professor, an author at fifteen and a creative genius at twenty; today [1793] my passion is to sacrifice myself for my country.'[2]

When he was only sixteen, he left home for France. Like Mercier, he spent a year or two tutoring in Bordeaux. He lived in Paris for a time and about 1767 began a long stay in England, where he practised medicine in London and probably in Newcastle. About the time that he left France, he began writing a novel, *Les Aventures du jeune comte Potowski*. This was the only one of his works about which he never spoke and it was not published until 1847. The novel was obviously inspired by the *Nouvelle Héloïse*, written in epistolary form, abounding in noble sentiments and moral dilemmas; it even included a boat trip on a lake during a storm. Marat occasionally managed to hit a genuinely Rousseauist note, as when a widow reflected on her

---

[1] Although his eulogist in the Jacobin Club in 1793 claimed him for France and said he was born in the Doubs, 'not far from that city that has been the home of liberty since she left Greece and Rome'. *Mélanges de Marat, dit l'Ami du Peuple*, Tokyo, 1967. *Oraison funèbre*, p.3. The biography of Marat by Gérard Walter (Paris, 1933) is as good as any. Dr. Cabanès, *Marat inconnu*, Paris, n.d., contains a good deal of original information on his pre-revolutionary career.

[2] Quoted in A.Bougeart, *Marat, l'Ami du Peuple*, Paris, 1865, p.5.

attempts – they were naturally unsuccessful – to seduce the young hero, 'In order to captivate him, I am trying to corrupt his heart ... It is his *belle âme* that enchants me and I am trying to make him unworthy of me.' On the whole, though, in marked contrast to Rousseau, the passionate language has a curious coldness and the whole thing reads like a literary exercise. It is still very much better than Mercier's frightful *Contes moraux*. A pointer to the future was the reference to the incorrigible vice of most princes: 'The evil is in the thing itself and the cure is violent. One must apply the axe to the root.'

This was Marat's only attempt at *belles lettres*. His next work, originally published in 1772 as an *Essay on the human soul*, was expanded in the following year and renamed *An essay on man*. Like Brissot in *De la vérité*, Marat claimed that his approach was empirical; this did not prevent him from asserting in the opening sentence that all animals had souls. He claimed to refute materialism, which could not provide any physical explanation for the existence of such 'passions' as patriotism or the love of glory. He thought that he had located the soul (by which he seems to have meant something very much like the brain), in the meninx. It was connected to the body by a 'nervous fluid'. Much of his argument about the passions was fairly conventional, but his denial of their physical origin led him to damn Locke with faint praise, to write off La Mettrie's *L'Homme physique* was 'a wretched collection of trivial observations' and to denounce Helvétius as 'false and superficial'. Rather oddly, he went out of his way to praise the 'sublime philosophy' of Montesquieu, 'that extraordinary man who combined so happily finesse, wisdom and depth of mind'.[3] The French edition concluded with an invocation of Rousseau that reads like an afterthought: 'Sublime Rousseau, lend me your pen to celebrate all these marvels.' If Marat took on the materialists, he had no use for religion or for 'priests whose task was always to blind the human race for their own advantage and to preach ignorance and error in the name of the gods'. A prudent footnote to the French edition explained that this referred only to pagan priests. Since it was impossible to imagine God except in a physical sense, 'all religions are buttressed by a crude cult that

---

[3] *De l'homme*, Amsterdam, 1775-76, 3v, I/xiv.

interposes material objects between creator and creature'.[4] He had already assembled most of the elements of his philosophy, including his lifelong devotion to Montesquieu and Rousseau.

When an edition in three volumes was published in France in 1776, it received quite a favourable review from Diderot, but Marat's contemptuous dismissal of Helvétius provoked the anger of the latter's friend, Voltaire. 'One should not indulge one's contempt for others and one's regard for one's self to an extent that revolts every reader.' 'One should not always be darting out of one's house to provoke a quarrel in the street.'[5] It was advice that Marat might have done well to heed. Granted Voltaire's authority as an arbiter of reputations, it was also an unfortunate start.

In 1774 Marat produced his first political work, written in English: *The chains of slavery*. The sub-title claimed this to be 'A work wherein the clandestine and villainous attempts of princes to ruin liberty are pointed out and the dreadful scenes of despotism disclosed'. Like his book on the constitution of 1789, and his revolutionary newspaper, it carried Rousseau's device: *vitam impendere vero*. Most of the book was an attack on despotism in general terms, but it began with an address to the British electorate, on the eve of the 1774 election. R.C.H.Catterall, in his investigation of the circumstances surrounding the publication of the book, came to the conclusion that the address and part of the book itself were written by an Englishman, the remainder being a translation of a work that Marat had previously written in French.[6] This may be so, but the advice to the electors to choose 'men whom an independent fortune secure from the temptations of poverty', was to be Marat's doctrine throughout his life.

The chains of slavery also expressed a point of view that Marat was never to abandon, except for a few euphoric months in 1789. All societies were founded and maintained by violence. Although sovereignty ought to reside in the people as a whole (a distant bow in the direction of Rousseau), in practice most nations were dominated by tyrants; princes, almost without exception, were

---

[4] Ibid. I/v, II/226.
[5] Paris, 1830 edition, XLVIII/226-34.
[6] 'The credibility of Marat' *American Historical Review*, 1910, pp.25-32.

on the lookout for means of extending their power. Being
ruthless and clever, or at least able to buy good advice, they
usually won. Marat envisaged two kinds of situation in which
their machinations could possibly be foiled. The first was the
familiar primitive society, in which a sound constitution was
maintained by the *vertu* of the citizens. This was the
Rousseauist scenario: such a society must be defended by
'vigilance, frugality, disinterestedness, love of glory and patria'.
Princes unable to overthrow it by force would try to corrupt it by
the theatre, entertainment of every kind and debauchery. All
'luxury' – in other words, commerce and industry – contributed
to their evil designs. Their task was made all the easier since the
mass of the people constituted 'a stupid animal whose affection
largesses ever secure'. 'A continual attention to public affairs is
above the reach of the multitude.' Free societies therefore
demanded Spartan habits and resistance to all innovation.

Unlike Rousseau, Marat was more concerned with the second
type of situation: the organisation of revolt against an existing
tyranny. Far from believing that peoples got the governments
they deserved, in the sense that the existence of tyranny was
proof of a lack of *vertu*, or, if not the consequence, would be the
cause of it, he maintained that 'liberty continually springs up
out of the fires of sedition'. 'By the efforts of the multitude only
are the projects of tyranny confounded.' Sedition might be
frequent and widespread, but it was rarely successful, since
princes could rely on the support of the Christian religion, with
its doctrine of passive obedience, on the greatest of their subjects
and on the 'prostituted herd'. Their only consistent opponents
were 'men of a middle rank, sensible and wise men, generous
souls who will obey the law only, and elevated minds who scorn
servility'. Such paragons would have all their work cut out, since
they could do nothing without popular support and princes could
always seduce the rabble with the prospect of loot.

Understandably, Marat found this situation both depressing
and confusing. Writing anonymously and as though he were an
Englishman, he advised the electorate: 'to select our
representatives from among wealthy men is prudent, if they are
not destitute of merit.' He had an uneasy suspicion that many of
them would be, and that they would see things from their own
point of view. In one of the few convincing passages of the book

he cried out 'Who are the friends of the poor in a senate composed of rich men only?'. It was therefore necessary to abolish the property qualification for MPs. Whatever one did was very unlikely to succeed, at any rate for long. Time was on the side of the princes.

The book concluded with a further diatribe against their evil ways. To have a pretext for expropriating traitors, the Prince 'denominates high treason an infinite number of guiltless actions and is wholly busy in contriving new crimes and finding out informers'. Princes 'maintain legions of spies among their subjects, they erect secret tribunals and inquisitions of every kind, the doors of which are for ever open to informers'. This was followed by an apocalyptic picture of life under such a tyranny. Marat admitted that it did not really look very much like England in 1774. He could not know how much it was going to resemble France in 1793.

His concern for the poor was probably genuine enough, but it went with a total contempt for the political wisdom, or even the *vertu* of ordinary people. His message was therefore essentially negative: tyranny was always to be attacked and all governments opposed, even those that emerged from a successful revolution, since they would soon be as bad as their predecessors, unless constrained by force. Power was always in the wrong hands and every political situation was one of conflict. The function of Parliament was not to pass wise laws but to oppose the executive. When it came to suggesting economic policies that might make the poor less poor, or constitutional ones that might guarantee civil liberty, Marat had nothing to say. All economic development was suspect as an instrument of princely subversion. England would be better off with a written constitution and no House of Lords since 'our deputies exercise their delegated powers without ever consulting us', but this scarcely amounts to a policy.

The chains of slavery was published in May 1774, in a rather elegant edition, priced 12/6. It was advertised in four periodicals and reviewed by two, adversely in the *Monthly Review* and favourably in the *London Magazine*.[7] Not surprisingly, at that price, it does not seem to have sold at all well. Marat sent two

---

[7] For a more detailed account, see Catterall, art. cit.

complimentary copies of the first, anonymous edition, to at least three of the Newcastle guilds. In the following year he seems to have reissued the unsold copies in Newcastle, this time with his name on the title-page. He himself gave a rather more dramatic account of what had been going on, when he published a French translation in 1793.[8] According to his own version, he was so prostrated by his attempts to get the book out in time to influence the 1774 elections, that he was confined to his bed for almost a fortnight. When he recovered, he found that nothing had been done. No periodical was prepared to advertise the book, though he offered to pay ten guineas instead of the customary five shillings. His printer was sending the sheets to Lord North as soon as they were ready. Informed of Marat's resolute character – he slept with pistols by his bedside for six weeks – North gave up the idea of violence and confined himself to guile. His spies corrupted Marat's host and servant and intercepted his correspondence. When he realised what was going on, Marat sent most of the copies of the book to various patriotic societies in the north and threw the Prime Minister's spies off the scent by crossing over to Holland and then making his way back to the north of England. He then discovered that three of the societies had sent him letters of affiliation in a gold box (*une boîte d'or* rather than *dorée* – i.e. gold rather than golden). Not knowing his name, they had addressed this to his publishers, which enabled the indefatigable North to intercept it. Although the 8,000 guineas he spent prevented the book from swinging the 1774 election, it did lead to the exclusion of placemen from Parliament and inspired an unsuccessful attempt at parliamentary reform.

Some of this is demonstrably untrue. *The chains of slavery* was advertised and reviewed in the normal way and it appeared six months before the election. The rest is wholly incredible. In the unlikely event of North's having heard of the book, he was not going to lose much sleep over the advice to the electors to choose wealthy candidates distinguished by their ability and integrity, and the rest of the book had no particular relevance to the election. Marat had no motive for inventing this cock-and-bull story in 1793. He had written to Wilkes in 1774 that his

---

[8] See the preface to *Les chaînes de l'esclavage*, Paris, l'an premier de la liberté, pp.6-10.

enemies, unable to suppress the book (i.e. it *had* appeared, after all, before the election), had somehow or other succeeded in getting it 'consigned to oblivion'.[9] It looks, in other words, as though Marat believed from the start that he had been the victim of a plot, even if it took him twenty years of brooding to concoct the melodrama that he served up in 1793. Whether or not this constitutes paranoia is perhaps a matter for specialists.[10] It certainly means one cannot believe anything he says about himself. His long stay in England has left hardly any traces.

All that is known for certain is that in 1775 he bought a medical qualification from St Andrews, the university that Dr Johnson predicted would grow rich 'by degrees'. In the previous year a Marat, who seems to have taught at the dissenters' academy at Warrington, offered his services to the director as a translator and his hand to the director's sister.[11] Both offers were refused. In February 1776, coins and medals to the value of £200 were stolen from the Ashmolean museum in Oxford by a John Le Maître, alias Mara. On the following day he offered some of them for sale in Norwich, where he was introduced to a jeweller by a local doctor who had been a pupil at the Warrington academy. The thief was captured in Dublin (where Marat later said that he had spent some time) and tried and sentenced in Oxford in 1777. This looks like rather a lot of circumstantial evidence. Understandably enough, Phipson, in his book on Marat's career in England, was inclined to take it at its face value, despite the existence of a letter from Marat, written from Dover in April 1776, by which time the thief had already been arrested in Dublin. Phipson even had an explanation for the fact that Marat is known to have been in France when he should have been serving his sentence in the Woolwich hulks: a small group of Woolwich prisoners is known to have escaped. Darnton's discovery of a letter by Marat, written from Geneva in May 1776, disposes of the whole business and suggests that the Marat who perhaps taught at Warrington may not have been Jean-Paul.[12]

[9] G.Walter, *Marat*, Paris, 1960 ed., p.45n[6].

[10] C.W.Burr, in 'Jean-Paul Marat, physician, revolutionist, paranoiac', *Annales of Medical History*, 1919, thinks that he was.

[11] *Notes and Queries*, 1922, p.53.

[12] See especially, Cabanès, ch IV and S.L.Phipson, *Jean-Paul Marat, his career in England and France before the revolution*, London, 1924, pp.52-82. The letter from Geneva is in *Annales historiques de la Révolution française*, 1966, pp.447-50.

Marat went back to France to rescue the French edition of his *De l'homme*, which was in difficulties with the customs. Although no question of censorship appears to have been involved, he convinced himself that he was the victim of a plot invented, not by the government, but by jealous philosophes. Before turning to his new career, it may be appropriate to look at the last production of his first radical phase, the *Plan de legislation criminelle* that he submitted for a prize competition in Berne and published in 1780. In the preface to the 1790 edition he described it as coming from 'the pen of an author who was famous in the republic of letters' and claimed that 'this excellent treatise' had circulated mainly in Switzerland and Germany, where the Habsburg Emperor, Joseph II, had adopted some of its proposals. It was a curious composition. The opening section was an elaboration, in extremely violent language, of the point of view expressed in *The chains of slavery*. Men were equal by nature but, in practice, law operated everywhere to the advantage of the strong: 'tyranny on the one side, servitude on the other.' All governments were founded on violence, murder and brigandage, and none could be regarded as legitimate. Unless prevented by law, wealth tended to accumulate in a few hands and the enrichment of some implied the impoverishment of the rest. The poor were entitled to 'an assured subsistence, proper clothing, complete security, care when sick and help in old age'.[13] In default of this they recovered the rights that they had initially enjoyed in a state of nature. Property rights were subordinate to the right of existence; in other words, no one was entitled to superfluity when others were in need. Crime was the fault of goverments which deprived the poor of the means of subsistence. Marat was more aware than most of his contemporaries of the fact that readiness to work was no guarantee of employment. He advocated an extensive programme of public works, to be financed by the property of the Church, and the provision of free education for the poor at the expense of the rich.

He then advanced the Rousseauist argument that ancient governments had regarded law as a means of stimulating *vertu*, whereas modern ones were concerned only with the punishment

---

[13] *Plan de législation criminelle*, 1790 ed, p.17. This was a paraphrase of *De l'esprit des lois* XXIII/29.

of crime. 'Let us leave those sublime institutions which are not made for our puny souls and since we cannot hope to make men *vertueux*, at least let us prevent them from being wicked.' He accepted his own advice: the remainder of the essay was moderate, reformist and humane, essentially concerned with the protection of the individual. It was also unusually conscious of the bias of law against women. Marat insisted on the equality of the sexes, in which context he discarded the anti-feminist Rousseau for 'the illustrious Montesquieu', to whom he was also indebted for the general shape of the essay. Such veneration for Montesquieu coexisted rather uneasily with a Rousseauist hankering after 'those governments where legislation tends only to inspire love of country and ... no one has any interest apart from that of the state'. Such classical perfection was naturally contrasted with present-day governments where 'everyone isolates himself and openly puts his particular advantage before the general interest'. For his conclusion he returned to Montesquieu, whom he plagiarised on the subject of the deterrent effect of harsh punishments: 'I was going to add ... [sic] But I hear the voice of lamenting nature, my heart contracts and the pen falls from my fingers.'[14]

The *Plan de législation criminelle* may have been derivative, but it was one of the best things that Marat wrote, and one of the most constructive. It also demonstrated his curious dualism. His respect for Montesquieu was genuine enough but it did not accord with his temperament, which could never resist the more violent chiaroscuro of Rousseau, which he interpreted in his own way, seeing all politics as a state of war, with popular violence (always directed from above) as the only answer to the hypocrisy and guile of governments. It was not a combination that appealed to the Bernese jury.

A year after Marat reached France, the abbé Filassier wrote to the *Gazette de Santé* describing the case of the marquise de l'Aubespine, a tubercular patient who had been miraculously cured by an unknown English doctor after several years of

---

[14] Montesquieu had been both more eloquent and more convincing: 'I was going to say that slaves in Greece and Rome ... But I hear the voice of nature crying out against me.' *De l'esprit des lois*, VI/17.

unsuccessful treatment by French practitioners.[15] Filassier was soon to be acting as Marat's demonstrator. At the invitation of the editor, Marat declared himself, described the symptoms of the marquise and the treatment he had used. This provoked a letter from a Dr Levi, to the effect that the symptoms, as described by Marat, suggested a nervous complaint rather than tuberculosis. (Brissot was later to assert ungallantly that the marquise had, in fact, been suffering from venereal disease, about which Marat had published a paper while still in England.)[16] Marat wrote again, recapitulating the symptoms, or rather, substituting different ones. The editor, who had initially extolled Marat, was now on his guard and he punctuated Marat's letter with sarcastic comments. A little later the abbé Tessier wrote to say that he had analysed the *eau factice* that Marat had prescribed, in default of *l'eau de Harrowgate*, and found it consisted of lime-water.

The whole peculiar business sounds like an ingenious advertising campaign. As such, it seems to have worked. Marat was installed for a time in the hôtel de l'Aubespine. According to his own story, the marquise secured him an appointment as doctor to the household troops of the king's brother, the comte d'Artois.[17] His commission described him as 'a doctor of several English universities.' He pretended that the post was created for him and that it was honorary. Neither statement was true. He received a handsome apartment and a modest salary of 2,000 livres a year. The story that he was actually employed as a vet is, however, an invention. To judge from a surviving letter to Artois's *Intendant des Finances*, Marat's services do not appear to have been purely medical and he seems to have been employed in buying off people who had written 'impertinent invectives' against Artois.[18] This would not have done Marat any good had it emerged during the revolution, when Artois was the leader of the émigré royalists. There is no means of knowing what Marat was like as a doctor – and no reason to accept his own statement that he was known as 'the doctor of the incurables'.

[15] See C.Vellay, *Supplément à la correspondance de Marat*, Le Puy, 1910, pp.1-13. These letters were originally printed in the *Revue historique*, 1910.

[16] Brissot, *Mémoires* I/199.

[17] Cabanès, op. cit. pp.114-5.

[18] C.Vellay, *Marat: correspondance*, p.90.

He was certainly expensive, charging 24 livres, or, if one can believe Brissot, as much as 36, for a consultation. He was always pressing prescriptions on his friends, for which they had to pay, and when Brissot presented Mercier to him, the latter was not very satisfied with Marat's treatment.[19] In an extraordinary letter printed by Vellay, who was not one of his detractors, Marat said that he was interested only in diseases where there was 'little to do and much to gain'.[20] It is hard to imagine anyone putting this on paper, however true it may have been, and even Brissot admitted that Marat wanted money, not for himself but for his research. He does, however, seem to have been very much of a society doctor. He had a fashionable address, he kept a servant and he wore a sword.

His passion was not medicine but physics. In the hostile words of Brissot, 'Insensible to the pleasures of the table and the agreeable things of life, he devoted all his resources to his experiments in physics. Night and day absorbed in them, he would have been content with bread and water in return for the pleasure of once humiliating the Académie des Sciences.' 'To fight and destroy the reputation of famous men was his dominating passion ' This was Voltaire's criticism all over again: Marat could not be convinced that he had won unless he had destroyed the reputation of everyone else. It is easier to evaluate his scientific activities than his medicine, since his publications have survived. Their interpretation, however, is a matter for specialists in the history of science. What matters is not that he was wrong, but how he fitted into the context of scientific knowledge and ignorance. Recent studies by two historians of science arrive at very similar conclusions.[21]

Marat conducted a series of experiments in the hôtel de l'Aubespine in 1779, to which he bombarded Franklin with invitations. 'Let the cabal be never so warm, it will certainly be silenced by the sanction of such a man as Dr Franklin.'[22] It was

[19] For Brissot's account of Marat at this time, see *Mémoires* I/196-212_

[20] Vellay, *Correspondance*, p. 90.

[21] J.W.Dauben, 'Marat, his science and the French revolution', *Archives internationales d'histoire des sciences*, 1969, and C.C.Gillispie, *Science and polity in France at the end of the old regime*, Princeton, 1980.

[22] Marat's letters to Franklin are in the *Revue historique de la révolution française*, 1910.

the old story of persecution. Franklin kept out of the way. When Marat published his *Découvertes sur le feu, l'éléctricité et la lumière* in 1779, the Académie des Sciences praised his experimental technique, without expressing any opinion as to his conclusions. In the following year he brought out *Découvertes sur la lumière*, in which he claimed to have refuted Newton. He was eager for endorsement by the Academy, but it delayed its report for eleven months, despite a series of letters from Marat to its secretary, Condorcet. This was certainly discourteous, but one can see why they did not take Marat seriously. He had presumably not been experimenting for more than a couple of years and he insisted that men with a lifetime's experience behind them should admit that he had surpassed them all. As Lalande put it, 'The greatest men only make one or two discoveries in the course of a long life, but Marat made hundreds.' 1780 also saw the appearance of *Recherches physiques sur le feu*, which Marat thought 'condemns to oblivion everything that the learned societies have ever published on this subject'.[23] In the *Recherches physiques sur l'éléctricité* in 1782, he once more claimed to have overthrown all existing theories – including those of the disappointing Franklin – and to have shown that lightning conductors were useless. His researches on air offered the prospect of taming the destructiveness of hailstorms.

As in the case of *The chains of slavery*, his reception was less hostile than he pretended. French periodicals noted his work as interesting and it was translated into German and commended by Goethe. Marat himself claimed that his memoir on fire created a prodigious sensation throughout Europe. Those who flooded to his laboratory included 'princes of the blood and the most eminent personnages in the state.' Visitors came from as far afield as Leipzig and Stockholm. This was naturally too much for the Académie des Sciences, whose members cried with one voice, 'If this man is right, what are we to do with the publications of the Academy?'[24] They therefore pretended that he was wrong and that was the end of that. When he won a prize from the Rouen Academy, the jury commented adversely on his

[23] Quoted in Dauben, art. cit. p.249.
[24] F.Chévremont, *Jean-Paul Marat*, Paris, 1880, 2v, I/47-51.

savage attack on a fellow-scientist, the abbé Bertholon. With his usual modesty, Marat said, 'In the opinion of all true connoisseurs, I am the only man who can bring this healing art [electro-therapy] to perfection' and claimed to be 'sought after by all the crowned heads' and to have turned down the offer of a pension of 24, 000 livres from a northern prince.[25]

It was all too familiar – apart from the change in his attitude towards crowned heads: Marat was the universal genius who exposed the errors of Franklin and of Newtonian optics ('this baseless system is merely a tissue of errors'),[26] as he had previously refuted those of Helvétius. He was acclaimed by the disinterested men of goodwill who rushed to honour him, but eternally foiled by the men in power whom he threatened, whether Lord North, the French philosophes or the Académie des Sciences. Common sense would suggest that if Marat had been right, someone would have rehabilitated him by now, and there might be fewer lightning conductors and hailstorms. A recent writer, C.C. Gillispie, after studying Marat's 'discoveries', concluded that his technique was 'to read voraciously, reject all previous theories and base his own on a *truc*, a gimmick'.[27] In every case, this amounted to the discovery of an unknown fluid: nervous (in the case of the *Essay on the human soul*), igneous, luminous or electrical. Gillespie's conclusion reinforces Burr's diagnosis of paranoia: 'Comparable hostility for science, or rather, what is at bottom the same hostility, has been manifested among the alienated from time to time throughout modern history.'

It is just possible that Marat's polemics may have brought him to the attention of Robespierre, in no favourable light. Robespierre was helping the Arras lawyer, Buissart, who became his friend, to defend a man who was being prosecuted for putting up a lightning conductor. Buissart enlisted the support of Parisian scientists, including Bertholon, who mentioned Marat's attacks on him, in a letter to Arras. 'This man is a madman who

[25] *Revue historique de la révolution française*, 1919, p.200; Chévremont, op. cit. I/54.

[26] L.R.Gottschalk, 'Du Marat inédit', *Annales historiques de la révolution française*, 1926, p.214.

[27] Op. cit. p.314.

thought he could achieve fame by attacking many great men and producing paradoxes that took no one in ... What makes this man furious is that no one talks about him or refutes him ... When a man, in this century, attacks lightning conductors, he merits nothing more than sovereign contempt and that is what he got ... He has to send two or three journalists letters signed by M. le chevalier de –, M. le marquis de –, to get them published in the papers in default of extracts that no one would print.'[28] Buissart is quite likely to have shown this to his collaborator and Robespierre had an excellent memory, especially for opponents. Since Brissot was trumpeting Marat's praises about this time, it was the first occasion when he and Robespierre found themselves on opposite sides.

Despite his prodigious acclaim by princes of the blood, state dignitaries and crowned heads, Marat's scientific reputation in 1783 left a good deal to be desired. This was all the more unfortunate since he was actively engaged in trying to obtain the post of secretary in a new academy that was to be created in Madrid. We know something of this from a number of letters from Marat to Roume de Saint Laurent, who was acting for him in Madrid.[29] Since more than scientific eminence would be required to commend him, south of the Pyrenees, Marat presented himself in a new rôle, that of defender of the faith. He told Roume, for onward transmission to the Spaniards, that when Marat was only 18 *nos prétendus philosophes* had tried to recruit him to their irreligious cause. His refusal was responsible for their constant persecution. The *Essay on man* was designed to refute materialism. (Since the Spaniards were very unlikely to have had access to a copy, there was not much danger of their finding out what he had said about religion in it.) The philosophes kept it out of France. Now he was worried in case their calumny should reach the ears of the Spanish ambassador in Paris. 'You know how much they bear a grudge against those, like me, who refused to swell their criminal sect and dared courageously to fight their pernicious errors.' Marat himself was

[28] *Revue historique de la révolution française*, 1912, pp.295-7.
[29] The most important letter, of 20 November 1783, is in Chèvremont, op. cit. I/41-63. Others are printed in Vellay's edition of Marat's correspondence, pp.18-19, in Gottschalk, art,cit. pp.210-11 and in the *Revue historique de la révolution française*, 1910 and 1919.

a man who frequented only those distinguished by piety and virtue – 'how many respectable clergymen could I quote as referees!'. Safe behind the Pyrenees, the Spaniards were perhaps unaware of the full extent of the danger from the philosophes. 'They have already formed the horrible project of destroying all the religious orders (something he had himself advocated in the *Plan de législation*) and annihilating religion itself ... if, one day, they come to entertain ambitious projects and direct their attention to political matters ... who will be able to prevent them from shaking governments and overthrowing states?' Times had certainly changed in 1793 when Roume wrote from gaol to beg Marat's help.

Brissot said of Marat, *Il fut en tout comédien* and one cannot help wondering how far he was consciously acting a part. It may have been innocent paranoia that led him to retail to Roume the story of his persecution by jealous mediocrities: how the Faculty of Medicine was so alarmed by Marat's competition that they denounced him in anonymous letters to his patients and the Académie des Sciences realised that it must destroy him before he destroyed it. Marat the *dévot* smacks of rational calculation. He knew that if the Spanish ambassador were to check his credentials in the scientific world, the game would be up. His only hope was to present himself as the victim of an atheist plot. He may well have believed in the plot himself, but his pious indignation at the threat of an attack on religion, and even of political subversion, was a deliberate invention.

His fears were justified. He did not get the post in Madrid and his position collapsed in France itself. He either left the service of Artois or was dismissed, in 1783 or 1784. He had been calling himself 'de Marat' and sealing his letters with a coronet and armorial bearings. This was innocent enough and in any case, it was not for 'de Robespierre' or Brissot 'de Warville' to cast the first stone, but, as usual, Marat went too far. He actually claimed noble birth, instead of merely trying to give the impression that he had it, writing to the *juge d'armes* to ask for recognition of the fact that the Marats enjoyed both French and Spanish nobility and arguing that his post in Artois's household made this a matter of general social interest. 'It is honourable for the state that the origin of a servant of princes should be established by certified documents.'[30] That would have come as rather a shock to the readers of the *Ami du Peuple*.

What happened to him between 1784 and 1789 is not at all clear but was probably not very pleasant. His scientific work seems to have petered out, although he reprinted some of his earlier papers and published a translation of Newton's *Optics* in 1788, which was rather curious if he really believed it to be 'a tissue of errors'. His feud with the Académie des Sciences did not prevent their awarding him half of a second prize, in 1785, in a competition for the improvement of the hydraulic machine at Marly.[31] There was nothing particularly unusual, in that cosmopolitan century, in his feeling no exclusive attachment to France. It was therefore not surprising that he should have written to Roume in September 1783 to tell him that he already regarded himself as in the Spanish service. In 1785 he claimed exemption from the poll tax on the ground that he was a foreigner and in the following year, remembering his birth on Prussian territory, he sent Frederick II a handsomely-bound copy of his scientific works, 'a feeble expression of my profound respect and admiration'. This may have been genuine: he was to go on praising Frederick during the revolution, but the hammer of princes could be a courtier too. If he hoped for a pension he did not get one; the king may have been dead when his letter arrived. Brissot said that in 1786 or 1787 he urged Marat to give up physics for politics, but his friend replied that he had no intention of going to the Bastille. There was certainly not much danger of that.

Phipson, in his account of Marat's life in England, repeated several stories from people who claimed to have recognised the revolutionary Marat as a man who had been arrested for debt in Newcastle in 1786 and again in Bristol in 1787.[32] Phipson's problem was that he had too many Marats, Maras, and Maratt Amiatts, including the children of the one arrested in Newcastle, when there is no evidence that Jean-Paul was married. Apart from these 'eye-witnesses' there is no evidence for his having been in England at this time.

In 1782 the academy of Bordeaux decided to offer a prize for

[30] *Correspondance, p.88.*
[31] *Bachaumont, Mémoires secrets*, 18 April 1787.
[32] Op.cit. pp.109-20.

the best eulogy of Montesquieu. There were more than a score of
competitors, all of whom were rejected. Marat fared no better
when the subject was re-advertised and he submitted an essay in
1785. The jury may have felt that no one *could* do justice to their
hero, but they certainly did not think much of Marat's effort,
which they found cold, languid, lacking in stylistic elegance and
vigorous thought and devoid of the *vues philosophiques* that the
subject invited.[33] They were quite right. Instead of saying why he
really admired Montesquieu, Marat decided to play safe. Most
of his essay consisted of an uninspired paraphrase that left out
anything remotely controversial, such as Montesquieu's defence
of a hereditary nobility as a check on absolutism, or his defence
of the British constitution. He insisted that Montesquieu's aim
was 'not to give [men] a blueprint of the best possible
government, but to make them as happy as the different kinds of
government under which they lived would allow. Unable to
remodel these governments, he concentrated on improving them,
cutting off abuses, correcting faults, bringing all parts of the
constitution into harmony, enlightening those who command
and giving those who obey reasons for admiring their laws, their
countries and their princes.' 'He never assumed the dogmatic
tone of a reformer.' This was more or less what Montesquieu had
said, for the benefit of the censors, but no one had been taken in.
Marat seemed to have confused the academy of Bordeaux with
that of Madrid. He said that Montesquieu was trying to bring
about a revolution 'which the century of true philosophy would
have realised if so many writers had not abused their freedom of
thought. Montesquieu was very different from those licentious
writers whose vanity is for ever carrying them beyond the bounds
of prudence, even more different from those mad writers whose
bold sacrilege overthows all barriers, shatters all restraints,
hands men over to the blind fury of their passions, plunges them
back into the horrors of anarchy, tears all remorse from the
wicked, all consolation from the wretched and, congratulating
itself in secret on the harm it has done them, proudly rests in
total destruction.' Marat had overdone it, as usual. There is no
need to suppose that the intellectual elite of the great sea port
felt in any need of a latter-day Bossuet. If Marat had actually

---

[33] Marat, *Eloge de Montesquieu* (ed. A. de Bretetz), Libourne, 1883.

believed all this stuff, 1789 would have found him on the conservative side.

In fact, he shared in the universal euphoria touched off by the convocation of the Estates General, so much so that his *Offrande à la patrie*, published in February 1789, the only optimistic thing he ever wrote, declared France's problems to be at an end.[34] His account of its composition and effect was a preview of what he was to write in 1793 about *The chains of slavery*. He was in a moribund condition when the news of the coming Estates General raised him from his sick bed to dash off a pamphlet whose arguments were taken up in 'practically all the *cahiers* of the deputies to the Estates'.[35] He does seem to have been ill – but in July 1788 – and very few of those who drafted the *cahiers* can have heard of Marat or his pamphlet.

The *Offrande* began on a sombre note: 'O my country ... I see you still covered in wounds and bathed in blood ... the excess of your torments at last drove you to cries of despair; they rung in the ears of your king and his paternal heart was moved with compassion.' The clergy, with honourable exceptions, were public enemies and the nobility insincere in their offers of fiscal equality. There were enemies everywhere, but the united efforts of the Third Estate would defeat them all. The financiers were 'too judicious to cover themselves with ridicule', the newly ennobled were estimable men, the lawyers intrepid defenders of the innocent, the parish priests respectable ministers of religion, and the intellectuals 'precious beings who dedicate their lives to your enlightenment'. The Third Estate was led by 'Gentlemen, magistrates, seigneurs, prelates, princes, all generous and magnanimous, who forget their prerogatives and espouse your cause'. Necker, the chief Minister, was 'A great statesman ... equally remarkable for his wisdom and integrity', the council of Ministers 'composed of wise and virtuous men'. As for Louis XVI: 'Blessed be the best of kings. Hope is reborn in our hearts ... Let the clergy and nobility continue to enjoy their honourable distinctions, but let all the Orders of the state draw together.'

As he warmed up, Marat's enthusiasm took on a hysterical note. 'O my *patrie*, how are you changed ... The people groan no

---

[34] Reprinted in C.Vellay, *Les pamphlets de Marat*, Paris, 1911, pp.1-37.
[35] *Ami du Peuple* No.382, 25 February 1791.

more under the crushing burden of taxation. Already the countryman has bread and clothing and can breathe again; so has the worker in the town; the artisan is no longer in need and the assiduous servant of the altar languishes in poverty no more. From the temple of liberty burst a thousand fertile springs. Prosperity reigns in every station' and so on, at considerable length. The Estates General had not even met when he published this.

Most people got excited in the spring of 1789, but they managed to keep one foot on the ground. Marat's concrete proposals were sensible enough: periodical meetings of the Estates General, freedom of the press (despite 'a multitude of libels ... which do not spare the throne, merit or virtue'), the abolition of *lettres de cachet* and the imitation of the British legal system. These were commonplaces in 1789 and Marat's customary advice to his readers to vote for men whose independent means put them beyond financial temptation was rather conservative. If he believed that the mere prospect of such useful improvements had already transformed France into an ideal society, when he came down to earth he was going to attribute all that was still amiss, not to the unreality of his vision but to the malevolence of the enemy. If the millennium fails to materialise, it is always someone else's fault.

When he published a supplement to the *Offrande*, a month or so later, things had already turned sour.[36] 'What, always imagining that princes actually have that love of the public good that they ought to have and practically never do!' He was now back in the mood of 1774, the last time that he had tried to influence an election. 'If the people have nothing to hope for except from their courage, to get them to break their chains one must not extenuate, in their eyes, the wrongs, the injustice and the outrages of their tyrants.' The king and Necker ('that wise man whose good intentions I shall always respect') still enjoyed his confidence but they were faced by 'a horrible conspiracy of the clergy, the nobility, the Parlements and the world of finance.' He had adopted the demagogues' creed that 'our misfortunes are due entirely to the incapacity and the vices of the proud men whose duty is to secure our happiness.' 'I ask myself, is it so

[36] Vellay, *Pamphlets*, pp.38-70.

difficult to do the right thing, if one genuinely wants to?' When it came to defining what the right thing was, he had little to offer, beyond the assertion that sovereignty resided in the nation, that legislative, executive, administrative and judicial powers should be in different hands and that the Estates General should insist on giving France a constitution before they agreed to new taxation. He approved of the king having a legislative veto, 'as is the present-day practice in England'.

He followed up the *Offrande*, in the summer of 1789 with *La Constitution, ou projet de déclaration des droits de l'homme et du citoyen, suivi d'un plan de constitution*. Once again he took Rousseau's device: *Vitam impendere vero*. His introduction defined his unchanging dual allegiance in the most striking way. 'If Montesquieu* and Rousseau were still with us, the best thing the Nation could do would be to implore them on its knees to give us a constitution.' '*Montesquieu, yes Montesquieu, the greatest man this century has produced ... He was the first amongst us to disarm superstition, to snatch away the dagger from despotism, demand the rights of man and attack tyranny.' If Marat had written like that in 1785 he might even have won the Bordeaux prize. He did quote a passage from his eulogy, to the effect that Montesquieu may have been more cautious than Rousseau because he had more to lose. Marat said that he was 'far from comparing himself to these great men', a rare instance of genuine modesty. The man who found it so hard to tolerate the reputation of anyone else was constant in his hero-worship of these two.

Marat had now reverted to his radical ideas of the 1770s. Everything, even cannibalism, was legitimate in the state of nature. Society was the product not of a contract but of force. Such concessions as rulers made to their peoples were extorted from them by revolt. Complete equality was an impossible ideal but inequality should be restricted to what derived from the unequal faculties of men, which presumably implied the abolition of inherited wealth. If the laws did not enforce relative economic equality, the man without property derived virtually no benefit from society. 'Liberty itself, which consoles us for so many woes, is nothing to him ... pinned as he is to crushing labour.' Then came a recapitulation of the right of the poor to food, clothing and shelter, that was quoted from his *Plan de législation* and probably derived in the first instance from Montesquieu. This was followed by a passage that echoed Rousseau on the starving man's right to take what he needed by force. 'Any authority that opposes him is tyrannical and the judge who condemns him to death is an assassin.'[37]

His sympathy for the plight of the poor (if not for their political competence) was probably genuine enough, but he had no idea what to do about it – beyond encouraging them to revolt against whomever happened to be in power. His constitutional proposals were in line with radical democratic thinking in 1789 and a good many of them were to be implemented by the Constituent Assembly.

All sovereignty resided in the people, who collectively embodied the general will and 'can never want what is bad for them, sell or betray themselves'. If this suggests that Marat had certainly understood his Rousseau, his assertion that the civil rights of citizens were 'even more sacred than the fundamental laws of the state' could be interpreted as pointing in the opposite direction. The electorate was entitled to impose imperative mandates on its delegates but, like Montesquieu, Marat thought this unwise, except in the case of fundamental laws. All legislation, however, should be subject to referendum. Like Montesquieu and unlike Rousseau, Marat praised the way things were done in England, whose government was 'the most celebrated for its wisdom'. He approved of the personal inviolability of the king, as professed across the Channel. Both king and Ministers were somehow responsible to the people, although Marat did not explain what this meant in practice. In one place he said that Ministers should be elected, the accused allowed counsel and treated as innocent until they had actually been convicted. Taxation should be proportionate to wealth, with indirect taxation adjusted to fall very heavily on such luxuries as servants, horses and carriages. Arguing that France had nothing to fear from her enemies unless she herself adopted an aggressive foreign policy, he wanted the army reduced to 60,000, with a militia of 200,000 disposing of its own artillery and

---

[37] Cf.Rousseau, 'A wretch who, to buy bread, steals an *écu* from a hard man stuffed with gold, is a knave who is hauled off to the gallows.' *Fragments politiques*, p.522.

stationed in all the major towns. The consent of the civil authorities should be required before troops were used against civilians. Despite the fact that 'public matters are scarcely within the range of ordinary people', all heads of families should have the vote, although, as usual, he advised them to elect 'men from the wealthiest class of citizens, whose fortune becomes a guarantee of their integrity'. On the subject of the clergy he was more violent and less realistic. 'The veil is rent, the mystical shadows in which they wrapped themselves are dispersed by the torch of reason.' This was more or less what he had told the Spaniards, but from a rather different point of view. Apart from those in charge of monastic finances, there was not a monk who would not jump at the chance of leaving the cloister, if offered a small pension.

It was all rather a jumble, which was not surprising since he was trying to squeeze both Montesquieu and Rousseau between the shafts of the constitutional coach. On the one hand he attacked those who professed 'a stupid respect for the institutions of our fathers, the ancient usages of the kingdom ... Why should we play at patching up an edifice that threatens to crush us in its fall and bury us beneath its ruins, when we can build anew?' On the other, he commended England as a model, still praised Louis XVI and thought that nobles and clergy were hastening to prove themselves citizens. He professed to detest 'licence, disorder, violence and irregularity', but said that the sufferings of the poor were all due to their pitiless exploitation by the agents of central and local government, who could only be tamed by the threat of revolt. He himself was probably hesitating over his choice of rôle, divided between the optimism of that unforgettable spring of 1789 and his deep-rooted convictions about eternal social war and the villainy of governments. If the latter won neither Montesquieu nor Rousseau would count for much.

Chapter 7

Robespierre

Maximilien Robespierre, or Derobespierre, or, as the more socially ambitious members of the family liked to spell it, de Robespierre, was born in Arras in 1758 only four months after the marriage of his parents.[1] His family circumstances were oddly reminiscent of those of Rousseau. His mother died when he was only six, while giving birth to a fifth child. His father, a reasonably successful barrister, was not present at her funeral and may have already left Arras; he was certainly to do so within a few months of her death. During the next eight years he returned from time to time, borrowing money on each visit, disappeared for good in 1772 and died in Munich five years later. Maximilien's sister said that he could never mention their mother without tears. There is no indication of what he thought about his father.

Unlike Rousseau, Robespierre was taken in hand by his family and received as good an education as was to be had in France. He and his brother were brought up by grandparents, the two girls going to their aunts. It probably meant a narrow and conventional life for them all, in a conservative and clerical town, but there is no reason to suppose it was not an affectionate one. Clerical influence secured for Maximilien a scholarship to Louis-le-Grand, perhaps the most famous school in Paris, where he remained for twelve years. Money was scarce: he must have found it humiliating to have to write to one of his teachers, the

[1] Of the many biographies of Robespierre, J.M.Thompson, *Robespierre*, Oxford, 1935, and G.Walter, *Robespierre*, Paris, 1936-39, 2v, are perhaps the best. For his early life, see J.A.Paris, *La jeunesse de Robespierre et la convocation des Etats-Généraux en Artois*, Arras, 1870. The most sensitive insight into his character is to be found in R.Cobb, *Tour de France*, London, 1976, pp.45-64.

abbé Proyart, as he did in 1778, that he would have liked to meet his benefactor, the bishop of Arras, but had no decent clothes in which to present himself. There were, however, plenty of other scholarship boys in the school and some of them may have been no better off.

There are two main sources for this period of Robespierre's life and they are totally contradictory. When she came to write down her recollections in the nineteenth century, his sister Charlotte presented him as the ideal schoolboy, good at his work and a favourite with his contemporaries. His first biographer, who called himself 'Leblond de Neuvéglise', described him as a monster.[2] In so far as one can reconcile them at all, they suggest that he was a boy of reasonable ability and great application. Even the venomous Leblond conceded so much: 'Consistent in his false idea of what constitutes real merit, he devoted himself wholly to work ... Stubbornly preoccupied with cultivating his mind, he seemed to ignore that he had also a heart to regulate.' Placed as he was, the head of the family, with reasonable prospects but no money, it would not be surprising if he had made work his refuge and his hope of a future.

The results were reasonably satisfactory. Between 1771 and 1776 he won three second prizes and six commendations. In 1775 he was the boy chosen to make a speech of welcome, in Latin of course, to Louis XVI and Marie Antoinette, as they returned to Paris after their coronation. When he left Louis-le-Grand in 1781, he was given a very generous 600 livres as a reward for his good conduct and success in classwork and examinations. Leblond tells the story of his being surprised in a lavatory when reading some *très-mauvais brochure* – presumably something 'philosophic' – but if the authorities were aware of this, and of his dislike of institutional religion, they took a more charitable view than his strait-laced and bigoted biographer.

When he graduated in law, there could be no question of his remaining to try his luck in Paris. His scholarship was passed on to his brother, Augustin, while Maximilien settled down to the

---

[2] Leblond de Neuvéglise, *La vie et les crimes de Maximilien Robespierre*, Augsburg, 1795. The author was almost certainly the abbé Proyart, who taught Robespierre in Paris and also knew him in Arras. Where his information can be verified, it is sometimes wrong and his viewpoint is consistently and improbably hostile, but he was very well informed about Robespierre's early life and his factual statements have to be taken seriously.

business of rebuilding his family's position in Arras. He got off to a good start. He was presented to the bar in 1781 and within a year he had been made a judge in the bishop's court, a position that normally went to a much older man. There is a little contemporary evidence – everything written after 1789 tends to reflect the political viewpoint of the writers – to suggest that he was regarded as one of the young hopefuls of the Arras bar. In 1783 he was elected to the local academy, a minor distinction perhaps, but one that probably seemed flattering enough to a man of 25. The lightning conductor case had already given him some local celebrity and even got his name into the Paris press.[3] His rôle then had probably consisted of not much more than presenting Buissart's case for him, but he endorsed Buissart's defence of science and the Enlightenment, praising Catherine II, Maria Theresa and Joseph II. He sent a copy of his speech to Franklin, presenting it as his own work. By 1783 he was doing rather well.

Like so many of his contemporaries – Mercier, Brissot and Marat, for example – he then set out on the academic trail that Rousseau had blazed with such remarkable success. In 1784 he competed for the prize offered by the academy of Metz for an essay on the subject of what should be done about crimes whose punishment involved 'corruption of the blood' (*peines infamantes*), in other words, the implication of a criminal's family and descendants in the consequences of his crime. Robespierre's essay was what might have been expected: an intelligent, if somewhat uninspired attempt to solve a particular problem by the application of Montesquieu's general principles. He began by arguing that the conception of *peines infamantes* depended on an attitude towards honour that was appropriate only to monarchies, and not to republics or despotisms. Like Montesquieu, he defined honour as a 'bizarre' amoral attitude, 'more preoccupied with grandeur than with justice, with show and dignity than with reason ... which has more in common with vanity than with *vertu* but which, in the political field, takes the place of *vertu* itself'.[4] After that, things got rather confused. Whereas Montesquieu had treated honour as the preserve of the

---

[3] See above, pp. 119-20.
[4] *Discours couronné par la société royale des arts et sciences de Metz*, Amsterdam and Paris, 1785.

nobility, Robespierre was up against the awkward fact that *peines infamantes* had been inflicted only on commoners. Montesquieu, in other words, did not fit. Robespierre may not have noticed; he had gone off into quite a fierce digression on the subject of judicial inequality, the fruit of a 'barbarous age, when it struck down with impunity an enslaved people, despised by a powerful clergy and a proud nobility who oppressed it'. Montesquieu would probably have found that somewhat lacking in historical perspective.

Robespierre shared Montesquieu's temptation to correct the moral flaws within a monarchy by the application of remedies that were appropriate only to republics. In the process, he got his lines thoroughly crossed. 'The mainspring of energy in a republic, as the author of *De l'esprit des lois* has proved, is *vertu*, in other words, political virtue, which is simply the love of one's country and its laws ... A man of principle will be ready to sacrifice to the state his wealth, his life, his nature itself – everything, in fact, except his honour.' In a *republic*, he did not have any to sacrifice. Having thoroughly mixed up Montesquieu's two *principes*, Robespierre went on to tackle the problem of *peines infamantes* from a moral, or 'republican' standpoint. Nothing that was unjust could be defended on grounds of social utility. '*Vertu* produces happiness as the sun produces light.' The maintenance of good *moeurs* would produce 'the reign of *vertu* on earth'. He came down against duelling which, for most eighteenth-century writers, was the touchstone of honour.

When it came to making practical suggestions, Robespierre was deferential but firm. He denied any intention of raising 'a profane hand against the sacred edifice of our laws'. Reform should be left to the authorities, the only men qualified to understand what needed to be done. Nevertheless, *peines infamantes* must be abolished root and branch and no distinction made between the punishment of nobles and commoners. Rather gingerly, he tried to extend judicial equality to the illegitimate: 'I could wish that public opinion would stop imposing a stain on bastards.' There were limits though: he did not think they should be allowed to inherit property. As befitted the champion of lightning conductors, he thought that 'Invincible prejudices are only for times of ignorance', not for 'an enlightened century, when everything is weighed, judged and discussed'.

The result was true to past form: he came second. The jury was sufficiently impressed to vote him a medal and a prize of 400 livres, which he devoted to printing his essay – with a title that *could* be taken to imply that he had come first. He got a brief mention in the Paris papers once again. His judges found his contribution 'well written, but without much warmth'. Despite its emphasis on *vertu*, the general tone was one of cautious pragmatism, with the odd hint that he might be accessible to more radical dreams. Most men are, at 26.

Presumably encouraged by this near-miss at Metz, he tried his luck again in the following year with a eulogy of the minor poet and local celebrity, Gresset, for the academy of Amiens. This was a disaster. Why he should have chosen such a subject, when other academies were offering more congenial social topics, is rather a puzzle. It could scarcely have been because he was something of a versifier himself, since he gave up Gresset's literary merits as a lost cause and concentrated on his virtuous life. He may have thought that being a local man might help. He was tipped off that Gresset was admired as much for his piety as for his poetry and he made this the basis of his essay, claiming to be 'a man who loves virtue even more than letters'.[5] What had been an 'enlightened century' when he was writing for Metz had now become 'corrupt', and the philosophes, the allies of yesteryear, were 'Proud and lofty spirits who trample underfoot what they call "prejudices"'. Since Gresset was 'much less of a philosophe than his enemies, he sacrificed glory to duty'. This was not so much the voice of the future Robespierre as a desperate attempt to play the right card. He praised the Jesuits (who had been expelled from France in 1764), Frederick II and the bishop of Amiens, Lamothe, who was, perhaps unjustly, believed to have been instrumental in getting the chevalier de la Barre executed for blasphemy. 'The healthy and upright heart of Gresset preserved those strong natural affections that are obliterated in most men by the taste for the false values of public opinion.' In this vein, it would have been easy for him to invoke

[5]*Discours qui a concourru pour le prix proposé par l'Académie d'Amiens en l'année 1785*, London and Paris, 1786.

the support of Rousseau, or if he had thought this risked offending the pious Amiénois, at least to strike a Rousseauist note of earnest moral exhortation. There was not a hint of this. On the contrary, he deliberately refused to take sides in the famous quarrel between Rousseau and the 'proud and lofty philosophes'. 'I make no pretence of deciding between those philosophes who have opposed the theatre and those who have praised it.' This could scarcely have been due to tactical caution, since a rousing attack on the corruption of the stage would not have been out of keeping with the rest of his piece. Gresset, it is true, had written for the theatre himself, but Robespierre made great play of the fact that he had abandoned his literary career in Paris for a life of exemplary retirement. If Robespierre opted for neutrality when Rousseau might have provided him with valuable ammunition, this presumably means that he had not come under his spell.

The Amiens jury decided that none of the competitors deserved the prize. If the others were no better than Robespierre, one can see their point. The experience perhaps discouraged him for, although he published this essay and prepared another one for Metz, on the treatment of bastards, and read it to the Arras academy in 1786, he never submitted it for the competition.[6] He himself never published it, though it was a good deal more substantial than his effort on behalf of Gresset.

Perhaps with the circumstances of his own birth in mind, Robespierre approached this subject with more feeling than he had put into his two previous essays. 'O humanity! Gentle and sublime *vertu*! How you would kindle the hearts of kings if you appeared to them in all the *éclat* of your divine beauty. How they would scorn the laws of false policy if you were to unfold the magnificent range of your power before their eyes.' This struck a note that was to become increasingly frequent: the rather formal declaration of his devotion to a somewhat marmoreal goddess – he could never rise to the warmth of Rousseau's passion, although he tried hard enough, but he was sincere in his own way. Despite his use of 'republican' language and talk of *citizens* and *patrie*, he continued to look to Montesquieu as his guide and

---

[6] The text was discovered by the abbé Berthe, who published it at Arras in 1971 under the title *Les droits et l'état des bâtards*.

to paraphrase him whenever appropriate. Policies must be designed to conform to existing *mores* rather than to transform them, since morals could not be reformed by legislation. What was regarded as scandalous was 'a relative idea, that depends on circumstances, time and place ... An absolute idea of purity and perfection can only be a source of political mistakes and the administrator must imitate the conduct of that legislator who gave his country not the laws that were best in themselves, but the best ones that it could tolerate.' This reference to Solon was taken straight from *De l'esprit des lois*.

Robespierre argued the case for cautious reform, 'to lop off piecemeal the different branches of an abuse that one cannot dig out by the roots'. Although he thought enforced celibacy was a prime cause of illegitimacy, he was careful to insist that he was not thinking of the clergy in this context. Even in the case of the army, he thought attempts to discourage soldiers from marrying were regrettable but 'there are abuses that are linked to so many circumstances, so many little habits, prejudices and passions that it would perhaps be absurd to attack them'. He advocated the introduction of adoption, but only for childless couples: 'where innovations are concerned, one should always show the greatest caution.' There was nothing to be done about the fact that public opinion saw nothing dishonourable about men having liaisons. One could, though, capitalise on that other fact, that it was regarded as bad form for fathers to refuse to support their illegitimate offspring, and it would help if the king made an example of some 'proud and cringing courtier'. Like Montesquieu, he put society before the state. 'It is undeniable that, as a general rule, it is better for children to be brought up by their parents than by some public administration.'

There were some hints of things to come, such as his enthusiastic tribute to Necker, especially for his recognition that religion was 'man's most salutary restraint and the most consoling of passions'. 'The people know nothing of philosophy; only religion can protect them from their poverty and their passions.' 'Poverty corrupts the *moeurs* of the people and degrades its soul, inclining it to crime by stifling the germ of honour and man's natural sentiment of his own dignity.' Despite his rejection of absolute standards of perfection, he could still write that 'Politics itself is nothing but public morality'. His message of cautious pragmatism was contradicted by the occasional flash of millenarianism. 'You who rule the earth ... Say just one word, command order to be reborn and it will be born again. Command poverty to disappear and it will disappear ... Be good, be just, in a word, behave like men, and there will not be much left for the orators and philosophes to do.'

With the historian's privilege of hindsight, one can see that Robespierre had the temperament of a moral crusader and the belief that people could be made good by act of parliament, allied to an education that had taught him the opposite. Which of the two would ultimately prevail would depend on circumstances, and in 1786 there cannot have seemed much of a future for the millenarian side. Leblond, speaking of his years in Arras, said that he 'always professed the greatest respect when speaking of Jean-Jacques Rousseau ... he praised the Philosophiste without reserve, because he shared some of his atrabilious temperament and democratic frenzy; he also thought that he had Rousseau's warm eloquence and magic style'. If there is any truth in this, it has not left many traces in what he wrote.

Other evidence suggests that he could have been evolving in a different direction. He seems to have lost interest in the Arras academy, after serving his time as director in 1786. In that year he was elected a member of the Rosati, a young men's literary society. If one can judge from the casualty rates during the Terror, the Rosati were rather more progressive, besides being younger than the academicians. They met once a year to drink to the rose and to compose more or less ingenious tributes to each other in eminently forgettable verse. One does not usually associate the Incorruptible with Bacchic odes, poems to young ladies (especially English ones) in praise of the pastoral life, or hymns to jam tarts, but that is perhaps a mistake. He wrote too much light verse for him not to have enjoyed it. Charlotte, who could easily have claimed that his attention was wholly fixed on higher things, insisted that he was an affable man, who enjoyed female company. His speech at the academy, welcoming Mlle de Kéralio, was quite a gallant, if a laboured effort. But for the revolution, he could conceivably have become a parlour radical.

He does seem to have established something of a reputation as a poor man's lawyer. Babeuf, in 1786, quoted someone who knew him as saying 'M. de Robespierre is not interested in making money. He is, and will always remain only the lawyer of the poor.'[7] The surviving evidence of the cases in which he appeared does not altogether bear this out and he was inclined to try to discredit hostile witnesses on the ground that they came from the 'dregs of the people'. Even his enemies conceded that he was disinterested in money matters. Perhaps this was why he did not make much of an effort to develop his legal practice, rarely appearing in more than a score of cases in any year. When he did get up in court he tended to be abrasive and to deliver harangues on matters of general principle, rather than to explore points of law. This got him into trouble with the legal establishment in Arras, but it would be wrong to regard him as a lonely rebel. He was supported by Buissant, his senior in the lightning conductor case, and by Dubois de Fosseux, a noble who was secretary of the academy.

Historians in a hurry to find traces of the future revolutionary, have implied that his alienation of his more senior colleagues was proof of some kind of political radicalism. This was not necessarily so. Too much has been read into the Deteuf case, of 1783, when he defended a man who was wrongly accused of theft, by a dishonest monk.[8] This led him on to accuse the monastic authorities of negligence and disciplinary laxity, in the kind of hyperbolic language to which he was becoming increasingly addicted. 'We who glory in the name of citizens ... Let us pray that it shall not be decided today that slanderers can bring down the sword of justice on our heads with impunity ... Never, on any kind of pretext, may the oppressor defy the cries of his feeble victim.' etc., etc. Robespierre's manner may have been aggressive and melodramatic, but his message was moderate enough. He had begun by going out of his way to repudiate any suggestion of anti-clericalism, contrasting the 'frivolous Philosophist' with the 'enlightened statesman who sees in the clergy of modern monarchies an intermediate body, whose existence forms part of the constitution, which cannot be

[7] V.Daline, 'Robespierre et Danton vus par Babeuf', *Annales historiques de la Révolution française*, 1960, pp.389-90.
[8] V.Barbier and C.Vellay, *Oeuvres complètes de Maximilien Robespierre*, Paris, 1910, I/120-59.

destroyed without disturbing the boundaries between monarchy and despotism'. This was not an attempt to make friends and propitiate judges; it was another tribute to Montesquieu. What did offend Robespierre's seniors was the fact that he printed and distributed his memoir during the trial itself and that, in an attempt to get damages for his client, he attacked the monastery when the only culprit was one of its erring monks. On the other hand, his old protector, the bishop of Arras, had not much time for the Benedictines, and neither had his friends, the Oratoriens. Public life under the *ancien régime* was a complicated business. Robespierre's handling of this case may have made him enemies but it does not prove anything in particular.

He was in trouble again, over the Page case, in the unpromising rôle of defence counsel to a woman accused of usury.[9] It was perhaps because he felt himself to be batting on a sticky wicket that he chose to launch a violent attack on the tendency of the judicial system to condemn on inadequate evidence. 'A feeble and timid creature ... can turn pale, stammer, contradict herself ... and still be innocent.' He was to change his mind about that in 1794. 'At the sight of so many scaffolds steaming with innocent blood ... I hear within me a powerful voice crying to me to renounce for ever that fatal inclination to convict on mere presumption.' There was a good deal more in the same vein, to which the *Conseil d'Artois* understandably took exception. It ordered the offending passages of his memoir to be deleted as injurious to 'the authority of the law, jurisprudence and the judges'. This cannot have been very pleasant for Robespierre – but he won his case. Towards the end of his speech he had looked forward to the 'happy revolution that the wise legislator, alarmed by so many ills, has been silently preparing for some time'. What this means is not at all clear, but it was certainly no call to arms.

In the Boutroue case of 1787 Robespierre, defending a Douai professor who was suing his vice-chancellor, paraphrased *Du contrat social* at one point, but this is hardly proof that he had forsaken Montesquieu for Rousseau.[10] Jean-Jacques would scarcely have agreed with his plea that men of letters in universities should be treated with 'decent liberty and the noble independence necessary to elevate their souls'. Like any other

[9] Ibid. I/274-352.
[10] Ibid. I/443-75.

barrister, he adopted the point of view that was most appropriate to the part he was playing in any particular case. When he defended the widow of the former lieutenant-governor of South Carolina, imprisoned for debt, he was respectful towards ladies, especially ladies of quality, and denounced the barbarity of putting them in gaol. When he appeared on behalf of a surgeon who was accused of abandoning his mistress in Brest, he was a good deal less chivalrous, and inclined to show more regard for honour than for *vertu*.

As late as the summer of 1788, when he joined in the local protest against Lamoignon's attempt to undermine the authority of the traditional courts, there is not much to suggest any strong commitment to radicalism. Leblond said that Robespierre sent his memoirs to unnamed 'philosophes' in Paris, corresponded with Mme Necker and was fond of boasting that her husband had adopted some of his ideas. That could be true. He certainly admired Necker, regretted his fall from offiice in 1781 and presumably hoped to see him back. The older Arras lawyers must have thought him a bit of a firebrand who was inclined to present every case as a melodramatic confrontation between pure innocence and improbable villainy. He liked to adopt the posture of the moralist, but that was fashionable enough at the time. When it came to the point, he generally came down on the side of Montesquieu, taking the values of his society for granted, even when he deplored their 'corruption', and assuming that one had to work within their constraints. By the standards of Mercier or Brissot, he looked like a provincial who had burned no boats. Buissart was using his influence to try to get him a job in the local royal court.[11] Charlotte thought it would not be long before he married.

It was the political crisis of 1789 that transformed his life. From the start he seems to have made up his mind to get himself elected to the Estates General. At the end of 1788 he had a convenient case for another of his judicial tirades. His client was a former soldier, Dupont, whose relatives had managed to have him imprisoned for twelve years by a *lettre de cachet*, in the hope of depriving him of a contested inheritance.[12] This allowed Robespierre to denounce 'this horrible system of *lettres de*

---

[11] *Annales historiques de la Révolution française*, 1930, p.76.
[12] Barbier and Vellay, I/573-681.

cachet, and to refer to the judicial crisis of 1788 and to Louis XVI as 'a sovereign who escaped from a frightful conspiracy against his justice, by taking refuge in the bosom of his people'. This version of the events of the previous year, even Robespierre's reference to 'the imprescriptible rights of nations and the sacred authority of kings' was not going to shock judges who had themselves joined in the defiance of 'ministerial despotism'. Robespierre indeed praised 'those courts renowned for their devotion to the public cause'. He concluded with a peroration in praise of the Paris Parlement whose recent actions outshone anything in antiquity.

What was new was his impassioned call for a revolution, but a moral rather than a political one. Everything that was happening was the work of God, although not of the God of the religious establishment. 'It is time that this idea of God, so long employed by flatterers to bestow on the rulers of empires unlimited and monstrous power, should serve at last to recall the imprescriptible rights of man. It is time to recognise that the same divine authority that orders kings to be just, forbids people to be slaves.' Providence, which was watching over France, had put on the throne a prince who was worthy to protect and cherish liberty. This was 'the unique moment vouchsafed to us by the goodness of that all-powerful being who regulates the destinies of empires. If we let it escape us, it is perhaps decreed that he will send us only days of trouble, desolation and calamity.' The social contract was written in heaven. 'There is the basis of that social contract of which men talk so much, which is no free and voluntary convention made by men, but whose fundamental terms, written in heaven, were for all time fixed by that supreme legislator who is the only source of all order, of all happiness and of all justice.' Providence had allotted a special rôle to the 'generous nation which, alone amongst the peoples of the world, without any fatal revolution or bloody catastrophe, by your own magnanimity and the virtuous character of your king, has recovered those sacred and imprescriptible rights that have been violated through the ages'. If France could preserve herself from disunity, 'the sceptre of Europe is yours', not 'the false and fatal glory of expanding territories wide enough already ... but through the irresistible empire of your wisdom and your virtues'.

All this called for a moral revolution and it was in this vein that he apostrophised the king. 'The glory of providing us with all the treasures of plenty, of embellishing your reign with all the *éclat* and enjoyment of luxury, such success – which seems to vulgar politicians the most admirable masterpiece of human wisdom – this is certainly not the most interesting part of the august mission which heaven and your own soul have entrusted to you. To lead men to happiness through *vertu* and to *vertu* by laws founded on the unalterable principles of universal morality, designed to restore to human nature all its rights and all its primal dignity; to re-form the immortal chain that should link man to God and to his fellow-men, by destroying all the sources of oppression and tyranny, which sow fear, mistrust, pride, baseness, egoism, hatred, covetousness and all the vices that carry men far from the goal that the eternal legislator has ascribed to society; that, Sire, is the glorious enterprise to which heaven has called you.' So much for the king. He then turned to the people. 'See, beneath that shell of imposing luxury and pretended wealth that fascinates administrators without *vertu*, the enormous fortunes of a few founded on the ruin and misery of all the rest ... See, above all, that lowest class, the most numerous, that pride seeks to brand with the name of *people* – a name so sacred and majestic in the eyes of reason – see it almost forced, by the extremity of its misery, to forget its human dignity and the principles of morality, to the point of regarding wealth as the first object of its cult and veneration.' It was a warning he might have heeded himself, for he had referred, yet again, in the opening of his speech to 'men from the scum of the people'.

All in all, it was an extraordinary performance and most of the future Robespierre was to be found within it: the belief in the special destiny of the new chosen people, provided that they heeded the voice of a jealous Providence that would inflict exemplary punishment on any backsliding; the concern – not for equality but for freeing the very poor from a life so hard that they were degraded into pining for wealth; the Manichean vision that placed all the human and divine virtues in one camp and tyranny and oppression in the other, so that any opponent was a monster of iniquity; the belief in 'frightful conspiracies' and the 'cabals of a corrupt court'. Robespierre was to stick to his initial viewpoint as firmly as Marat. It was a very long way from Montesquieu, in its insistence that the millennium was merely a matter of will, and its assumption that the elect knew what was best for the majority, but it was not very close to Rousseau either. Robespierre found his God in the Old Testament where Rousseau had sought him in the New. Nevertheless, the moral fervour, the consciousness of his own rectitude and the confidence that his faith *could* move mountains, that, in the last resort, everything depended on will, aligned him with Jean-Jacques.

In Artois, as in much of France, the elections to the Estates General shattered the unity of the reformers. In Arras the clergy, as they said themselves, not without smugness, 'did not allow their attention to stray in the direction of either their corporate interest or the personal interest of their constituent members'.[13] The nobility and the third estate had no such inhibitions. 'Liberal' nobles like Dubois de Fosseux fought a successful campaign to wrest control of the affairs of their own order from those who had previously monopolised power, but they were defeated when they tried to extend their influence to the Third Estate as well. This resulted in a temporary estrangement between de Fosseux and Robespierre. Despite the plea for unity that he made in the Dupont case, Robespierre took the offensive from the start. In an anonymous *Adresse à la nation artésienne*, probably published in the latter part of 1788, he denounced the way in which the local establishment had exploited the constitution of the province to its own advantage.[14] In the process, he used some of the arguments that he was to advance in court about the same time. 'We are approaching the moment that must decide for ever between our liberty and our slavery, our happiness and our misery. The choice depends entirely on the character and principles of the representatives to whom we entrust our destinies in the general assembly of the nation and on the zeal we show for the recovery of the sacred and imprescriptible rights of which we have been despoiled.' While dangerous enemies of the province were active in the preservation of their power, 'we sleep beneath the chains they

---

[13] Archives Nationales, H.38.

[14] The Bibliothèque Nationale possesses only the second edition, which seems to have appeared during the spring of 1789, in the middle of the electoral campaign.

have piled upon us'. This was the unique opportunity offered by Providence. The poor were degraded to a point where self-preservation left them no time to think about 'the causes of their misfortunes and to understand the rights that nature has given them'. There followed a long diatribe against the nobility and the clergy and their abuse of the local constitution, and Robespierre ended with the customary passage in praise of Necker.

During the course of the elections he reprinted this pamphlet and reinforced it with a second one, *Les Ennemis de la patrie démasqués*.[15] Most of the new pamphlet consisted of an account of the battle for control over the election of the deputies of the Third Estate in Artois. As usual, the crisis was 'the war of prejudice against reason, of humanity, honour and patriotism against pride, vanity and personal interest. What will be the prize? The safety, glory and happiness of generations present and to come, or their humiliation, their enslavement and their eternal misery.' He concluded, in a vein worthy of Marat, by boasting of his own 'salutary example of courage, generosity and disinterestedness'. With obvious reference to himself, he spoke of the 'Eternal Founder of human society' imprinting in men's hearts 'that generous sensibility that leads them without hesitation to help the oppressed, that courage, unshaken amidst danger, calm amidst the storm, in a word, all those divine virtues that make a man worthy to immolate his whole being to the glory and happiness of his country. Citizens, the nation is in danger. Domestic enemies more fearsome than foreign armies, are secretly plotting its ruin ... They are planning already to make martyrs of all the defenders of the people.' If it should come to that, 'Who is the citizen who, after conceiving in vain the enchanting hope of seeing humanity relieved and the nation triumphant, can complain if his destiny is to suffer with it and to be spared the misfortune of outliving its ruin. Ah then, may the tears of friendship mingle on his tomb with those of the unfortunates whom he helped. May his memory be dear and precious to all men of goodwill, while his soul journeys to enjoy, in the immortal abode of order and justice, the happiness that

---

[15] *Les ennemis de la patrie démasqués par le récit de ce qui s'est passé dans les assemblées du tiers-état de la ville d'Arras*, n.p., n.d.

the tyranny and injustice of men shall have banished from the earth.' He had hit the Rousseauist note at last, but it made an odd kind of electoral address and it was typical of Robespierre, when he was fighting a fairly ruthless electoral campaign, that he should have appealed to his constituents, not so much to see him through, as to mourn the immolation of their would-be saviour at the hands of the unrighteous. The accent of self-righteousness and self-pity was to be heard many times in the next few years. The time would come when it was to sound less absurd than it must have done in Arras, in that memorable spring of 1789 when no one else was thinking of martyrdom.

There is not much point in trying to investigate Robespierre's electoral tactics. Little can be known for certain, and the abuse that his enemies showered on him when he was dead is only moderately persuasive. It was always his belief that Providence helped those who helped themselves, and he was in no hurry for the martyrdom whose prospect he found so moving. He was probably not alone in using whatever means came to hand, and they secured him his election as fifth of the province's eight deputies.

It was presumably about this time that he wrote the strange *Dédicace de Maximilien Robespierre aux mânes de Jean-Jacques Rousseau*, which seems to have been intended as the preface to a work that was never written or has not survived.[16] It was addressed to 'the most eloquent and virtuous of men'. 'Divine man, you taught me to know myself; when I was still young you made me appreciate the dignity of my nature and think about the mighty principles of the social order.' 'I saw you in your final years and the memory is a source of joy and pride.[17] ... I understood then all the pains of a noble life devoted to the cult of truth. They did not frighten me. The wages of the virtuous man are his confidence that he desired the good of his fellows. Then comes the people's gratitude, which envelops his memory, and the honours from his contemporaries. Like you, I would buy these rewards at the price of a laborious life, even at the price of a

---

[16] The text is reprinted in H.Fleischmann, *Charlotte Robespierre et ses mémoires*, Paris, n.d., pp.290-2.

[17] Rousseau died when Robespierre was only twenty. There is nothing to suggest that the two actually met.

premature death.' 'Your admirable *Confessions*, that bold and open emanation of the purest soul, will go down to posterity, not as a model of art, but as a prodigy of *vertu*. I should like to follow in your honoured path, even if I were to leave a name unknown to future centuries; happy if, in the perilous career that an unheard of revolution has just opened up to us, I remain constantly faithful to the inspiration I have found in your writings.'

Like Brissot and Mercier, Robespierre claimed to have been converted by Rousseau when he stood on the threshold of adult life. In their case there is plenty of evidence to confirm it; in his, virtually none. This is not to doubt his sincerity when he wrote the *Dédicace* but merely to suggest that he may have been less affected by Rousseau in his youth than he imagined later. In his case, it seems to have been the political crisis that completed the conversion. Whereas Mercier came to Rousseau through the sensibility of the *Nouvelle Héloïse* and Brissot through the deism of *Emile*, Robespierre chose to single out the *Confessions*, with their emphasis on their author's self-regard, his consciousness of moral superiority and his suffering at the hands of wicked men who had pretended to be his friends. It was a dangerous choice.

PART 3

The Revolutionaries

Chapter 8

Revolutionary Circumstances

Almost everything in the summer of 1789 combined to convince most Frenchmen that the millennium had actually arrived. During the early spring, men from every village and every guild in the towns had been invited to list their grievances, so that the good king could put them right. The result was a collection of complaints and aspirations so complicated and voluminous that it still defies the computer. The more educated dreamed of constitutions, the humbler of bridges repaired and seigneurial habits reformed. The excitement built up through March and April as each of the three Orders of society – clergy, nobility and commoners – elected its representatives to the Estates General. These were France's first national elections for the best part of 200 years and they were generally regarded as the beginning of a new order rather than the revival of an ancient practice. As in most elections, there was a good deal of acrimony as the more ambitious competed for the privilege of becoming the Founding Fathers of the new France. Historians, both blessed and cursed with hindsight, tend to emphasise the conflicts at the expense of the hopes that gave birth to them. When the Estates General at last met at Versailles, on May 4, they like to draw attention to the contrast between the splendid plumage of the first two orders and the sartorial sobriety enforced on the Third Estate, whose members Court officials tended to treat as second-class citizens. This contrast was noted and resented, but it was only one side of the picture.

The marquis de Ferrières, an obscure deputy of the nobility, was so moved by the occasion that he wrote, not for public declamation, but in a private letter to his wife, 'O France ... never will I betray the confidence with which I was honoured when your interests were entrusted to my hands. Never shall anything alien to the general good determine my judgment or my will.'[1] Wordsworth was looking back to a slightly later period, but his reminiscence recaptures equally well the mood of 1789, when he wrote of his belief

> .... that a spirit was abroad
> Which could not be withstood, that poverty,
> At least like this, would in a little time.
> Be found no more, that we should see the earth
> Unthwarted in her wish to recompense
> The industrious, and the lowly child of toil,
> All institutions for ever blotted out
> That legalised exclusion, empty pomp
> Abolished, sensual state and cruel power,
> Whether by edict of the one or few –
> And finally, as sum and crown of all,
> Should see the people having a strong hand
> In making their own laws, whence better days
> To all mankind.[2]

Most people agreed with him that it was bliss in that dawn to be alive, and those who were not can only form a dim guess as to how it must have felt.

Conflict came quickly enough, when the Third Estate defied the king's attempt to impose his own will, and it led to revolts in many French towns in July, when power passed, almost without bloodshed, into the hands of the revolutionaries. What gave an epic quality to this national movement was the revolt in Paris and the capture of the Bastille, the perfect symbol of the overthrow of both the 'Gothic' Middle Ages and royal absolutism by the popular will. The event was acclaimed in this sense throughout the civilised world. On July 23 the House of Lords debated whether or not to appoint a day of thanksgiving for the French revolution; if the vote had gone the other way, 'Bastille Day' might have begun as a British celebration.[3]

On the night of August 4, in an attempt to appease widespread peasant revolts, the Constituent Assembly (to give the Estates

---

[1] Marquis de Ferrières, *Correspondance inédite, 1789, 1790, 1791* (ed.H.Carré), Paris, 1932, p.43.

[2] *The Prelude*, 1805 ed., IX/521-34.

[3] I am indebted for this information to my friend, Dr. John Addy.

General their new title) abolished some seigneurial dues without compensation and made provision for the buying-out of the rest. What had begun as a tactical manoeuvre got out of control, as deputies of the first two Orders competed with each other to renounce privileges, and by the end of the sitting the Assembly had committed itself to the transformation of the legal system, local government and, by voting to abolish tithes, to the reorganisation of the Church. Here again, modern historians have chosen to stress the limitations of what was offered and the readiness of some to renounce the privileges of others. There is some truth in this, but it was not how contemporaries saw it. Ferrières thought it was 'the most memorable [session] ever held in any country. It is typical of the noble enthusiasm of the Frenchman. It shows the whole universe his generosity and the sacrifices of which he is capable when honour, love of the public good and heroic patriotism are concerned.'[4] Even the king, who had no reason to share Ferrières's enthusiasm about the way things were going, concurred: 'With one mind, prelates, seigneurs, gentlemen, the rich of all ranks were in hot competition to contribute to the greater happiness of the people. To this end they made sacrifices that no one had any right to expect of them.'[5] Looking back from a harsher future, Bailly, who had been made mayor of Paris in July, commented sadly, *Beaux moments, qu'êtes-vous devenus?*[6]

What was immediately – and rightly – perceived as one of the great revolutions in the history of the world, had taken place with very little bloodshed, and such casualties as there were arose from mob violence rather than from fighting between revolutionaries and royal troops. This had important consequences for what men made of the tremendous events. When the Assembly had committed itself to such far-reaching changes and even Marat believed for a time that social relationships had been transformed and desperate poverty abolished, it was impossible not to talk in terms of regeneration. When the impossible had just happened, it was also implausible

---

[4] Ferrières, loc.cit. p.113.
[5] Louis XVI, Marie Antonette and Mme Elisabeth, *Lettres et documents inédits* (ed. F. Feuillet de Conches), Paris, 1865, 4 v., III/194.
[6] J.S. Bailly, *Mémoires*, Paris, 1821-22, 3 v., II/216.

to dwell on the limitations to what was politically practicable and the constraints imposed by a primitive economy. The events of the night of August 4, when compared with the interminable manoeuvring in defence of vested interests that had been the rule before the revolution, seemed to prove that human nature itself had been regenerated too. If this was not *vertu*, it looked very much like it. Those of a religious turn of mind thought that so many miracles could only be the work of Providence. That included men as different as Mercier and Robespierre. Exalted and bemused at living through events of such magnitude, men were going to think again about what they might previously have dismissed as impracticable Rousseauist dreams.

It was tempting, if not altogether accurate, to think that these manifold blessings had been achieved by consensus, or at least by consent. It was typical of Marie Antoinette's defective political judgment that she wrote to her friend, the duchess de Polignac, 'Everyone is taking flight'.[7] This was not even true of court circles. Only a handful of those who were particularly unpopular, Marat's old employer, the comte d'Artois, and a few of the queen's friends, left the country. With the exception of this tiny group which chose to exclude itself from the nation in the most literal sense, to speak of the French community as a whole accepting the revolution was somewhat optimistic but not demonstrably untrue. In the Assembly, the Right, as it came to be known since the clergy and nobility sat on that side of the president, with varying degrees of conviction and commitment, played the parliamentary game and by participating in debates implied their acceptance of the outcome. Most important of all the king, when pressed hard enough, was always prepared to give his assent to revolutionary legislation and even to profess his general approval of the way things had gone, despite his forcible removal to Paris in October. It was therefore just possible to construct a political fiction that 1789 had seen the triumph of the people and of the Enlightenment by the conversion of their basically well-meaning but hitherto misguided opponents. The Queen of the Night might lament that everyone had fled but within Sarastro's sacred halls men loved their fellow-men, no traitors lurked and enemies were forgiven.

[7] Louis XVI etc. loc.cit. III/186.

In more prosaic, and ideological, terms, there was no difference between the *volonté générale* and the *esprit général*. The nation as a whole knew where its duty lay and the privileged were prepared for the necessary sacrifices and in some cases even welcomed their chance to make a special contribution to the general interest.*Fraternité* was more than a slogan and it implied membership of a single national family. Since men wanted what they ought to want there was no need to choose between the gradualism of Montesquieu, with its respect for vested interests and venerable prejudices, and the enforced rectitude of Rousseau. When all, or almost all, sought the common good, no one needed to be coerced or compulsorily re-educated. This was, of course, rather an optimistic way of looking at things, but it was more true of 1789 than of most years and it could acquire reality by the mere fact of being believed. Few political fictions can stand up to rigorous critical analysis but this does not prevent their serving as the foundation for tolerable working arrangements. In fact, the king had very serious reservations about the whole business, the clergy and nobility could only be pushed so far and the Assembly was to show itself not very good at judging the limits of consent. Nevertheless an attempt *was* made to transform the country by agreement and it had more success than it is fashionable to acknowledge.

In the event, everything went tragically wrong. *Volonté générale* and *esprit général* were, if not wholly irreconcileable, extremely awkward bedfellows. Faithful to what were believed to be Rousseau's ideas, the Declaration of the Rights of Man proclaimed that 'the law is the expression of the *volonté générale*. All citizens are entitled to participate in its formulation, either personally or through their representatives.' This certainly seemed to imply universal suffrage. In fact, the Assembly divided the population into 'active' and 'passive' citizens on the basis of the amount of taxation they paid. Since a majority of adult males was enfranchised and most of them did not bother to vote, the infringement of democratic principle was of more symbolic than practical importance. Time and again, however, as when they excluded passive citizens from the National Guard, or punished army and navy officers by the loss of their honour, and other ranks by more physical penalties, the deputies showed that they regarded some citizens as more equal than others. They were, in fact, substituting something like the British concept of the gentleman for the former noble. Montesquieu would probably have recognised this as corresponding to the social and economic facts of life. To the deputies, it must have seemed as natural as the profession of political opinions that implied the opposite.

Where the constitution was concerned, they were in a dilemma. Montesquieu instructed them to construct a political system in which legislative and executive powers were evenly balanced. In practice they suspected that, despite his and their professions to the contrary, the king had not resigned himself to the revolution. It was therefore not safe to entrust him with the powers that, in theory, they thought a constitutional monarch should have. This made him all the less willing to content himself with what he was given. Each side was calculating the political odds, but in a situation for which there was no precedent, the Assembly had to legitimise its stand by an appeal to abstract theory. This meant that it came to regard itself as the sole embodiment of the general will, with the king no more than the chief agent of government. Similar attitudes prevailed when the time came to settle the future shape of the Church. Rousseau had taught them to be suspicious of corporate bodies, and they were impatient with the idea that canon law could serve as a source of moral obligation exterior to the national will. Although their intention was merely to reform the Church, and not to challenge the position of religion in society, they imposed an oath of allegiance to the new order that was rejected by about half the parish clergy and almost all the bishops. In the summer of 1791 a parliamentary enquiry revealed that, in the Vendée and the Deux-Sèvres, the religious issue had split the local population into two hostile factions which used political terminology (*aristocrate* and *patriote*) to describe their religious allegiance.

As positions hardened the assumption of consensus contrasted more and more with the facts of political life, which were pointing in the direction of civil war. The deputies had little sympathy with attacks on châteaux and mutinies in the armed forces but the Assembly was reluctant to repress too forcibly those on whose support it might come to depend. Most people on both sides probably regretted the drift towards confrontation and believed their own contribution to the process to have been dictated by the unreasonableness of the other side. The political leaders, Mounier and the Monarchiens, Mirabeau and the triumvirate that had guided the initial Left, successively looked for a compromise with the king. These attempts seemed to the extreme Left a surrender of the victories of 1789 and alarmed many uncommitted deputies who were inclined to lend an ear to the insinuations of journalists that principle was being sacrificed to the pursuit of office.

Contrary to the expectations aroused in the blissful dawn, life became harder for ordinary people. The Assembly hoped to liquidate the enormous debts of the *ancien régime* by the sale of Church property, which was used as the backing for a new paper currency, the *assignat*. As tax returns fell under weak and unstable governments, declining confidence in the *assignat* produced a rise in prices. A growing stream of *émigrés* transferred wealth out of the country and men of property who remained in France were unlikely to advertise their wealth by conspicuous consumption. Unemployment increased in the towns. For the very poor, the provision of relief and medical care, which had been patchy and inadequate at the best of times, declined with the secularisation of Church property and inflation.[8] The Assembly and its *comité de mendicité* did all they could to translate their benevolent intentions into material improvements but there was never enough money and the slackening of the economy multiplied demands.

In June 1791 the constitutional fiction of a united country was brutally exposed when the royal family fled from Paris and the king left behind a message repudiating what he had previously appeared to endorse: 'The result of all the operations is the destruction of the monarchy, the violation of property, the breakdown of personal security, total anarchy in every part of the country.' When the king was caught and brought back to Paris with his family, his personal authority had been fatally compromised. Despite a popular campaign for his dethronement, the leaders of the Assembly still hoped to strike a bargain with him, which meant pretending that his flight had

[8] On this subject, see A.Forrest, *The French revolution and the poor*, Oxford, 1981.

been an 'abduction'. This policy involved the imposition of martial law in Paris, with National Guards firing on peaceful petitioners – the 'massacre' of the Champ de Mars.

The king's subsequent acceptance of the constitution and the election of a new Legislative Assembly offered no more than the illusion of a new start. By now there were substantial *émigré* forces in Germany, including considerable numbers of army and navy officers, preparing for invasion and trying to enlist the support of the European Powers. Austria and Prussia made threatening noises, which increased the feeling of insecurity in France, although neither was contemplating action. When Louis XVI vetoed legislation against *émigrés* and refractory clergy, he was acting within his constitutional rights but seemed to a good many of his subjects to be demonstrating his hostility to the revolution. Within the Assembly the majority remained forlornly faithful to a compromise that had broken down. They mistrusted the king but would agree to no action against him. A radical minority, led by Brissot, decided to coerce him by the expedient of a limited foreign war which was intended to force him either to capitulate or to come out as an open opponent of the revolution. Others in the Jacobin Club, notably Robespierre, believed the war policy to be a dangerous gamble that would endanger all the gains of the revolution. In a number of debates at the club, the two moved from courteous disagreement to allegations that their opponents were secret agents of the Court. This produced a permanent division within the radicals, between Brissotins or Girondins and those who were called Montagnards, that was to have catastrophic consequences.

France declared war on Austria in April, and Prussia came to Austria's support. By the end of July the initial French offensive had petered out ignominiously and a Prussian army was approaching the frontier. The Girondins and their opponents now reversed rôles, with those who had initially gambled on war trying to negotiate yet another compromise with the king, and the former peace party, reinforced by popular forces in Paris and National Guards from Brest and Marseilles, staking everything on an attack on the royal palace. On 10 August 1792 the attack succeeded, although not without heavy casualties. The royal family fled for protection to the Assembly, where Louis was 'suspended' until the election of a Convention to decide his fate and the future of the country.

August 10 was one of the decisive *journées* of the revolution. It can be quite easily explained in political terms. Each party to the constitutional deadlock had resorted to force, either foreign or insurrectionary, and the revolutionaries had won. Paris, if one disregards the men from Brest and Marseilles, who could only be said to represent the rest of France in a symbolic sense, had acted against both the king and the Assembly that had refused to dethrone him. The Parisians therefore claimed to speak in the name of the country as a whole. There could be no question, in the summer of 1792 or at any subsequent date, of putting that claim to the test. On the other hand, no one, either then or now, could be sure that free elections would not have returned some kind of royalist majority. Since the victors of 10 August were not going to apologise to the king for having, in all innocence, mistaken the general will, and to put him back on the throne, they could not risk such a verdict. Royalism of any kind, whether constitutional or cavalier, could not be tolerated in the press or on the hustings. The elections to the Convention were therefore 'democratic' in the sense that the fiscal qualification for voting was abolished, but they were less representative than those of 1791. In Paris, where whole categories of suspected royalists were excluded, fewer people voted than in the previous year. This was the inevitable consequence of the resort to force. If the king had won, he would have claimed to incarnate the legitimacy of the restored monarchy. The republicans were in a more awkward predicament: they claimed to derive their authority from popular sovereignty, but they could not risk extending to the whole of society the free democratic institutions in which they believed. For thoroughly practical reasons, they had to behave as though monarchists had excluded themselves from the national community. This fitted rather nicely into a Rousseauist view of things. The monarchists had excluded themselves from the new social contract and although, for the most part, still physically present in France, they no longer counted as part of the French people. The general will was something that concerned only republicans; it was not to be equated with a simple majority of the population. For the time being, it could be assumed that most people did accept the *fait accompli* of August 10 and one could speak as though the Convention reflected the will of the majority, but its legitimacy would not be in question even if this proved to be untrue. The full consequences of this were to emerge over the next two years.

Within this Rousseauist framework, different conclusions could be drawn from the same situation. The Girondins, while quite happy to accept the verdict of the insurrection of 10 August, sought to minimise its significance and implied that the elections to the Convention endowed the revolutionary regime with a new kind of legitimacy that retrospectively indemnified the insurgents who had anticipated the national verdict. Since the Girondins at first controlled a majority in the Convention they naturally considered that there could be no possible justification for repeating the process. Their opponents, smarting at having pulled the Girondins' chestnuts out of the fire for them, saw the situation in rather different terms. The Paris Commune, as the vehicle of the general will, had enjoyed a kind of legitimacy that the Legislative Assembly had forfeited when it ceased to represent the real interests of the nation. Such a situation could recur. Since the Montagnards, as they became known because of their seats on the top benches, virtually monopolised the Paris deputation and could normally rely on the support of the Commune, this was a situation that they could contemplate, not exactly with enthusiasm, since they did believe in representative government, but with more equanimity than their opponents. They therefore emphasised the uncon-stitutional nature of the insurrection, defended the right of the Paris Commune to dictate terms to the Legislative Assembly during the rest of August and implied that its popular election did not automatically guarantee the legitimacy of anything that the Convention might subsequently choose to do.

One of the first things it did was to declare France a republic. To regard this as merely a form of government without a king would be to ignore all the ideological and emotive associations that the word had been accumulating since the publication of *De l'esprit des lois*. For contemporaries, the republic was a regime whose principle was *vertu* and the overthrow of the monarchy meant the end of the attempt to strike an uneasy compromise between *vertu* and honour. Henceforth the state was dedicated, not merely to the pursuit of the general interest, but to the promotion of republican values and the eradication of every form of moral and political vice. The stakes had been raised and, for some Frenchmen at least, the objective was now the full Rousseauist utopia in all its glory. For the time being, since royalists were unlikely to make much noise, except in the more remote parts of the country, it was still just possible to imagine that they were a small minority who had excluded themselves from the national community, which would henceforth be unanimous in pursuit of its republican goal. Everyone was agreed that it ought to be unanimous since the general will, like the republic itself, was *une et indivisible*. Disagreement could only be due to faction and faction meant the search for sectional advantage at the expense of the general good. Political rivalry was therefore not so much about specific policies, although they provided the battlegrounds, as about competing claims to embody the general will. About that there could be no compromise and no pardon for the defeated.[9]

The Convention split into two warring groups of Girondins and Montagnards, with perhaps half of the deputies committed to neither side. Debates tended to degenerate into slanging matches, with each side convinced that any proposal from the other was intended to secure some party advantage. When most of the Girondins, for a variety of reasons, opposed the execution of the king, towards the end of 1792, it was not difficult to present them as crypto-royalists. This implied that they were not legitimate members of the new republican family. During the spring of 1793 a military crisis developed, with civil war blazing in the west and the main French army in Belgium defeated by the Austrians. The attempt of its commander-in-chief, Dumouriez, to negotiate an armistice that would allow him to turn his army against Paris, understandably created the impression that the most serious threat to the revolution came from lukewarm and self-interested people who were primarily intent on using it for their own advantage. This was the crisis of the previous summer all over again and the dénouement was somewhat similar, except that this time the Parisian coup d'état could only be directed against the Assembly itself. On 31 May and 2 June a popular insurrection browbeat the majority of the

[9] See F.Furet, *Penser la révolution française*, Paris, 1978. (Eng. trans. *Interpreting the French revolution*, Cambridge, 1981) esp. chs I and III.

deputies into voting the arrest of the Girondin leaders. This was widely interpreted in the provinces as the imposition of the will of Paris on the representatives of the country as a whole. From this time onwards there could be little doubt that the government and the majority in the Convention represented only a minority of the electorate.

Although the silencing of the Girondins produced something like unity within the Convention, it was six months or so before the new revolutionary government, under the general supervision of the Committee of Public Safety, could vindicate itself by military victory. During this time a new radical opposition, some of whose leaders had been disappointed in their hopes of election to the Convention, used their positions within the Commune and the War Office to stir up more popular discontent, in the hope that a third *journée* would bring them to power. To ensure its survival, the government had to accept most of the radical programme: conscription, the direction of labour and requisitioning of war materials, wage and price controls and the arrest of 'suspects' who could be detained indefinitely without trial. Although the government was ready enough to make use of exceptional powers for the prosecution of the war, few if any of its members regarded this 'alternative economy' as more than a temporary concession to misguided popular pressure. As politicians, they could scarcely admit that they had no confidence in the policies they had been forced to accept. As ideologists they had to convince themselves that they represented the 'real' will of the country, which was assumed to correspond to the interests of 'the people' who tended to be identified, in practice, with the Parisian sansculottes.

Such attitudes were not confined to one or two theorists. They provided the only basis on which the policies of a minority could be enforced in the name of democracy. In August 1793 some argument arose as to whether a majority of the population of Savoy had actually voted for incorporation into France. This produced the revealing comment from Prieur de la Marne, a member of the Committee of Public Safety, 'If it were true that only a minority had accepted the constitution, one would have to conclude that, in this respect as in many others, the people have been deceived'. Tallien, a fellow-Montagnard, concurred, 'It is the *vertueux* minority that has always sought the interests of the people'.[10] A few months later another member of the committee, Barère, told the elected representatives of the sovereign people that 'Electoral assemblies are monarchical institutions'. This struck his colleague, Couthon, as unnecessarily blunt. 'The right to elect is an essential part of the people's sovereignty. No one can interfere with it without committing a crime – unless extraordinary circumstances make it necessary for the welfare of the people themselves.'[11] The circumstances were certainly extraordinary, but then they often are.

As the military situation improved, the Committee of Public Safety developed into a kind of War Cabinet. It was then challenged, both by extremist groups in Paris and by the moderate wing of the Montagnards themselves. Once again, it is not difficult to explain what followed in purely political terms. When, in the spring of 1794, the radicals began threatening another *journée*, the government, after failing to talk them out of it, had them arrested, tried and executed. Soon afterwards it struck down Danton, the hope of the moderates. Each faction, however, was accused, less of specific crimes than of 'counter-revolution', which implied the total opposition of evil men, not so much to the policies of the government as to the idealised community that it represented. When all the opposition leaders were dead, they were accused of having formed part of the same plot, which went back to 1789, if not before, and embraced all those who had ever opposed what hindsight now declared to have been orthodoxy. This only made sense if one saw the revolution as a kind of religious war between good and evil. In some ways it anticipated the Soviet treason trials of the 1930s, with the significant difference that, in France, the accused were vociferous in protesting their innocence.

With the popular forces in Paris now under control and French armies victorious on all fronts, the Committee of Public Safety might have been expected to wind up the Terror and begin a phased return to normal constitutional government. During the summer of 1794 the opposite happened: the revolutionary tribunal had never been so murderous and the Convention was terrified into silence. One can explain this in conventional political terms, as a frightened dictatorship clinging to power to

[10] *Moniteur*, 25 August 1793.   [11] Ibid. 4 December 1793.

protect itself from the vengeance of the allies of those whom it had destroyed. The dictators themselves would have had to be curiously dispassionate cynics to have thought of things in this way. Robespierre and Saint-Just at least had become aware of a widening gap between the government and all shades of opinion. Only one conclusion was possible: the one advanced by Prieur in the previous summer. The 'people' had been deceived and it was the responsibility of those who knew better to re-educate them. The general will, which had once been located in the Convention, after being identified with the Montagnards and then with the Committee of Public Safety, after the committee broke up under the intolerable stresses to which it was subjected, was finally located within a group of half a dozen men.

In July 1794 the break-up of the committee gave the majority in the Convention the chance to overthrow the revolutionary dictatorship. The revolution then went into reverse: the Terror was quickly abandoned, economic controls gradually repealed, surviving Girondins restored to their seats and most of the Montagnard leaders who were still alive imprisoned, deported or executed. In the summer of 1795 a new constitution was drafted. Superficially, this looked like a belated victory for the ideas of Montesquieu, in the sense that government was understood to be a reflection of society rather than a vehicle for its transformation. Warned by the experience of 1793-4, the deputies provided for a bicameral legislature and a weak executive. Montesquieu would no doubt have welcomed the precautions against over-strong government but he had seen politics as the pursuit of absolute moral goals, within the limits of what public opinion could be induced to accept. For the men of 1795 it was mainly about the provision of political defences for the economic status quo.

Irrespective of anyone's intentions, the French were now too bitterly divided for there to exist any kind of *esprit général*. The Convention was still the prisoner of the situation created in August 1792: if civil war were to be avoided, it would be necessary to proscribe every kind of royalism and to suppress those Catholics who rejected the Church settlement of 1790. The deputies therefore voted that, when a new assembly was elected, in the autumn of 1795, two-thirds of its members must initially be drawn from their own ranks. This attempt at self-perpetuation produced an insurrection in Paris which was put down by regular troops, under the command of Bonaparte. When subsequent elections threatened to produce royalist or Jacobin majorities, the government rectified the inconvenient results by purges, which increased its dependence on the army. Eventually, an attempt by a group of politicians to put an end to this see-saw and revise the constitution by a coup d'état, in 1799, allowed Bonaparte to seize power for himself and put an end to ten years of revolution.

This was the political context within which all the republicans had to act: confused, complicated and, from 1792 onwards, desperately dangerous. How they reacted to it depended on various factors. In so far as ideology mattered to them, they all shared a similar heritage, compounded of veneration for Montesquieu and emotional attachment to Rousseau. Attempts to explain their enmities in terms of class loyalty or conflicting principle defy all the evidence.[12]

The extent and nature of their political ambition counted for something. Mercier saw himself primarily as a man of letters. Brissot bustled around as usual, with a finger in many pies, more concerned – although he would probably have been reluctant to admit it – with doing things than with thinking about them. Marat saw himself as a front-line fighter, endlessly exposing the machinations of those in power. Robespierre, though a skilful political tactician, was primarily an ideologist, a man who never held any departmental responsibility but hoped to enlighten the Assembly and the Jacobin Club about the moral implications of what looked like political choices. Saint-Just was too young to have played a major political rôle before 1792, when he was elected to the Convention at the minimum age of 25. In some respects the most interesting of them all, he revealed himself to be both a man of action, in his missions to the armies, and a man who, like Robespierre, tried to find the solution to specific problems in the general principles that he thought must underlie the construction of a genuinely republican government.

If will and personality counted for much, circumstances also had their part to play. What people made of situations depended to some extent on whether they experienced them as journalists, deputies or members of central or local government, with

---

[12] See Appendix for a comparison between the ideas of Brissot and Robespierre.

practical responsibility for getting things done. This in turn was a question not merely of ambition and ability, but also of chance. Of the men with whom this book is concerned, only Robespierre was elected to the Estates General. This gave him a status denied to the rest in 1789 and encouraged him to see things from a national perspective. He was a legislator, and for any devotee of Rousseau, that word was charged with almost as much significance as 'republic'. As such, he could aspire to no higher position and he was aware that he occupied a place in history and shared in the collective responsibility for creating a new kind of society. At the same time, as one of a tiny group of ultra-radical deputies, he was in permanent opposition and not personally responsible for the decisions of the Assembly, most of which he opposed. It was a situation that encouraged criticism from the standpoint of abstract principle. Not having an active part to play on any of the Assembly's committees, he was not called upon to compromise and not responsible for making anything work. Both temperament and situation inclined him to the rôle of public watchdog and frequently of Cassandra.

Brissot failed to win election to the Assembly in 1789 and had to settle for the Paris Commune, where he was made a member of the police committee. In July 1789 he also launched one of the more successful revolutionary newspapers, the *Patriote Français*. As a journalist he was even more free than Robespierre to criticise, challenge and denounce, since there was no one who could tell him to sit down and shut up. As a member of the Commune he shared the responsibility for governing a restless city with a population of over half a million. Faced with a challenge to the ill-defined authority it had created for itself in 1789, from the 60 Districts into which Paris was divided, especially from that of the Cordeliers, the Commune was bound to see itself as a kind of government. It rejected the claim of the more revolutionary Districts to political autonomy and was inclined to treat their activities as demagogic rabble-rousing. As a member of the police committee, with responsibilty for the enforcement of law and order, Brissot found himself, willy-nilly, something of a government man in a small way.

When the Assembly failed to respond to his attempt to become its unofficial adviser, Marat opted for journalism. In September 1789 he created the newspaper that became famous under the title of *L'Ami du Peuple*. It soon became one of the most violent of all the revolutionary organs, endlessly denouncing, exposing and inviting its readers to lynch the enemies of the revolution. Marat soon moved to the protection of the Cordeliers District and early in November 1789 he went into hiding. This allowed him to disregard such flimsy defences against libel as the law still afforded. The reputation of his paper rested on the violence of his polemics and he was free to make such innuendoes as he chose, to write himself letters in the name of imaginary correspondents and to make charges without being called upon to substantiate them. His immediate enemy was the Commune, whose policemen were on his heels. This cannot have improved his relationship with Brissot.

Mercier, who was busy bringing out a 37-volume edition of Rousseau's works and writing the odd play, also started a newspaper, the *Annales Patriotiques*, which carried as its banner the quotation from Rousseau: 'Liberty may be won, but once lost it can never be regained.' Mercier soon lost interest in his paper and handed over its effective direction to Carra. Later in the revolution he was associated with another paper, the *Chronique*, but he never became an important revolutionary journalist. Since his contribution to the revolution was so slight, it may conveniently be disposed of within the present chapter.

He published a brief *Adieu à l'année 1789* which celebrated it as 'a unique year when the august French brought back to Gaul equality, justice and liberty, which aristocratic despotism (sic) had held captive'. 'The space of a few months made good the misfortunes and the faults of centuries; man recovered his primal dignity.' Mercier claimed some of the credit for himself, congratulating 1789 on its resemblance to his own 2440 and concluded, 'It is enough to *will* ... and God protects every generous revolution.' Robespierre could not have put it better.

In June 1791, just before the king's flight, which was bad luck for him, Mercier brought out a two-volume work, *De Jean-Jacques Rousseau considéré comme l'un des premiers auteurs de la révolution*. The title was promising enough, but even by his own not very exacting standards, this was a sloppy, rambling and self-contradictory work. It consisted of reminiscences of Rousseau, disjointed comments on some of his works and reflections on the current political situation, with no

attempt to relate them to each other. He provided his readers
with a reasonable summary of the gist of *Du contrat social*: 'The
sacrifices demanded by a nation become qualities; positive laws
and natural rights, without being stifled, are reduced to silence.'
Nations were not bound by formal contracts. 'To be general, a
will must be unified.' Mercier then advocated, in complete
contradiction to Rousseau, democracy and the separation on the
powers, the need for a balance between the king and the
Assembly, and for opposition as a safeguard against political
stagnation. His old heroes, the *gens de lettres*, had prevented
ancien régime France from ever being a tyranny; despotism, in
fact, had never existed in the west. Later on he said that Louis
XVI *had* been a tyrant before 1789 and, despite the fact that he
had gained more than anyone else from the revolution, would try
to recover his old powers.

   Mercier seemed unable to stick to one point of view about
anything. At times he appealed for an alliance between king and
people against the nobility, at others he praised the parlements
for their resistance to the royal government. He said that trade
was good for liberty and Sparta had been despotic because it had
no navigable rivers. Then he argued that the French revolution
would promote industry and agriculture at the expense of
commerce. Although Sparta had been despotic, thanks to the
formidable lungs of the revolutionary orators, 'We will soon
breathe again the air of ancient Rome'. He was obviously much
excited by the times in which he was living but not at all clear
about what people ought to do. 'O land of desolation, Europe,
hear my prayer! A citizen, a humble disciple of Rousseau,
prostrates himself before you; his eyes bathed in tears, in the
silence of his grief and indignation, he implores you, in the name
of the Eternal and of the generations to come, to honour
man.'[13] Amongst all the verbiage and confusion one thing stood
out, in sharp contrast to Mercier's pre-revolutionary effusions.
Despite his profession of internationalism – 'The Assembly will
create a natural form of politics that will go round the world' – he
had become a French patriot who was very suspicious of
foreigners; such 'vermin' were advised against daring to meddle
in French affairs. His view of the British, his former idols, had
undergone a complete transformation. His most violent abuse

[13] II/125

was reserved for 'the rich and cruel inhabitants of London, pale worshippers of gold, the hardest, most inhumane and the most coldly vicious of all mortal men.'[14] At a time when the relations between the two countries were still friendly, Mercier's venom was quite extraordinary. Rousseau would at least have approved of his exclusive patriotism, though not of his long-standing antipathy towards anything that came out of Geneva. Despite his title, he had very little to say on the relationship between Rousseau's writings and the revolution. He did comment that *Du contrat social* was 'the least read of all Jean-Jacques's works. Today every citizen is pondering it and learning it by heart.' 'The *Contrat social* is the rich mine from which our representatives have drawn the material for the great work of the constitution ... and so Rousseau's maxims are responsible for most of our laws.'[15]

When the Legislative Assembly was elected in the autumn of 1792, Brissot and Robespierre changed rôles. Brissot became a deputy, and Robespierre, as a result of his own motion excluding former deputies from the new assembly, was without a seat. In the previous July he had taken a major part in steering the Jacobin Club through the difficult period that followed the king's flight. From that time onwards it had become his base, although he had to struggle very hard to maintain his position there against the challenge of Brissot's popular war policy. Through their affiliated clubs, the Jacobins were a national organisation and Robespierre remained a national figure. In the spring of 1792 he too began editing a newspaper, the *Défenseur de la constitution*. The *journée* of 10 August transformed his situation. He became a member of the Paris Commune and conveyed some of its threatening messages to the Legislative Assembly. During the prison massacres of early September he denounced some of his Girondin opponents, presumably in the hope that, once arrested, they would share the fate of the other prisoners. This did not make for subsequent political co-operation. As a leading Jacobin, he was one of those responsible for the efficient management of the Parisian elections to the Convention, which returned an almost solidly Montagnard team.

Brissot, despite a venomous pamphlet by his old London

[14] II/91n.   [15] II/99n[1], 306-7.

associate, Théveneau de Morande, who was presumably paid by someone, managed to get himself elected to the Legislative Assembly. He at once became a committee man, specialising in foreign policy, on which he had always fancied himself to be something of an expert. He was largely responsible for the adoption of the war policy and when Clavière and other political allies were made ministers in April 1792, he was very close to the government itself. Louis soon dismissed these Girondin ministers and Brissot then found himself in an uncomfortable situation, hoping that renewed pressure would force the king to recall his friends to office, and consequently opposing plans for the coming insurrection. He nevertheless welcomed the *journée* of 10 August, though his experiences during the September massacres, when an attempt was made to arrest his editor, Girey-Dupré, and he himself was threatened, cannot have reconciled him to the Montagnards. He was elected to the Convention for the Eure-et-Loir.

Marat continued as before. According to his own account, he asked Pétion, the mayor of Paris, to get him a passport just before 10 August, which suggests that he was not very confident about the outcome of the insurrection.[16] He did not emerge from hiding until the 15th, which was perhaps carrying caution rather far.[17] He then got himself, quite illegally, added to the *comité de surveillance* of the Commune, of which he was not a member. In this capacity he made his only material contribution to the revolution by helping to start the prison massacres, which he had already advocated in his paper. The Parisian electors did not seem very keen to put him in the Convention and it was only after Robespierre's intervention that he was eventually returned.[18]

In the Convention itself, Brissot was generally regarded as one of the leading Girondins, or Brissotins, as they were often called.

---

[16] *Ami du Peuple* No.685, 21 September 1792. According to the Girondin, Barbaroux, a hostile witness, in early August Marat begged him to take him with him to Marseilles, disguised as a jockey. This sounds too good to be true, but too improbable for Barbaroux to have dared to invent it. C.A.Daubon, *Mémoires inédits de Pétion et mémoires de Buzot et de Barbaroux*, Paris, 1866, p.357.

[17] *Journal de la République française* (the new title of Marat's paper), No.39. 7 November 1792.

[18] Archives Nationales C 180. Sessions of 7, 8 and 9 September 1792.

He supported them in his paper and in pamphlets, but took little part in debate, confining himself to the work of the diplomatic committee and keeping out of the dog-fights between the rival factions. When his arrest was ordered on 2 June, unlike several of his colleagues he did not withdraw to a sympathetic province in the hope of organising resistance to Paris, but tried to flee the country. He was caught at Moulins, brought back to Paris and tried and executed with the other Girondin leaders.

Marat found himself for the first time a member of an elected body. As he complained repeatedly in his paper, he was for much of the time in a minority of one. The Girondins hoped to use him to discredit the Montagnards and the latter were reluctant to be associated with him and made few attempts to get him a hearing. Not without some moral courage, he soldiered on, endlessly clamouring to be heard about urgent matters of national importance, which invariably turned out to be new plots that he claimed to have uncovered. He got a rather more friendly reception in the Jacobin Club. Eventually the intensification of the faction fighting forced the Montagnards to come to his support, notably in April 1793, when the Girondins foolishly sent him before the revolutionary tribunal without having a proper case against him. His acquittal gave him the only popular triumph of his life. By now he was a very sick man, 'who would give up all the dignities of the earth for a few days of health'. He was murdered by Charlotte Corday in July 1793.

Robespierre was one of the leading Montagnards and the hero of the Jacobin Club. For a long time he sat on no committees in the Convention and started another paper, *Lettres à ses commettans*, which allowed him to concentrate on general issues. He was probably sincere in saying that it was against his will that he was put on the Committee of Public Safety in July 1793. Even then he never exercised any departmental responsibility, apart from a few weeks in charge of a police bureau, and he remained to the end the man who tried to reconcile the exigencies of political tactics with the justification of revolutionary government *sub specie aeternitatis*.

Saint-Just quickly made his mark with impressive speeches on the measures necessary to bring government practice into line with revolutionary theory. He was put on the Committee of Public Safety in May 1793 and thereafter acted as both government spokesman and military commissar. This did not prevent him from continuing to see the detailed work of administration as something that must be made to conform to republican principles, indeed, as fear and suspicion grew on all sides during the deadly summer of 1794, he came to see France's only possible salvation as dependent on the adoption of what he called 'republican institutions'. He and Robespierre perished when the Committee of Public Safety itself split into two hostile factions in July 1794.

That left Mercier. For reasons best known to himself and his constituents, he stood for the Convention and was returned by the Seine-et-Oise. Once in, he seems to have done almost nothing, apart from drawing attention to the *vertu* of his friend Carra in resigning from a paid office when he too was elected, and explaining why he thought the king should be imprisoned rather than executed. No doubt he was busy with his edition of Rousseau, which he finished in 1793. He also published three volumes of *Fragments on history and politics*, a pamphlet on the *assignats* and a couple of plays in 1792. Whatever his faults, they did not include idleness. Arrested in the autumn of 1793 for having protested against the purge of the Girondin leaders, he spent the next year in gaol, After his release and return to the Convention, he was elected to the Lower House of the new assembly in 1795, but for only one year, after which he withdrew into private life until his death in 1814 at what was, for a revolutionary, the remarkable age of 74.

If one looks at the course of the revolution as a whole, the experience of these men was significantly different. Brissot was generally in some sort of office, in contact with those who were, or at least a member of an important parliamentary committee. Robespierre remained essentially a political guide, not much of a policy-maker and no administrator. Marat was in irascible opposition to almost everything that happened before June 1793 and died soon afterwards. Saint-Just played a leading part in the actual running of the revolution and also tried to see it in more abstract and theoretical terms. For all of them political perspectives were influenced by the positions they occupied and outlooks altered when these positions changed.

Chapter 9

Brissot II

At no stage during the revolution did Brissot make a clear choice between Montesquieu and Rousseau. As late as the spring of 1792 he argued in his paper that if Rousseau deserved a place in the Pantheon, Montesquieu should have one too. 'Jean-Jacques Rousseau developed the bases on which different kinds of governments ought to rest. Montesquieu described them as they existed, but in his description he disseminated that philosophy which, by perfecting reason, inevitably brought about the present revolution.'[1] If this suggests that he did not understand very much about either, at least he paid his respects to both. Rousseau was 'the greatest philosopher of the eighteenth century' (29 October 1790). His *Emile* and *Du contrat social* would last as long as the French constitution itself (2 January 1791). That was rather an under-estimate. In July 1791, in a kind of profession of faith, he argued both that representative republics would be free from the errors of the direct democracy of classical times – a contention of Montesquieu's that Rousseau rejected – and that philosophy had been working to '*dishonour honour* in order to put *vertu* in its place', which was pure Rousseau.

On occasion, Brissot criticised them both, Montesquieu for his alleged pride in his noble lineage (21 November 1789) and for intellectual snobbery (4 June 1791), Rousseau for being too utopian (9 October 1789). He dismissed a proposal for an international court as 'too far above this sublunary world, only fitting for that of Jean-Jacques' (19 May 1790).

More important than specific references of this kind was the

---

[1] *Patriote Français*, 11 February 1792. Unless otherwise indicated, all quotations in this chapter are taken from the same source.

fact that he saw politics in the theoretical terms that the two men had bequeathed to the revolutionary generation. When he wrote, on 19 December 1790, that France was not ready for a republic since there was 'much ignorance and corruption, too many towns and industries, too many people and not enough land' this only made sense in terms of a peculiarly Rousseauist conception of what a republic should be; it was not merely classicism, since it would have eliminated Athens. When he came to consider the problem, to which Rousseau had provided no satisfactory answer, of how *moeurs* could be reformed in a people already corrupted by despotism, Brissot included, together with law, education, good examples and the multiplication of men of principle – of which Montesquieu would have approved – the encouragement of rural life, the breaking up of big landed estates and more respect for tradesmen. On 31 August 1792, in words that would have delighted Jean-Jacques, he argued that the theatre, which up to then had been merely a school of corruption, would have to become 'the school of *bonnes moeurs* and of all the virtues.'

Reconciling his political theories with the facts of revolution involved him in some mental acrobatics. It was all very well to explain in 1790 why the French people were as yet unworthy of a republic. *La forces des choses*, as the revolutionaries liked to call it, was soon to force republicanism upon them. When the king fled, in June 1791, Brissot insisted that there could be no question of restoring him to his throne, whether the country was ready for a republic or not. At that time, he accepted the Jacobin policy of leaving the decision to the Assembly, which reinstated Louis. By the end of the year, when he had been elected to the Legislative Assembly, he had become more impatient and inclined to put the cart before the horse. 'The enemies of the revolution say that our *moeurs* are too corrupt for us to be free: the foundation of liberty is morality. We reply, by turning their own argument against them, let us once be free and our *moeurs* will purify themselves ... A free regime, even a representative one [i.e. one not based on direct democracy] leads men to *vertu* through self-interest: public esteem is the ladder that leads to honour' (18 December 1791). This was a more ingenious than convincing way out of a dilemma that only existed because he took it for granted that a free society had to be based on *vertu*:

something that Montesquieu had denied. At the time he wrote this, Brissot was also claiming that French society could be regenerated by the ennobling experience of war. Within a fortnight – and long before war was declared – the miracle had already happened and the French had become 'this people which, in two years, has already progressed by almost a century'. Rome had been left far behind and past examples were irrelevant since 'We are creating new eras, new revolutions'.[2]

This was very satisfactory so long as one was sure of having the regenerative movement securely under one's control. After the overthrow of the monarchy on 10 August 1792, Brissot and his allies became less confident of the support of those popular forces that could be described as 'the people' when they were on one's own side. It was probably no accident that, from then onwards, he appealed rather more to the Enlightenment in general and less specifically to Rousseau. He had previously made unkind comments about Franklin (too fond of the word 'populace'), Voltaire, who feared Rousseau's influence and tried to poison people's minds against him, and men of letters as a whole, who were inclined to 'crawl before those in office'. By the end of 1792 he was changing his views. When the Jacobins, who had expelled him in the autumn, destroyed a bust of Rousseau's *bête noire*, Helvétius, Brissot did not approve. 'To pass from despotism to liberty we had to go through a century of enlightenment; people are trying to lead us from liberty to despotism through ignorance and barbarism. Already the busts of philosophers are falling beneath the hands of stupid demagogues; already ... the word *philosophe* is being used as an insult; already the beneficent influence of the Enlightenment is being described as another aristocracy to be overthrown' (14 December 1792). He came back to the same theme a fortnight later, complaining that the agitators were describing arguments of principle as *de la philosophie toute pure*. 'They accustom the multitude to despise its benefactor [the Enlightenment] and to idolise ignorance. That is why they are always denouncing elitism (*l'aristocratie du talent*)'. He had a point – but it was one that could have been made against Brissot himself when he had believed that the big

[2] *Second discours sur la nécessité de déclarer la guerre aux princes allemands*, delivered at the Jacobin Club on 30 December 1792, pp.21, 15.

battalions were on his side.

Any attempt to justify policies or claim rights in terms of abstract theory – and one can scarcely appeal to precedent or prescription during a revolution – is likely to raise insoluble problems about sovereignty, which politicians are prone to answer in terms of their day-to-day convenience. What distinguished one revolutionary from another was not so much his inconsistency as the form it took – which was largely dictated by circumstances. Brissot's view of the political situation in April 1789 was stern and gloomy; the future seemed to offer a choice between slavery and civil war. Despotism, even in its death-throes, was still formidable and 'the party of perverse men who sustain it is still manoeuvring night and day to delay that long-sought day of our regeneration'.[3] A week after the 'miraculous' fall of the Bastille he sounded a very different note. Despite all the odds and all the difficulties, including both the habits of deference engendered by the former regime and 'the perfidy of our enemies', three days had decisively overthrown 'the despotism of many centuries'. What had happened was a sudden metamorphosis of the French people. The need now was for reconciliation: 'Let us have the generosity to forgive all, since we are the conquerors.' At the time he made this speech he had failed to get himself elected to the Estates General but was in the process of becoming a member of the Paris Commune. This may not have been wholly irrelevant to his argument in favour of municipal sovereignty. He saw local authority, not as power delegated by the body that represented the nation, but as a parallel emanation of the general will. Every municipality was therefore entitled to draft its own constitution. Paris, however, held a special position, since no other city included 'the men most renowned for their knowledge' and 'such an imposing and independent mass of people'.[4]

In a commentary on a draft constitution for the Commune, he developed this argument that the national assembly did not enjoy exclusive sovereignty.[5] The popular will had delegated to it

[3] *Discours prononcé à l'élection du District de la rue des Filles-St.-Thomas*, pp.12, 2-3.

[4] *Discours prononcé au District des Filles-St.-Thomas le 21 juillet 1789*, *passim*.

[5] *Motifs des commissaires pour adopter le plan de municipalité*, read to the Commune on 10 August 1789.

certain specific powers, such as the right to determine the level of taxation. Other powers, such as the distribution of taxation, had been similarly delegated to the Paris Commune. On 18 August 1789 he went on to make claims for Paris that are rather ironical in view of what the Girondins were going to say about the city a couple of years later. 'Cities have the right to draft their own municipal constitutions ... they have no need of the sanction of the legislative power ... the legislative power has no right to interfere with municipal by-laws ... these municipalities will keep a constant watch on [future] assemblies. It is the aristocracy of the Long Parliament of England that forfeited the fruits of the revolution of 1650 [sic].' All municipal governments enjoyed this kind of sovereignty, but Paris had a special position of its own. 'One hears everywhere that Paris has too much influence over the national Assembly. People are trying to arouse the fears and jealousies of the provinces against the capital. We must beware of this ruse of our enemies ... either the Assembly will always vote in accordance with the general interest or it may sometimes diverge from it ... in the latter case its rôle as censor will save both Paris and the country. Paris keeps watch for all' (20 August 1789). This was a splendid specimen of Rousseauist logic: there is always a single general interest, which can be correctly identified by the right people; once they have recognised it, they are entitled to promote it by whatever means may be necessary and their actions will have a kind of legitimacy that transcends mere constitutional legality. It is a point of view that has commended itself to other people since then. Among other things, it implied that the correct policy was never a compromise that tried to reconcile conflicting interests and points of view. Brissot himself spelled this out on 20 January 1790: 'Agreement is no doubt an excellent thing, but it exists only in heaven or under a despotism ... To propose an agreement between the democratic and aristocratic parties is to want to unite the principles of good and evil.' On that, at least, most of the revolutionaries were agreed.

Brissot had no intention of sharing the Commune's authority with those lower down. Paris was divided into 60 Districts, some of which – notably the Cordeliers where Marat went to live – were inclined to claim the same position in relation to the Commune that Brissot claimed for the Commune vis-à-vis the

Assembly. Brissot would have none of this. On 21 November 1789 he told the Districts to get on with their real job of looking after their poor, instead of challenging the Commune. He had no use for the practice of electoral recall when applied by the Districts to their men on the Commune (24 November 1789) and he denounced their 'continual clamour' and 'the anarchy they have produced within this city' (16 April 1790). What was sauce for the goose was emphatically not sauce for the gander. He did, however, make an exception in favour of political clubs, which he recognised as legitimate censors of both municipalities and Departments (19 June 1790). He publicised the foundation of the Cordelier Club in his newspaper (3 August 1790) and the Cordeliers read extracts from the *Patriote Français* at their inaugural meeting.

Brissot's belief that what mattered most about the government was that it should be in conformity with the general will, rather than that it should comply with legal forms, led him to conclusions that he shared with all the radical revolutionaries. Although he maintained on 6 February 1790 that the *comité des recherches* of the Commune did not employ police spies, 'that method is perhaps not so blameworthy when used in times of crisis in order to safeguard *la chose publique* ... Anyone who trembles under the new regime must be a really bad citizen.' Although he disapproved of Marat's rages, slanders and speculative 'facts', 'I believe that his scourge has more than once proved useful and necessary to repress enemies of the revolution and secret traitors'. Since Marat and Desmoulins were *des auteurs patriotes*, they must be allowed liberties that would not be extended to the other side, where matters of libel were concerned (2 August 1790). The use of the term *exagérations du patriotisme* was 'the hallmark of the moderate ... Despotism may be exaggerated ... but never *patriotisme* ... Distrust is the eternal basis of a free regime ... the reason is simple: *all power, even delegated power, is essentially corrupting* ... in a free regime distrust must therefore be tireless and pitiless' (4 May 1791). 'The people's instinct is worth more than all your dialectic; that instinct has saved you a dozen times and will save you again, for the people know very well that everything is not over yet ... Let us have a good laugh at that scarecrow of anarchy' (10 May 1791). In general, no doubt, the Assembly was to be obeyed – he accepted its refusal to extend the vote to the free coloured population in the West Indies, much as he deplored it – but not in times of crisis when the future of the revolution was at stake. When a crowd prevented the royal family from leaving for St Cloud in April 1791, because of fears that the king might be trying to escape, Brissot argued that the Parisians were acting within their rights. *'The citizens of Paris* know that they are *only one section of the French people.'* Circumstances, however, gave them special responsibilities which entitled them to use more forceful methods than petitions and addresses (23 April 1791). This was a principle that made good political sense in time of revolution but it could be extended indefinitely and those who invoked it when they were in opposition thought it had served its purpose once they themselves were in power and, of course, governing in accordance with the general will.

When he was himself elected to the Legislative Assembly, it was some time before Brissot abandoned his original point of view. On 6 February 1792 he accused his moderate opponents of being hypocritical: 'They pretend that the people is only sovereign and can only be heeded in the mass, but since one can never find it *en masse*, it is clear that this sovereign is an abstract idea, without any real sovereignty ... once they restrict the national will to the clearly expressed will of 14 million men, and that majority is impossible, it clearly follows that they are entitled to trample on petitions, even from substantial sections of the population.' As he and his associates began to sniff power, however, he started to argue that, in times of crisis, the government, as well as the 'people', could break the rules. It was therefore entitled to control people's movements by the issue of passports 'when the interest of liberty in general and the safety of the state make this essential' (31 January 1792).

Once his friends entered the government, in March 1792, the situation began to look rather different. On 3 April he warned 'the deputies who seat themselves *à la montagne'* (i.e. the most radical deputies) against being too suspicious of Ministers. 'One cannot repeat it too often to the *patriotes* that giving free reign to suspicion threatens to destroy everything through mistrust.' He was still prepared to condone popular violence, when it was harmlessly employed in burning the châteaux of seigneurs who could be presumed to have provoked it by their insolence, but not when it was invoked in Paris and could be turned against his own side. 'Men who are always calling for popular vengeance are very blameworthy; they are invoking anarchy' (7 May 1792). Logically, if not very consistently, he now approved of another attempt to prosecute Marat, even insinuating that it was no coincidence that the government was being attacked by both royalists and 'demogogic agitators' who could well be in secret alliance (4 May 1792). When the radicals, true to Brissot's former belief in the virtues of *défiance*, encouraged troops to mistrust their officers, the *Patriote Français*, as a ministerial paper, naturally emphasised the need for military discipline, 'the secret of Greek and Roman armies'. Both sides were the prisoners of circumstances. The Montagnards encouraged mutinies which might wreck the armies; the Girondins preached obedience to generals like Lafayette who hoped to use the troops to get rid of them.

The dismissal of the Girondin Ministers in June 1792 involved a difficult couple of months for Brissot and his friends. They possibly hoped that the Assembly could be induced to dethrone the king, or perhaps they never intended to do more than frighten him into recalling them to office. With this objective in view they opposed the insurrection of 10 August, though Brissot, at least, welcomed it wholeheartedly once it had succeeded. They then found that the Paris Commune, which had been renewed during the insurrection, was rather too keen on the notions of popular sovereignty that Brissot himself had been preaching a couple of years earlier, and rather inclined to dictate to the discredited Assembly. The September massacres, when the despised Commune did its best to have some of them murdered, and the elections to the Convention, which deprived any of them of a seat in Paris, completed their disenchantment with popular politics in the capital. If Brissot's political theories had not been affected by these complicated and desperately serious pressures, he would have been a very remarkable man. Despite some oscillations, his experience during the summer of 1792 inclined him towards conservatism.

His initial reaction to the exclusion of his friends from office was revolutionary. It was up to the Assembly to raise itself to the level of the people (29 June); the Assembly might refuse to act but the people were on guard and only awaiting the signal to make liberty secure (30 June); 'The people can save itself, without its representatives and even despite them, but its representatives cannot save it, despite the people or without its support' (27 July). He welcomed the coup d'état of 10 August without any inhibitions: 'Crime was on guard at the palace, *patriotisme* everywhere in the city' (11 August). Two days later he told his readers 'The people is responsible only to itself in the exercise of its sovereignty and no power can *prescribe* rules of conduct to it.' On 27 August he made his last pronouncement in this vein, to the effect that, even when the form of the people's demands was irregular, the demands themselves always rested on a sound basis.

By this time the tide had begun to ebb. On 24 August he had objected to the Commune's attempt to veto the revival of the Paris Department, its superior in the hierarchy of local government. On the next day he remonstrated with petitioners from the Gobelins Section for presenting their 'petition' to the Assembly in the form of a threat: 'You are being misled; enemies of popular sovereignty are making use of your hands to undermine it, while you swear that you are strengthening it.' He still thought that the insurrectionary Commune had done a good job on 10 August but 'The powers created to give a revolutionary movement to the political machine must come to an end with the movement itself'. The object of overthrowing royal 'despotism' was not to instal an 'even harsher and more malevolent one' (30 August). He himself was denounced by the Commune on 2 September – the day the massacres began – and his papers were searched on the following morning. After this unpleasant experience and the loss of his Paris seat at the hands of the effiicient Montagnard political machine, he became a convert to order and legality. 'The worst of tyrannies is that exercised in the name of the people' (18 September). That was what some of his more conservative opponents had been telling him for a long time. 'Your most formidable enemy, the only one that can prevail over you, is anarchy.' (21 September). It was no longer the laughable scarecrow of May 1791. When he was expelled from the Jacobin Club, he made a new assessment of the situation.[6] The anarchists were, of course, not the voice of the

[6] *A tous les républicains de France, sur la Société des Jacobins de Paris.*

people, but a violent minority that had usurped the title to act in the name of the sovereign people. One of their crimes was to 'invest one municipality with the whole power of the nation ... they tell one fraction that it is the whole people, the true people, the only sovereign ... in practice they elevate Paris above all [the other Departments]'. If this was not exactly what Brissot had been doing earlier in the revolution, it sounded remarkably like it.

When the Convention met it promptly became a battleground between Girondins and Montagnards. Brissot took no part in this trench warfare, for which his own side must take most of the responsibility. His own preference, which was not shared by the man to whom he had handed over the editorship of the *Patriote Français*, Girey-Dupré, was the very sensible one of detaching Danton from the Montagnards and concentrating the attack on Marat, whose implication in the September massacres made him virtually indefensible.[7] On 7 September Brissot wrote, 'The name of that man should be included amongst those shameful words that no one can speak without blushing'. This did not prevent his Girondin allies from taking on the Parisian deputies as a whole and their shrill and ineffectual attacks on too wide a front soon alienated Paris and gradually lost them support in the Convention. Although Brissot took no part in these faction fights, the Montagnards had a particular dislike for him and were inclined to refer to their opponents as Brissotins rather than Girondins.

Brissot remained a Rousseauist at heart but he was moving in the direction of Montesquieu, to the extent that he was more inclined to locate the general will in what the majority actually wanted, rather than in what a self-styled revolutionary vanguard believed to be good for it. On 23 September he said there were two tendencies in the Assembly: 'One tends towards the destruction of all existing institutions, towards general levelling ... the other tends to maintain provisionally whatever exists and towards progressive reform, without sudden disorganisation. One is always prating about the sovereignty of the people, but by doing so tends towards anarchy which destroys the people. The other does not flatter the people but serves it better by promoting

[7] Ibid. p.22.

order, the only means by which the people can exist.' What was
actually new was not so much the tendencies, which could be
said to have existed since 1789, but the one to which Brissot
chose to belong. He was still careful not to condemn the
Parisians *en bloc* – he was, after all, more of a Parisian than most
of the Montagnards – and he still insisted that the 'anarchists'
were supported by only a small minority of the inhabitants of the
capital.

On 18 October he opposed submitting the punishment of the
king to a national referendum, on the ground that the
Convention was a sovereign body. There were limits, however, to
the free play of representative institutions. Like all the
revolutionaries, he was caught in the trap of 10 August. The
Paris Sections should not be allowed to meet every night, in case
they fell into the wrong hands. On 6 December he supported
Buzot's motion that even the *assemblées primaires*, the meetings
of voters where, if anywhere, a democrat could be expected to
locate sovereignty, could not be allowed to discuss the
restoration of the monarchy. According to Brissot, Robespierre
went a good deal further and gave the deputies a good laugh
when he proposed that the Convention should vote that no
nation was allowed to give itself a king. On 1 January 1793
Brissot reversed his opinion about a referendum on the king's
fate, presumably on tactical grounds, since this was the most
likely way to save his life. He justified his new view on the ground
that 'The real check on the despotism of agitators lies in the
frequent exercise of the sovereignty of the entire people', which
he contrasted with 'partial and local sovereignty, the sovereignty
of certain clubs, certain Sections, which allows certain men to
dominate the rest of France'. In terms of pure logic, this was as
defensible as his earlier view. What it meant in practice was that
he was no longer confident that the Convention, exposed to the
intimidation of Paris, would spare the king's life. The 'entire
people' to whom he wished to appeal, would only be allowed to
exercise their sovereignty within limits – to imprison the king
rather than to execute him, but not to put him back on the
throne. Brissot was no more of a democrat than his opponents;
he was simply playing the national card because they had
trumped his Parisian one.

On 12-13 January he reprinted in his own paper an article that he had previously published in the *Chronique*. One again he argued, as he had done in July 1789, that the revolution had finally succeeded, this time with the establishment of the republic. Now, however, he was being challenged by men who claimed to be better revolutionaries than he was, 'men without talent or virtue', who were posing as the real spokesmen of the people. This led Brissot to draw some rather nice distinctions. 'They say that the people are never wrong and I believe that too, but *the multitude which is not the people* is often wrong, often misled.' This implied a shift from his previous assertions that his opponents in Paris were a small factious minority. 'When a revolution has been accomplished, men have to improve or liberty disappears. If enlightenment and virtue do not prevail, cruelty and ignorance reign and rend. There is no middle way.' They were all agreed on that: there never *was* a middle way. The ignorance of the masses was a consequence of the old order. Brissot's side wanted to end it by education; their opponents, to exploit it for their own purposes. It was a long time since he had been saying that the people's instinct was worth more than the dialectic of the moderates, but all attitudes changed with circumstances. Before 10 August, 'order' was merely 'a passport to facilitate plots.' Now it was 'the thermometer of the free man'. But if Brissot had become a conservative he had not stopped being a Rousseauist. Politics was still a Manichean conflict of values rather than the adjustment of competing interests, and if he insisted that 'the aristocrats and the agitators are hand in hand', this was more than a clumsy attempt to discredit the Montagnards. If all the right is one side, the wrong must all be on the other.

By April Brissot had assumed a defensive, almost a defeatist tone. For a Rousseauist to recognise that he is losing popular support must be very hard to bear. Defending himself against Robespierre, Brissot now turned to Rousseau for consolation rather than for guidance, beginning his article with a quotation from the Master. 'I am growing old amidst my savage enemies, without losing either courage or patience. For my only defence I present to heaven a heart free from fraud and hands that no evil stains.' As always, the quarrel was not so much about the wisdom of specific policies, but about who was morally right. 'They think they have the general will and all they have is the will of a handful of tribunes, taken up by slaves or idiots.' His last word was another brochure, written only a week before the overthrow of the Girondins.[8] There is a certain weariness about it, reminiscent of Robespierre's last speech to the Convention. Once again, it was all a matter of absolutes. The anarchists had controlled affairs since 10 August and everything had naturally gone wrong. They were responsible for the lot: 'the multiplication of crime, attacks on property, dear bread, fiscal deficit, the fall of the *assignat*, the almost universal collapse of the administration, troubles in the Eure and the Orne, in Orleans, in the Vendée.' It was they who had extended the war to England, Holland and Spain – and they who had rejected his advice to attack Spain! *He* now used the argument that Robespierre had thrown against him a year before: 'It is not with swords that one engenders the love of liberty.' The Belgians did not want to be liberated. 'Paris has rendered immense services to the revolution, but it would be paying them too dearly to sacrifice the liberty of France to Paris.' 'Those who compose the present Convention hate each other too much not to keep up their obstinate fight against each other for ever.' There was only one way out: a dissolution and new elections. Rather more than a year later Robespierre and Saint-Just were to propose the opposite way, but they had retained the control over government that Brissot had lost.

When Brissot wrote about the 'people' he was never referring merely to the population in general. Some people were more popular than others. This was not merely a matter of recognising that the poor were in a special situation, in the sense that they depended on positive action by the state if they were to survive. For the Rousseauist, the 'people' were special in the sense that, because of their closeness to 'nature', they were relatively uncorrupted by false social values, a repository of *vertu*, not necessarily better than the Rousseauist himself, of course, since he shared the values they personified, but qualitatively as well as quantitatively superior to the general run of the educated and the wealthy. Brissot believed both in the special needs and the special virtues of the poor and he was rather more consistent in

[8] *J-P Brissot, député du département d'Eure-et-Loir, à ses commettans*. The preface is dated 22 May 1793.

the conclusions he drew from this than in his attitude towards sovereignty.

The policies he advocated were intended to go beyond philanthropy and to bring about a gradual levelling of wealth, without involving the expropriation of the rich. On 12 November 1789 he proposed dealing with the shortage of bread in Paris by allowing the price to rise, while supplying the poor at the old price, on production of ration cards. If the money needed for a bread subsidy could not be found in any other way, it should be raised by a special tax on the rich. Something very much like this was actually put into practice, but not until the spring of 1793. On 22 December 1789 he printed a letter from a correspondent who suggested that when the property of the Church – which included a great deal of land – was put on the market, something could be done to help the poor. 'It would be madness to try to get back to the original causes of the unequal division of land but if ever an opportunity presented itself for remedying this, at least in part, it is now.' His correspondent wanted to give one-third of the Church lands to the poor, in smallholdings that would be inalienable for three generations. If this was too expensive – since the object of the sale was to reduce the National Debt – at least the Church lands should be sold in small lots that could be paid for over a period of years. On 24 November 1791 Brissot complained that the debts of the ancien régime were being liquidated to the advantage of the rich and he supported a proposal by Clavière to suspend all payments above 3,000 livres, in order to support the *assignat*, while making special arrangements to protect the smaller creditors.[9] Although a free trader in principle, he wanted to ban the export of raw materials in order to bring down the price of manufactures. In the Convention, perhaps because he was now appealing to the country as a whole, rather than to the urban sans-culottes, he opposed price controls (30 November 1792) and insisted that internal free trade should apply to food as well as to other commodities (17 November 1792). On 29 December he printed a letter on the general subject of economic equality. 'In any democracy the laws should destroy and prevent excessive *material* inequality amongst the citizens. Otherwise their

---

[9] This speech was reported at some length in the *Moniteur*.

equality of *rights* will only be an illusion.' To achieve this, legacies should be restricted to direct heirs, with the property of the childless being given to virtuous and hard-working young men. Even children's right to inherit was no more than a concession by society. The minimum that a family needed to support itself should be exempt from taxation. This was about as far as any of the revolutionary leaders was prepared to go.

Brissot's initial remarks on the subject of popular *vertu* were fairly moderate. On 24 May 1790 he quoted Roland, 'Let us tell the merchants that the people who really matter in trade are the *artistes* who invent and the workmen who execute'. Always aware of the international dimension, he took advantage of the opportunity to refer his readers to an earlier work of Roland's in which he had argued that western imperialism had done more harm than the crusades to non-European peoples. Attacking the restriction of the vote to those who paid a certain level of taxation, Brissot wrote, rather patronisingly, on 2 July 1790, 'There are already among our working men ... men up to the level of our revolution, who understand and speak the language of liberty'. On 5 February 1791 he went much further. 'It is admitted today that it was the most despised, the most wretched section of the people that, almost alone, began the revolution on 14 July. It was only later that the working class and those of the wealthy who happened to be *patriotes* added their strength to these first efforts. The writers, none of whom, however brave, would have dared to recommend or even hope for what the people undertook and carried out on their own, could only applaud and celebrate their victory.' The enemies of the people then hoped to discourage them by engineering a slump that would deprive them of the work they needed to live. Brissot did not deny that things had got worse under the new regime and he thought the people's patience under these hardships even more praiseworthy than their former courage. In the last resort, the welfare of nations and societies always depended on 'this immense and unfortunate class. Philosophers and truly religious men exhaust themselves in thought; *patriotes* wear themselves out in vain resistance; only the people, at certain times, knows what to say and what to do. This is the order established by providence itself, which brings everything to pass by immutable law: when tyranny is at its height, when insurrection has become *the most sacred of duties*, if the people did not follow its own natural inspiration, all would be lost.' Robespierre would have found it hard to disagree with that.

Time and again Brissot denounced the elitism of clubs like the Jacobins. When Desmoulins complained that this was to discredit the revolution, Brissot replied that the latter depended on the people as a whole. 'Do the Jacobins not exclude *passive* citizens [those who paid less than a certain amount of direct taxation]? Those are the only ones who make revolutions.' The people were the natural friends of order (13 August 1791); too much so perhaps, when compared with those who 'try to hide behind these words of order and peace their hatred of equality and of the people' (19 March 1792). 'It is within the class of citizens called *people* that one finds the most sincere republicans. Why? Because the people have more good faith, more good sense, fewer prejudices, less self-seeking calculation than the other classes' (22 September 1792). His faith in the 'people' had evidently survived his disenchantment with the Parisian sans-culottes.

In this Manichean world, the *vertu* of some necessarily implied the wickedness of others. Brissot began, harmlessly enough, by saying on 5 June 1790 that the enemy was no longer the king and his Ministers but the prejudice in favour of the rich. By 5 February 1791 he was arguing that 'Profound corruption reigns amongst the rich; even the most self-aware of philosophers cannot keep his habits, his ideas and his inclinations from being affected by wealth, or even by modest comfort'. On 25 January 1792, without altogether excusing sugar-rioters, he said that the profiteers who provoked them were just as guilty 'and they would deserve no pity if they became their victims'. This was not a direct incitement to lynching, like Marat's pronouncement a year later, but it was leaning in that direction. Brissot printed a letter from Pétion to Buzot, on 10 February 1792, deploring the fact that 'the bourgeoisie, that numerous and wealthy class, is cutting itself off from the people, placing itself above them, being taught to believe that the revolution is a war between the haves and have-nots'. The people, for their part, were being told that they were worse off than before 1789. Pétion admitted that this was true, but claimed that everyone else was suffering as well – which threw a rather curious light on the revolution. He appealed for a return to the alliance of 1789 of all the Third Estate against the privileged. 'If our will is strong enough, we are more formidable than ever.' If Brissot too wanted to reconstitute the old alliance, it was scarcely tactful of him, on 18 March, to denounce 'that corrupt class of hardened egoists known as *capitalists*'. On 23 June he complained that 'While the rich are conspiring against liberty and working to replace the aristocracy of titles with an aristocracy of big estates, the poor are shedding their blood for their country and depriving themselves of part of their livelihood on its behalf'.

It is fashionable amongst historians of the French revolution to describe Brissot and the Girondins as not merely politically conservative but as the representatives of capitalism and property and the natural enemies of the sans-culottes. This is demonstrably untrue of the period before 10 August 1792. Once in office, both Girondins and Montagnards changed their tune. The challenge of a radical opposition inclined the former towards conservatism; more generalised discontent drove the latter towards the endless concentration of power in their own hands.

One of the constants of politics is that policies fail to work and electorates prove fickle. It is only human if the politicians concerned think this must be either bad luck or someone else's fault. For the Rousseauist the problem is rather different. The object of political action is the implementation of the indivisible general will. Once he, or his associates, are in office, there can be no doubt that this is the actual policy of the government. Since the general will reflects what is to the real advantage of the community as a whole, it is, as Rousseau said it was, infallible. If things do not work according to plan, policies fail or people do not like them, this cannot be the fault of either the government or the general will. The most satisfactory explanation of this unfortunate state of affairs is that the whole beneficent process has been thwarted by the Enemy. The *émigrés*, men so vicious that they could not bear to live in a country that was being regenerated, had almost nominated themselves for this rôle. The trouble was that they did not look threatening enough, unless one could see them as merely the vanguard of an ideological crusade whose main forces were those of the European 'tyrants'. Burke's *Reflections on the Revolution in France*, which Brissot reviewed on 2 January 1791, was rather helpful, since Burke advocated precisely this. Brissot was wrong to call it 'Gothic from start to finish'; Burke had more in common with Rousseau than either he or Brissot would have cared to admit.[10]

So long as things were going well, Brissot did not need the Enemy, whose menace rose and fell, not with the actual danger of foreign intervention, but with Brissot's political and ideological needs. For a long time he insisted that there was no danger from abroad; the recovery of prosperity demanded peace and it was counter-revolutionaries who pinned their hopes on war (19 May 1790, 9 June 1790, 3 November 1790). Rather ominously though, Brissot's pacific policy was accompanied by the kind of chauvinistic tub-thumping in which most of the revolutionaries liked to indulge. French Ministers must not 'debase the majesty of the first nation in Europe' (24 October 1789). In view of 'the superiority of a free nation over those countries that contain only petty tyrants and slaves', the conduct of French ambassadors should be 'proud and republican'; they should 'make the glory of the French revolution respected by the whole world' (18 September 1790). As the months went by, Great Britain declined from the natural ally of a free France to a nation whose people would restrain the tyrannical intentions of its corrupt government, and eventually even this became doubtful.

Brissot sounded the alarm early in 1791. There was no serious foreign threat but he was worried by growing conservatism at home and adopting a more radical stance all round. What made him worry about foreign troop movements was the fact that France's leaders were not like Ludlow and Ireton, who would have stood no nonsense from counter-revolutionaries (1 January 1791). By now the danger came, not from warmongers but from 'those who want to lull us to sleep on the edge of a precipice' (1 February 1791). When the domestic crisis intensified with the king's flight, foreign intervention for the first time became a serious possibility. Full of the hope that France was heading for a republic, Brissot dismissed it. This did not prevent him from striking a defiant stance at the Jacobins on 15 July 1791. 'Who are you? A free people? And they threaten you with a few

[10] On this subject, see David Cameron, *The social thought of Rousseau and Burke, a comparative study*, London, 1973.

crowned brigands ... Did Athens and Sparta ever fear the innumerable forces that the despots of Persia trailed behind them?' Nevertheless, his message was that there was no danger of foreign attack unless the revolutionaries weakened, and no question of France attacking anyone else.

Once elected to the Legislative Assembly his policy changed. His first speech was on the *émigrés*.[11] After proposing the confiscation of the property of the king's brothers and of all royal officials who had left the country, he turned to the *émigrés'* backers. 'It is across the Rhine that you must strike.' This was followed by the first of a number of thumbnail sketches of the European situation that were to become a feature of his speeches. Foreign policy, for which he seems to have regarded himself as especially gifted, actually saw him at his worst. Every *tour d'horizon* was a pretext for airy optimism, an assurance that, despite their malevolence, none of the despots was in a position to threaten France. The moral was not, as it had been formerly, that they could therefore be ignored, but that 'you must force the foreign powers either to expel the *émigrés* or to give them open protection'. In the latter event, France would of course go to war. For the time being he left it at that.

Towards the end of the year he launched his war campaign in earnest, with five major speeches in as many weeks. He claimed afterwards that his intention was essentially tactical: to exploit a limited war to force the king off the fence so that he would either capitulate to the revolution and appoint *patriote* Ministers or reveal his support for France's enemies – in which case he would presumably be deposed. It was quite an accurate calculation, even if the Girondins lost their nerve at the vital moment and the limited war took on nightmarish proportions. Brissot could not, however, justify his policy in quite such blunt terms. He first told the Assembly that it was a matter of defending French honour. When the minor German princes told the *émigrés* to decamp he could no longer use this argument or talk about national defence when there was no danger. The objective now became war for its own sake. On 29 December he wanted to break off diplomatic relations with Sweden, Russia, Spain and Rome and to threaten both Spain and Austria. On the following day he favoured

[11] *Moniteur*, 20 October 1791.

invading Holland – which would have meant war with England and possibly Prussia as well. On 17 January he proposed sending an ultimatum to Austria. To the Jacobins he gave a rather more ideological view of the situation. 'A people that has conquered its liberty after twelve centuries of slavery needs war to consolidate it; it needs to show that it is worthy of liberty, to purge itself of the vices of despotism, to get rid of men who can still corrupt it.' Faith in foreign support was the last hope of the enemies of the revolution. 'The war of liberty is a holy war, ordained by heaven and, like heaven, it purges men's souls. It is amidst the terrors of war that egoism disappears and a common peril unites all souls ... After the fight we shall have a nation regenerated, new, moral.'[12] A fortnight later he had changed his tune. France was already regenerated and its revolution surpassed anything in ancient history. The war was now a crusade for universal liberty. 'Everywhere they know that sublime saying that to be free, all a people has to do is to will it.'[13] His last speech to the Jacobins was mainly a defence against Robespierre,[14] who had torn his windy rubbish to pieces in some of his most impressive speeches. This was the parting of the ways between the two men. When the debate began they were studiously polite to each other. By the time it ended each professed to believe that the other was out to destroy the revolution.

Delessart, the Foreign Minister, did his best to frustrate the Assembly and to preserve peace. In a quite remarkably vicious speech, Brissot persuaded the deputies to impeach him on a charge of high treason.[15] Delessart was still awaiting trial, at Orleans, in September, when he was butchered during the prison massacres. His blood was therefore partly on Brissot's head. In the course of this speech Brissot anticipated some of the Montagnard attitudes of the following year, which he found less persuasive when *he* was on the defensive. 'You know the people's rights. They come before the law. You can punish their abuse but you cannot prevent the people from using them.' 'People have

---

[12] *Discours sur la nécessité de déclarer la guerre aux princes allemands*, 16 December 1791.

[13] *Second discours sur la nécessité de déclarer la guerre ...* , 30 December 1791.

[14] *Troisième discours sur la nécessité de déclarer la guerre ...* , 20 January 1792.

[15] *Moniteur*, 10 March 1792.

tried to discourage denunciation; all that needs discouraging is its abuse.' 'Let us never forget ... that indulgence may compromise the fate of 25 million men.' Delessart had written in one of his despatches that the great majority of the nation was in favour of the constitution. That was a subtle form of heresy. He should have said that, with the exception of the *émigrés*, it was unanimous. Brissot also used that argument by insinuation that was to do yeoman service for both sides in the battle between the Montagnards and the Girondins: if Delessart had been secretly acting on behalf of the Austrian Emperor he would have done just what he actually did. Therefore ...

When the war resulted in defeat and invasion, Brissot might have been expected to have learned his lesson. The victories of Valmy and Jemappes and the occupation of Belgium in the autumn of 1792 seem on the contrary to have convinced him that he had been right in presenting the 'despots' as paper tigers. He urged an attack on Spain.[16] It was he who presented the reports from the diplomatic committee in favour of declaring war on England, even if he pretended afterwards that he had been opposed to it.[17] There was, as usual, no danger. France could defeat England at sea. The Irish would revolt, the English soon weary of the war and overthrow their government. It was, in fact, all *too* easy. The less the danger, the less plausible it was to justify the war as either necessary to remove an obstacle that was preventing the revolution from fulfilling its promises, or a means of regeneration through sacrifice and the sharing of common dangers. Enemy No. 1 seemed to have outlived his usefulness.

Brissot was ready with a substitute. As early as 30 December 1791 he had warned the Jacobins that the only remaining danger, once war had been declared, would come from anarchy. 'The men who are most dangerous to this Society ... are those who call themselves your brothers and yet really attack the constitution in a society dedicated to the defence of every part of it.' (The official title of the Jacobins was 'Friends of the Constitution'.) As we have seen, this was a note that he sounded with increasing urgency in the autumn of 1792. During the

[16] See his letters to general Miranda and to the former War Minister, Servan, in *Correspondance* (ed.C.Perroud), 3v., Paris, n.d., III/312-7, 321-3.
[17] *Moniteur*, 12 January 1793, 1 February 1793.

military crisis of 1793, when an Austrian army began invading northern France and there was a real danger from Enemy No. 1, Brissot, who always treated the war as a political convenience, concentrated his fire on Enemy No. 2. His final pamphlet, as we have seen, blamed everything that had gone wrong on the Montagnards. Like Robespierre a year later, he thought it all went back to 1789: each of the three Assemblies had been motivated primarily by fear. The division of society into two hostile classes was due not, as Pétion had said in the previous year, to the selfishness of the bourgeoisie, but to the self-interest of the Montagnards. Brissot had always tended to see the outside world in terms of his own preconceptions. When the *force des choses* broke through, on 2 June 1793, there was, quite literally, nowhere for him to go.

Chapter 10

Marat II

To begin with, Marat seems to have seen his revolutionary rôle as that of adviser to those in power. He sent a presentation copy of his *Offrande à la patrie* to Necker, 'that great statesman ... distinguished both by his wisdom and his integrity'.[1] On 29 September 1789 he said that he had already written a score of letters to the Constituent Assembly. If that of 23 August is typical, these were unlikely to have had much effect: ostensibly about the danger of copying the British constitution, this letter consisted mainly of Marat's version of the British government's attempts to suppress *The chains of slavery* in 1774.[2] He went on writing to the Assembly for quite a while, letting the deputies know, in May 1790, that he had been 'born with an inclination towards study' etc., etc.[3] In this authorised version of his career he admitted that when he had returned to France 'the kind of censor's rôle that I had played in England seemed too dangerous', which rather weakened his claim to have been 'the apostle and martyr of liberty'. No one took any notice of him.

His respectful letters to the Assembly were rather different from the one that he wrote to the Paris Commune on 25 September 1789, ordering it to purge itself of its less worthy members – he was particularly worried about 'men without any situation, living in furnished rooms and without any means of support apart from their work.'[4] 'I am the eye of the people; you are at most its little finger.' 'The incorruptible defender of the

---

[1] *Offrande à la patrie*, p.14 n[1]. For the presentation to Necker see *Les pamphlets de Marat* (ed. C.Vellay) Paris, 1911. p.78 n[1]. Unless otherwise indicated, all the quotations in this chapter are from Marat's newspapers and are indicated by the date only.

[2] *La correspondance de Marat* (ed. C.Vellay), Paris, 1908, pp.100-3.

[3] Ibid. pp.141-4.

[4] Ibid. pp.103-8.

rights of the people', he alone had saved liberty during the July crisis. This did not make any impression on the Commune.

Since no one was disposed to listen to his advice, he founded a newspaper of his own. The prospectus described it as the creation of a society of *patriotes*, which allowed Marat to refer to 'the purity of views, the breadth of knowledge and well-earned success of the political works of the editor, a zealous citizen who for a long time neglected his own reputation, the better to serve his country, and whose name will be inscribed amongst its liberators'. This excellent man had saved Paris on the night of 14 July by halting single-handed 'several regiments of German cavalry' that were trying to move into Paris while its feckless inhabitants were still celebrating the fall of the Bastille.[5] His paper, with the uninspiring title, *Le Publiciste Parisien*, carried Rousseau's device: *Vitam impendere vero*, and its editor promised his readers 'freedom without licence, energy without violence and good sense without excess'. All the other aspiring editors promised much the same thing.

Marat began moderately enough, but on 16 September he changed his title to *L'Ami du Peuple*. This was a stroke of genius: the paper *was* Marat and he was soon using the title to refer either to it or to himself. The tone changed too. On the following day he told his readers, 'We make a great song and dance when a few villains whose extortions have ruined whole provinces, fall beneath the blows of the populace [sic], in legitimate revolt, and we keep silent when the satellites of the Prince go in for the military butchery of thousands of his subjects'. It had not taken long for Marat to find his style and his message was scarcely to alter during the next four years. The tone of the paper did fluctuate: when he was living in the open he was relatively moderate; when he went underground – as he did in November 1789 to avoid prosecution for a libel directed against the wrong man – he became violent. He was on the run for most of the time. This was no doubt unpleasant, perhaps even dangerous, but it gave him a freedom to defy the law that was denied to his competitors. It may also have had an effect on his mental stability. The violence of his writing varied both with

---

[5] Although Marat was to repeat the story of his lifelong services to liberty over and over again, he dropped this one from the canon after 1789.

the political situation and with his own state of mind as well. The king's flight in 1791 brought on a particularly vicious paroxysm, when he demanded the shaving of Marie Antoinette's head, the burial alive of imaginary armies of invading *émigrés* and the impaling of the majority of deputies. Where verbal ferocity is concerned, one can easily concede his claim to have been unique.

The issues of 18-20 September contained a *discours au peuple* that was a kind of profession of faith. The French were a frivolous people whose liberation in 1789 had been a temporary accident. Paris in particular was the home of luxury and vice. The provinces were marginally less corrupt, 'But what can one expect from an egoistic people that acts only from self-interest, lets its passions dictate to it and responds only to vanity? Let us not deceive ourselves: a nation without understanding, without *moeurs*, without *vertus*, is not made for liberty.' The cardinal mistake of the Parisians was not to have taken advantage of their lucky victory, in order to exterminate their enemies. This had allowed 'them' to recover and to win over the majority of the deputies. As a result, 'You are further from happiness than ever'. Bad as things already were, in the future they could only get worse, and all this was due to people neglecting Marat's warnings. 'What regrets you would have spared yourselves if you had followed the wise advice that the *Ami du Peuple* gave you nine months ago [i.e. in the *Offrande*].' 'There is only one way to save the state, that is to purge and reform the National Assembly, to expel with ignominy all its corrupt members ... to convene [to a new assembly] only men distinguished by their enlightenment and their virtues, and to supply it with a detailed plan of action, in accordance with a well organised constitutional plan.' A footnote explained that this was no other than his own work, published in the previous month. What he wrote during the next four years amounted to little more than variations on these themes.

Throughout the revolution Marat's attitudes were the product of a megalomania so monstrous that it sometimes struck people as funny. When he said to his fellow-deputies in the Convention, on 4 October 1792, 'You can't prevent the man of genius from projecting himself into the future. You don't understand the man of learning whose knowledge of the world anticipates events

... Where would you be if I had not prepared public opinion ... '
the general hilarity must have taken him by surprise for he was a
totally humourless man.[6]

He was the only one of the people's defenders who had never
been deceived (22 December 1790), the only one capable of
judging men, who had never relaxed his guard but always
immolated himself for the salvation of the people (20 April 1791).
'I believe I have exhausted just about all the combinations of
morals, politics and philosophy that the human spirit has
devised, to arrive at the best conclusions' (14 January 1793).
Turning on his political allies in the Convention, he told them, 'I
am not like you, only born yesterday, where liberty is concerned.
I sucked in love of liberty with my mother's milk and I was free
forty years ago when France was still peopled only by slaves' (1
March 1793). If he really started at ten, he must have been a
kind of political Mozart. His delight in proclaiming his own
virtues and giving his readers the edifying story of his life became
even more of an obsession with him in 1793. By then he was
seriously ill and perhaps concerned to get the record straight
before he died. A month before his assassination he wrote that
his energetic contribution to the revolution would be a source of
'profound reflection' to posterity which would be amazed, both
by his firmness, courage, etc., and by the fact that no one took
any notice of him (17 June 1793).

In so far as the revolution had actually achieved anything, it
was virtually his own work. *All* the *cahiers* of the Third Estate
had reflected the ideas in his *Offrande* and *Constitution* (25
February 1791). This was positively telepathic, since the latter
was not published until long after the last *cahier* had been
handed in. He had saved the *patrie* both on 14 July and on 4
October 1789, when he had exposed an aristocratic plot.[7] When he
fled to England in January 1790 the *patriotes* were frozen with
fear (4 May 1791). When he got back he held the Constituent
Assembly in check until the time of the Champs de Mars
massacre (29 May 1792). After the massacre, he was the only
man to remain on his feet (27 January 1793). In short, 'Not many

---

[6] *Moniteur*.

[7] For the fullest account of his victory over the German cavalry, see the *Ami
du Peuple* for 12 November 1789.

great events since the taking of the Bastille have happened
without my preparing them; how many of them were not due to
me alone?' (5 May 1791). In the roll-call of his battle-honours he
never included the only event where his intervention may
actually have had some effect: the prison massacres of
September 1792. What he *could* have done, if only he had been
given the chance, was even more impressive. 'If I were the
tribune of the people, supported by a few thousand determined
men, I guarantee that within six weeks the constitution would be
perfect ... the nation free and happy; in less than a year it would
be powerful and flourishing, and it would stay like that so long as
I lived' (26 July 1790). If only he had been fit enough to travel, he
would have led a small force to the Vendée and finished off the
civil war there in a single day. 'I am no stranger to the art of war
and, without boasting, I can guarantee success' (6 July 1793). He
never mentioned any problem that he could *not* solve.

It was understandable if the thought of so much talent running
to waste sometimes made him sad, or even bitter. 'Poor people!
You tremble at the dangers your defender runs. A thousand
swords of steel are suspended over his head at every moment.
But he will never abandon you. Strong in the purity of his heart,
when the fatal moment comes he will fly to his execution with
the joy of a martyr' (16 January 1790). There were times when he
could not help losing his patience. 'Perish then, stupid and
cowardly citizens, since nothing affects you. And you, their
unfortunate defender, die of grief at the sight of your powerless
efforts. Why force yourself once again to pull back your unworthy
compatriots from the edge of the abyss? No, it is not with a
people of vile slaves that one can make a nation of free men' (16
January 1791). The authorities at least knew what he was worth.
'The enemies of the revolution would give ten million for my
head' (13 January 1790). Necker – always parsimonious – had
offered one million livres in gold to buy his silence (24 April
1793). This was at least an advance on Lord North's 8,000
guineas. In January 1791, 10,000 assassins were after him; in
September, five spies and 2,000 assassins. It does not seem many
spies.

He was curiously jealous of anyone else's reputation. When
Desmoulins told his readers of an attempt to buy him, Marat
immediately replied that *he* had been offered a million (1 July

1790). When Desmoulins talked of giving up his paper because of threats to his life, Marat tried to cheer him up by telling him how much more he himself had suffered from persecution (23 July 1790). He praised a speech by Saint-Just on the financial situation, only to continue 'I myself go much farther ... ' (1 December 1792). During the early years of the revolution he had consistently praised Robespierre to the skies, as 'perhaps the only true *patriote* in the Assembly', even on the rare occasions when he had disagreed with him. When both were elected to the Convention he may have seen Robespierre as a rival. For the first six months he scarcely mentioned him in his paper and when he commended Robespierre's initial opposition to the war, he was careful to point out – correctly – that he himself had been converted to a defensive policy before Robespierre (28 March 1793).

His political verdicts owed something to personal considerations. It was Brissot's plan for a municipal constitution that convinced Marat that he was no more than 'an ambitious little man and a smooth intriguer' (19 August 1790). That was when Marat was fighting a personal war against the Commune. By 11 September 1791, when that quarrel was no longer relevant, Brissot was 'far above his successful rivals [for election to the Legislative Assembly] both in feeling and in understanding, even though I don't regard him as a very frank patriot'. What turned him against Brissot once again was not his old friend's campaign for war, of which Marat approved at the time, but his association with Condorcet – Marat's old enemy, the secretary of the *Académie des Sciences* – in launching a new newspaper (28 November 1791). From then onwards he sneered at all Brissot's speeches, even when he agreed with their conclusions. On 17 December 1792 he warned the Montagnards that unless they supported him in the Convention he would 'not spare them any more than the enemies of liberty'. Four days later he told readers that 'base jealousy has even led [the *patriotes*] to abandon those with the best means of foiling plots ... No good is to be expected of them'. The Convention was therefore useless and would have to be purged.

The question that immediately arises is how one is to account for Marat's influence when the evidence for his paranoia is so overwhelming. Where the politicians were concerned, the extent of that influence is easily exaggerated. One Montagnard deputy, Thuriot, said in the Assembly 'There is no one here who can let himself be influenced by Marat or believe that he influences the Convention'.[8] Another, Levasseur, said much the same thing in his memoirs. Marat himself complained a good deal, towards the end of 1792, that he was completely isolated. Things changed in the following spring, when the quarrel between Montagnards and Girondins reached a new intensity and the Montagnards had to defend anyone who was attacked by their opponents. Marat was then too useful as a hatchet-man for his services to be rejected. Unlike Robespierre and Saint-Just, he rarely offered any constructive suggestions about policy but confined himself to exposing plots and denouncing individuals. At the time, he did not appear to stand for anything very much. Things became different when his murder by Charlotte Corday made him a genuine victim, if not exactly the martyr he had always pretended to be. He was now irreproachable, canonised by the Cordelier Club, and as the revolution itself entered the bloody impasse of 1794 he made posthumous converts.[9]

His most faithful clientele had always come from the streets. Dutard, an observer employed by the Minister of the Interior, summed this up with his usual intelligence. The *petit peuple* could not condemn Marat for things like the September massacres, without condemning themselves. 'They don't respect him, they even think he is slightly mad, but whether because his predictions have sometimes come off, or because of his opposition to parties that the people themselves hate, or because their idea of his integrity (the people's god) had earned him supporters, he has won their protection.'[10] If Marat prided himself on one quality above all others, it was on his ability to smell out plots and to expose counter-revolutionaries, which may have impressed those whose political education was on the rudimentary side. He did have some undeniable – and well-publicised – successes. Since he denounced virtually everyone in office, the law of averages was bound to guarantee him that. He predicted the king's flight – but he began six months too soon

---

[8] *Moniteur*, 3 March 1793.

[9] For the case of Saint-Just, see below, pp. 257, 259-60, 262.

[10] A.Schmidt, *Tableau de la révolution française*, Leipzig, 1867, 3 vols, I/283-4.

and when it happened he got the details badly wrong, inventing an Austrian invasion in the east and an *émigré* landing in the west. This was presumably a question of his taking the will for the deed. His luckiest stroke was a prediction in the autumn of 1792 that Dumouriez, the military hero of the hour, would have fled the country within six months. When this happened, he naturally drew the Convention's attention to the fulfilment of his prophecy. He did not remind them that, only three weeks before, he had expressed the view that Dumouriez was 'bound to the *salut public* since 10 August' and had denounced as counter-revolutionaries some men from one of the Paris Sections who wanted to have the general arrested.

Marat's predictions of what did *not* happen were much more numerous. In a famous pamphlet, *C'en est fait de nous*, that gave rise to a warrant for his arrest, he said that Artois and 25,000 Piedmontese troops were about to invade France.[11] Some of his other shots were equally wide of the target: there were 40,000 brigands hidden in Paris, merely waiting the signal of the king's flight to murder the *patriotes*; the Constituent Assembly would keep postponing the election of its successor; Lafayette was planning another St. Bartholomew's massacre, etc. Some of the plots were so tortuous that only a Marat could have got to the bottom of them. England and Spain were preparing to fight each other in order to threaten the revolution in France. The French government should therefore ally with England, which would 'secure European peace for ever' and might well produce a revolution in Spain (19 May 1790). The law against the *émigrés* was a ministerial trick. When the Ministers then persuaded the king to veto their own law, the Assembly should have suspended him for his hostility to the revolution (11 and 15 November 1791). In February 1793 the Girondins organised both a shortage of food (to force up the prices) and petitions from the Sections to bring them down by way of price controls. He did not care much what he said, provided that the sans-culotte in the street got the general impression that Marat was on his side. He changed his mind about individuals to an extent that did not say much for his perspicacity, but since this was generally to attack former idols, it could pass for insight.

---

[11] *Pamphlets*, pp.201-9.

He himself made a big fuss of his exposure of Necker, 'that wise Minister whose good intentions I shall always respect', in January 1790.[12] The case would not be worth lingering over if reputable historians had not leaned over backwards to give Marat the benefit of what ought not to be doubts.[13] He made five charges against the Finance Minister: Necker had been responsible for the concentration of troops near Paris in July 1789; he had exported good grain and imported bad, in order to force up prices and create unrest; his 25 per cent income tax was a bad measure since it could easily be evaded by financiers; he was behind the session of 4 August 1789, a reactionary diversion intended to relieve pressure on the king to accept the declaration of the rights of man and the constitution; he had failed to prevent the march on Versailles of 5 October. On the last occasion, 'Necker compromised the honour of the Prince ... by forcing the king to divest himself of the natural goodness of his character and appear as a despot'.[14] (For a long time, Marat was curiously ambivalent about Louis XVI and inclined to blame wicked Ministers for abusing a weak but well-intentioned king.) The income tax may have been open to criticism: most attempts to increase taxation usually are. Necker's handling of food supplies may not always have been wise, although it was certainly well-meant. The remaining charges are too absurd to have imposed on anyone.

Marat's attack on Lafayette was no more convincing. On 25 September 1789 he was 'that generous citizen whose spirit is open only to those feelings that exalt humanity'. On 19 December, 'You fought to break the shackles of the Americans. How can anyone believe you would forge chains for your own countrymen?' By May 1790 Marat had his doubts and on 28 June he published a full-scale denunciation that was the prelude to a systematic character-assassination. Lafayette had only gone to America to escape his creditors (11 July 1790), as an agent of the Court and to further his military ambition (19 October 1790), because the countess de 'Nolstein' (he could not even spell her name correctly) had preferred the duc de Chartres (26 April 1791). When he got there he kept out of the fighting: 'A few

[12] *Supplément à l'offrande à la patrie. Pamphlets*, p.51 n[1].
[13] See, for example, G.Walter, *Marat*, Paris, 1933, p.129.
[14] *Dénonciation contre Necker. Pamphlets*, pp.76-120.

campaigns without danger made him an imaginary hero.'[15] (When Lafayette was wounded at the battle of Brandywine in 1777, Marat had just entered the service of the comte d'Artois.) During the revolution, Lafayette had helped Necker to starve Paris (4 October 1790), attempted to get the king away to Metz and start a civil war (6 October 1790) and promised Marie Antoinette (who loathed him) that he would restore absolutism (11 December 1790). It is true, of course, that Lafayette's attitude to the revolution changed. One could, if one fancied that kind of language, say that 'objectively' he had become a reactionary. To argue that this justified the kind of lies that Marat told about him is to accept Marat's own argument that what matters in politics is not the nature of the methods used, but who uses them.

Marat's reputation could scarcely have rested on such distasteful rubbish. When he wanted, he could be a shrewd, even a statesmanlike observer. Like Mirabeau, he understood how the destruction of the intermediate bodies so dear to Montesquieu had potentially increased the power of the central government (16 December 1790). Unlike almost everyone else, he foresaw the danger of a breach with the Church. 'This is perhaps the only occasion since the taking of the Bastille when you need moderation in dealing with the enemies of your peace. One should not violate consciences and no power on earth can tyrannise over souls' (9 January 1791). He consistently opposed the abolition of noble titles: 'Instead of waiting for reason to do its work, the Assembly has barbarously undermined a stately edifice, built by glory and respected by time' (25 September 1791). Burke could scarcely have put it better. He had quite an acute understanding of the king's character and behaviour (1 October 1791). He could have made his reputation as a different kind of journalist but, as he told Robespierre at what may have been their only meeting, his influence was not due to his 'close analysis', but to 'the frightful public scandal' that his paper created, 'to the effusions of my soul, the outbursts of my heart, my violent denunciation of oppression, my violent attacks on the oppressors, my accents of grief, my cries of indignation, fury and despair' (3 May 1792).

---

[15] *Pamphlets*, p.156.

Beneath the emotional self-indulgence, there is a clue here to
the real reason why Marat stood out from the anonymous mass of
journalists who made the revolution such a bonanza for the
printing trade. He alone offered a coherent alternative to the
orthodox interpretation of the revolution.[16] What had happened
in 1789 was not the reaffirmation of the rule of law but its
defiance by force (23 February 1791). 'To what do we owe our
liberty if not to popular insurrection?' (10 November 1789). This
had been a lucky accident: 'The people rose in revolt and the
other classes joined in only to prevent plundering' (12 April
1791). There was no conversion of the more conservative, no
compromise and no national regeneration. The Enemy (it was
never very clear whether this meant the king, his ministers, the
nobility and upper clergy or the wealthy in general) immediately
set about recovering the ground they had lost. They quickly
bought the majority in both the Constituent and Legislative
Assemblies. Indeed, since it led to the bribery of almost all men
of talent, the revolution had corrupted *moeurs* rather than
regenerated them. 'We are at war with the enemies of the
revolution ... Concern for the salvation of the *patrie* and our own
safety therefore makes it imperative that we treat them as
traitors and exterminate them as base conspirators' (21 May
1791). Whatever good had been done had been achieved by force.
'Follow its work and you will see that the Assembly has only been
pushed into action by popular revolt. It was revolt that
subjugated the aristocratic faction in the Estates General,
against which the arms of the philosophers and the king's
authority had fought in vain' (11 November 1789). It was
therefore absurd to protest against 'those popular executions to
which you owe the revolution and the only good laws that ever
came out of the National Assembly' (26 September 1790).
Official law was the weapon of the enemy. The people's reply,
which was equally legitimate, was mob violence. 'The
government is the mortal, the eternal enemy of the peoples' (31
December 1789). Marat was never quite sure whether this was an
unchangeable law of nature or whether the French revolution
might not offer an escape from the endless cycle of revolt, new
tyranny and further revolt. Since princes were always the

[16] See above, p. 152.

enemies of their subjects, 'any Minister who has been in office for some time is necessarily suspect' (21 December 1789). 'To imagine that a Minister could be a *patriote* is folly; to pretend that he actually is one is madness' (28 June 1790). On the other hand, if the right action were taken, everything would be possible. The purge of the Assembly 'would release the springs of plenty and bring back peace and happiness at a stroke' (25 September 1789). 'A few guilty heads paraded in the streets from time to time would have kept the senate in a state of holy terror ... already the reign of justice would have been established; alarms would have given way to peace, competition would have released the springs of abundance and you would already have been free and happy' (20 October 1790).

Marat then found himself faced by the contradiction that has afflicted a good many subsequent revolutionaries: how was a degraded people, corrupted by centuries of servitude, to sustain the effort needed for its liberation? It was not until 1790 that he found the answer, during his stay in England. 'The only way to restore order is to nominate for a time a supreme dictator, to arm him with public force and to hand over to him the punishment of the guilty ... A few heads struck off will check the public enemies for a long time and will preserve a great nation from the horrors of poverty and civil war for centuries.'[17] There was not much doubt about who the man should be. Once he had got hold of this idea, Marat repeated it over and over again, until it got him into trouble in the early days of the Convention. The job specification varied: sometimes three days would have been enough; in his own case, life-tenure would be necessary to preserve the benefits he could bring.[18] Sometimes the leader's function was to draft a constitution or to win the war; more often it was to organise the slaughter of counter-revolutionaries – the fatal omission that had ruined the work of July 1789. The range of the guilty grew all the time; by 22 October 1790 it included the Ministers and their followers in the Assembly, Bailly, the mayor of Paris, Lafayette, the commander of the National Guard and almost all of his staff officers, most of the members of the Commune and the agents of the royal administration throughout the country. On 28 August

---

[17] *Pamphlets*, p.155.   [18] See above, p.197.

1790 it had included all the nobility and upper clergy. This was a lot of people. On 17 September 1790 Marat came up with an idea to which he became very attached: in July 1789 it would have been sufficient to murder only 500 people. False humanity then meant that 10,000 would have to die now. For a year or so this figure remained constant but inflation set in and by the autumn of 1791 it had risen to 2-300,000.

No one else followed Marat in his bloodier fantasies. If the treatment he recommended was a prescription for anarchy and civil war, his diagnosis of why the revolution had failed to fulfil the expectations of 1789 was another matter. Beneath Marat's lies, slander and hysteria there was enough truth in his version of events to make it sound as plausible as the official interpretation. The constitutional compromise that almost everyone professed was one in which few believed. When most people hoped for the best without really expecting it, Marat successfully predicted the worst. To the extent that he contributed to the atmosphere of hatred and fear – and his appeals to the mob to lynch political leaders were unlikely to increase their attachment to the revolution – he may have given events a push along the road, but it was a road they would almost certainly have taken in any case. His own resolute pessimism may have been due to paranoia but pessimism is an even safer bet during a revolution than in normal times. By the spring of 1794 everyone was trapped in a suffocating atmosphere of terror and hysteria – which was *not* due to the pressure of external events, since the war was going well – and Marat's view of things began to seem more credible. Saint-Just, who had not previously paid him much attention, began bringing his name into one speech after another and took over the *Maratiste* argument that all France's ills were the product of conspiracies that could have been prevented by more violent repression in the past. He even suggested to his colleagues on the Committee of Public Safety that they should appoint a dictator. This raises the disquieting question of whether *Maratisme* should be considered, not as the aberration of an individual, but as the natural destination of anyone who tried to adapt Rousseauist principles to the circumstances of revolution.

So far as Marat himself was concerned, his political theories were of the most rudimentary kind. All his life he retained an extraordinary veneration for Montesquieu. On 4 July 1791 he wrote that, if he had still been alive, he was the only man who would have made a suitable tutor for the Dauphin. And yet it would be difficult to think of a single idea of Montesquieu's that Marat accepted. Temperamentally, he was much closer to Rousseau, 'the most mortal enemy of absolute power' (28 December 1790), 'the sage whose virtues I respect even more than his talents' (4 July 1791). He shared Rousseau's contempt for the decadence of urban society, especially that of Paris, 'the sewer of all the vices' (5 February 1791), 'the only rotten part of France' (12 October 1791), 'the most corrupt [city] in the whole of Europe, the most venal and the most worthless' (27 July 1791). Like Rousseau, he loved to abuse his readers for their effeminacy, sharing his dislike of society women. The French were unworthy of democracy which was only possible in a free society like that of Sparta, some of the Swiss cantons, the United States and – a picturesque touch – San Marino. Marat obviously considered himself to be on a par with his two heroes. When Desmoulins reminded him of Voltaire's review of *De l'homme*, Marat replied that Voltaire had criticised Montesquieu and Rousseau too. He thought that the three of them would have been slumming it if they had been sentenced to the Pantheon.

When it came to offering theoretical guidance to his readers, Marat's thoughts were few and predictable. Democracy was inconceivable in France, 'a nation of vile egoists, without *moeurs*, energy or soul, men corrupted by soft living and vice, old slaves, consumed by their passion for gold and always ready to sell themselves to any master who could pay them ... Even if the poorest part of the population is healthy, without any resources how can it bring the rest of the nation to subscribe to this healthy form of government?' (7 July 1791). Not merely did those he was inclined to describe as the 'plebs' or the 'populace' have no political power; they were also 'bad at judging things, they rarely see things as they are ... because of their lack of understanding' (8 November 1790). For their enlightenment they needed journalists – but not too many, for Marat had the true revolutionary's suspicion of the media. Royalist journalists should be lynched and only a few *patriote* papers allowed. Eventually he thought that one would be enough (25 April 1792).

One political party would be sufficient too. If the Assembly were composed of honest men, 'it would be neither expedient nor necessary to allow the minority to protest against laws, or even to record their objections or negative votes, since men of good sense and pure intentions can never take decisions contrary to the national interest' (20 May 1793).

There could, of course, be no question of parliamentary sovereignty in the abstract. It was all a question of who was right. The intimidation of deputies by the public was 'a crime when all those who speak are enlightened and well-intentioned. But it is a good deed when they are factious conspirators' (25 January 1791). The poor did not know how to vote (and they were disfranchised in the 1791 election) and the rich voted only to protect their privileges. It was no wonder if the Convention was worse than the Legislative Assembly and that had been worse than the Constituent (26 November 1792). The laws of war applied as much to the deputies as to anyone else. They must be lynched as soon as they failed to do their duty (15 September 1792).

There is a kind of logic to all this. If the revolution was an actual war, it made sense to argue that 'liberty exists only for the friends of the *patrie*, chains and torments for its enemies' (6 March 1791). If the Assembly was controlled by the Enemy it was natural to argue that its laws were not morally binding on the other side. Marat dressed this up in rather fancy language: 'The law must be the expression of the general will, but of an enlightened will, based on the rules of eternal reason; a law that is obviously unjust is no law, even if it is endorsed by the whole nation' (10 January 1793). The obvious question is who was to decide that it was unjust if the whole nation agreed with it, and the answer is presumably either God or Marat. Since we are all against sin — at any rate as a general proposition – it is pleasant to denounce injustice and to demand righteousness of our governors, and how could one criticise a man who was doing precisely that, unless one had something to conceal. This line of argument may have commended itself to some of Marat's 'plebs'. What he was actually doing was to locate the general will within his own person. Some members of the revolutionary government were to do much the same in 1794.

One might have expected the People's Friend to have paid a fair amount of attention to improving their living conditions. Behind his posturing, verbal barrages against the vicious and corrupt rich and rather patronising sympathy for the virtuous and benighted poor, there was some awareness of actual problems and some genuine sympathy for real people. He knew and he was less inhibited than most of the revolutionaries in admitting, that for the urban poor, life had become more difficult since 1789. He saw that alcoholism was in part the response to grinding and unpleasant work for low wages (14 June 1790). He repeated his old arguments: the one originally derived from Montesquieu, that the poor were entitled to a decent livelihood (27 October 1790) and the assertion that 'those without property, who can claim no employment, who derive no benefit from the social pact' had no *patrie* (24 November 1789). It was when he came to explain why this should be and what could be done about it, that the trouble began. In one mood he reverted to his old pessimism: almost all wealth was the product of violence, favour or fraud (18 November, for 19 November 1789; *Ami du Peuple* No.52). The rich were incorrigible, but intelligent self-interest, reinforced by judicious intimidation, might induce them to palliate by their philanthropy what the state was powerless to cure (18 November 1789, 28 February 1793). If not, the poor might demand the 'agrarian law' : in other words, the redistribution of land (27 October 1790). In a fit of temper, he said this would advance the cause of enlightenment. Generally, however, he was a violent opponent of anything more than the traditional restraints on the grain trade. Price controls were 'the height of folly and wickedness' (12 February 1793). 'No doubt the blind multitude was bound to enthuse over the doctrine of perfect equality' (25 September 1791). He told his readers that he himself had reassured the Swiss banker, Perregaux, that he was a firm opponent of 'strict equality' (3 March 1793). He was not very keen on other people supping with bankers, and six months later Perregaux seems to have been acting as a secret British agent.[19] It is tempting to think of how Marat could have used such 'evidence' against someone else.

---

[19] Archives Nationales, AF II 49 which indicates that Perregaux was transmitting funds to British agents in the Jacobin Club.

Striking a more optimistic note, he sometimes argued that all economic problems could be quickly solved by political means, which in his case meant popular violence. Since the food shortage was due to hoarding – either because of greed or to provoke disorder that would offer a pretext for repression – it could be dealt with very quickly. We have already seen that purging the Assembly would produce plenty at a stroke. Hoarders should be strung up outside their warehouses for a second offence (8 October 1789). By 25 February 1793 his economic thinking had progressed to the point where he saw no need to give them a second chance.

He had no clear or consistent economic principles. Despite a passing reference to the virtues of competition, he opposed the abolition of the old guilds on the ground that consumers would suffer if there was no control over bad workmanship. 'When every workman can work for himself, he stops wanting to work for anyone else. If desire for betterment is divorced from desire for a reputation for good work, one can say goodbye to good faith. Look at the endless development of the passion for gain that torments all classes in big cities.' His solution was in the best Rousseauist tradition and would have delighted Mme de Wolmar: craftsmen should be made to serve an apprenticeship of six or seven years under masters responsible for their good conduct. Those distinguished by their skill and *sagesse* should eventually be helped to set up in business for themselves – but they would have to repay the money advanced if they had not married within three years. 'The only way to make society prosper is to reward talent and good conduct. It is nature's will that the ignorant should be guided by those with knowledge and men without *moeurs* by respectable people' (16 March 1791). Those who have welcomed Marat as a preacher of class war have not read him very carefully.

He printed a letter commending enclosures in England as a practical demonstration of the fact that property was a social institution whose distribution could not be left to the caprice of individuals (5 September 1791). After insisting on the need for large farms, the writer suggested that any land not farmed by the owner himself should be leased in small units only. Marat favoured communal grazing in 1791 and the division of the common lands two years later. Even he did not claim to be an expert on agriculture.

Despite his Rousseauism and his respect for Sparta, he had a curious hostility to compulsory military service, especially for the middle classes. The poor too were fools if they volunteered for the army – and that was after France had become a republic, in 30 October 1792. This applied equally to service in the National Guard. The poor should not be made to give up working time to protect 'the houses of the rich who oppress them' and 'merchants, men of letters, savants and *artistes*' should be exempt (24 November 1789). He went rather further than this on 13 April 1791, arguing that military service might 'upset the organs and destroy the delicacy of touch of *artistes*'. The Assembly had no right to conscript peace-loving philosophers, *dévots* and priests. Things had been better under the *ancien régime* when military service was only for peasants and anyone who could afford it could buy a substitute.

What emerges from all this is that Marat was perhaps rather more aware than men like Robespierre and Saint-Just of the poor as people with problems and not just as an abstract category of the population. Unlike Saint-Just, he never seems to have thought at all seriously about economic policy and he fitted everything into a simplistic view of the world where all problems could be solved by the revolt of the poor under the leadership of men like himself and the intimidation – but not the expropriation – of the rich. The *petit peuple* might be 'the only healthy part of the nation' but this was only because 'they have neither the time nor money to deprave themselves and so have to remain close to nature' (7 October 1790). This must have prompted the thought that it might be kinder to leave them that way and from time to time Marat did ask himself why he went on working so hard to save men who were not worth the trouble.

It was only during the last year of his life that he became something more than a journalist, and this period is worth a brief examination. July 1792 found him in one of his blackest moods. In several consecutive issues of his paper, from 7 to 12 July, he summed up the situation. The revolution had turned against the people and become a colossal disaster. This was because successful revolutions, like those of Switzerland, Holland, England and America, required the co-operation of all classes. On their own, the mass of the people were incapable of making any progress. 'Political discourse is, always has been and always will be beyond its grasp.' In other words, the people could never understand the need to exterminate traitors when they had the chance. Political liberty was meaningless to men enslaved to labour and since 'love of domination is innate in men's hearts', nothing was to be expected from their social superiors. 'Love of liberty acts only in spasms: for the plebs that feeling does not exist at all. Let us not deceive ourselves; what led our plebs to make certain expeditions [Maratese for lynching parties] was the pleasure of acting a part; for them the revolution was no more than an opera.' There was a flicker of hope: something might yet be achieved by popular executions and a leader – 'You know a man who aspired only to the glory of immolating himself for the salvation of the state'. This was soon extinguished. 'Liberty will never be established in France. Of all the peoples on earth the French are perhaps the ones that love it least.' On 22 July he told his readers that he was giving up and a fortnight later he asked Pétion to get him a passport. This was not a particularly clairvoyant approach to the *journée* of 10 August.

When he was quite sure that the revolutionaries had won, Marat emerged from hiding to claim some of the credit. 'the country has been pulled back from the abyss by shedding the blood of the enemies of the revolution, which I have never stopped saying was the only effective way. If the sword of justice at last strikes the plotters and prevaricators you will not hear me speak any more about popular executions' (16 August). It was all a matter of how many needed to be struck, and his most recent estimate was 2-300,000. He did not give the sword of justice much time. On 19 August he said that since the Assembly had resumed its 'infernal machinations' the people should massacre traitors, even if they had been acquitted by the courts, or better still, storm the Abbaye prison since it was 'madness to want to give them a trial'. 'On your feet, and let the blood of traitors begin to flow!' Between 21 August and 13 September his paper did not appear. He was presumably fully occupied, for part of the time at least, as an illegal member of the Commune's *comité de surveillance*, helping with the prison massacres. For Marat this was July 1789 all over again and if the second victory of the people was not to be thrown away like the first, it was essential to exterminate as many enemies of the revolution as possible, while the opportunity lasted. No doubt he did his best, but the total casualties in the prisons did not reach much more than a thousand – most of them minor common law criminals – and the provinces failed to follow the Parisian example. Once again the people let him down and the chance was lost. 'All my efforts to save the people will lead nowhere without a new insurrection ... You are crushed for ever, fifty years of anarchy await you and you will only emerge with the help of a dictator, a true patriot and statesman. O people of babblers, if only you knew how to act!'[20] His subsequent attitude to the massacres was curiously equivocal. Generally they were one of the *journées* that had saved France (29 September), an example of popular justice (12 December), a general insurrection (22 January 1793) or the popular execution of a handful of traitors (25 February), but they were sometimes 'disastrous although necessary events' (6 October). On one occasion they had been provoked by the counter-revolutionaries themselves, in order to get rid of their accomplices (17 November). There are times when one wonders whether Marat knew or cared what he was writing.

When the Convention met, the Girondins rather foolishly tried to get rid of Robespierre, Danton and Marat at one blow by accusing them of aspiring to form a triumvirate. Marat *had* advocated this, probably with the other two in mind as his only eligible partners, on 26 August, but it was not an idea that was likely to appeal to either of them.[21] Understandably, they dissociated themselves from Marat and left him to look after himself, which may explain why he became rather less enthusiastic about Robespierre. He defended himself with some courage and a touch of melodrama, refusing to disown his opinions and, pulling out a pistol, threatening to blow his brains out if anyone proposed to impeach him. For the next few months he was entirely on his own. He was continually clamouring to be heard on matters of the highest public importance. Somehow or other he generally got a hearing, though the plots that he revealed never amounted to anything.

Early in the new year he found himself in the unfamiliar position of helping to defend the revolutionary establishment against a threat from below. As in the case of Brissot, this led him to revise his views about parliamentary sovereignty. On 7

[20] *Pamphlets*, pp.341-5, 20 September 1792.
[21] Ibid. pp.302-3.

January he and Desmoulins got Chaumette, the Paris *procureur*, summoned to the bar of the House for having presumed to call before the Commune a deputy who was not merely a marquis and a Girondin, but whose offence was an article in the paper edited by Marat's old enemy, Condorcet.[22] On 18 January Marat argued in his paper that the people were incapable of understanding *raison d'état*, which meant that the king's fate must be decided in their name by the Convention. Worse was to follow. In February petitioners from the Sections began demanding that the Assembly control the price of food. Instead of applauding this popular initiative and revolutionary surveillance of an assembly that he himself had written off as useless three months before, Marat thought that proposals 'so excessive, so strange, so subversive of all order' could only be counter-revolutionary. When the frightened petitioners tried to sneak away, the Convention was treated to the unusual spectacle of the furiously anti-Montagnard Louvet seconding Marat's motion to have them arrested.[23] As late as 15 March he tried to reassure his colleagues about Dumouriez's intentions and denounced talk in the Sections about purging the Assembly as an atrocious crime.

With their usual tactical ineptitude, the Girondins chose this time to send Marat before the newly-created revolutionary tribunal on the flimsiest of charges: his signature, as president of the club, to a Jacobin circular that was somewhat implausibly said to hve called for an insurrection. Marat made the most of his opportunity. He went into hiding, rather than allow himself to be locked up, appeared for his trial, was triumphantly acquitted and carried back to the Convention shoulder high. It was the only time in his life when he really was a popular hero – even if the crowd amounted to rather less than the 100,000 that he pretended – and it perhaps helps to explain his growing obsession with his own importance. 'Once rid of Marat, what would Dumouriez's accomplices have to fear?' (18 April).

Relations between the Montagnards and their opponents had now reached breaking-point, and Marat reverted to his old ideas about the need for the people to purge their representatives.

[22] *Moniteur.*
[23] Ibid. 12 February 1793.

When the insurrection of 31 May looked like petering out, he went to the Commune and urged it to bully the Assembly into getting rid of the Girondins. When the president asked if it would not be advisable to remain within the law, Marat, according to his own version, replied that this was not necessary when the people were oppressed (5 June). He greeted the ensuing purge with the reflection that the measures he had been proposing for the past four years had at last been adopted (6 June). The question, of course, was whether they would prove as disappointing as the September massacres. By 7 June he was already worrying about the Convention's refusal to ban the Sections from meeting every night, and about rumours that voting was to be made compulsory; this was logical enough if the Convention was now on the right lines and the plebs were as easily misled as he always maintained. He thought the coup d'état had not done much good and invited the Montagnards to assemble on the following day at the Champ de Mars, apparently to purge the administration – since no one turned up it is not quite clear what they were supposed to do. He did, however, approve of the new constitution. By now he was seriously ill and confined for much of his time to his bed or his bath. Most of his attention was given up to personal denunciations, notably of Roux, Varlet and Leclerc, who were reviving the threat from the streets. Despite moments of optimism – the *patriotes* were working away zealously – the prospects did not seem to have improved very much. 'We are in a state of total anarchy, in a frightful chaos' (22 June). 'We have been talking about liberty for four years and we have still not got the first idea about it. Pitiless prattlers, when will you learn that it is neither for the false, the furious nor the wicked, but for men of goodwill who don't want to abuse it' (23 June). 'To establish the rule of justice, why should we not use the methods the despots use to destroy it?' It was the same old story: what was wrong was not a matter of what was done but of who did it, and violence was the only way.

As always, one is left wondering how far Marat believed himself. He certainly manufactured evidence. When Desmoulins reproached him for this he replied 'How do you know that what you took to be false news was not a text that I needed to parry some fatal thrust and achieve my purpose? ... To judge men you always need positive, clear and precise evidence ... the general current of affairs is enough for me' (5 May 1791). When the Committee of General Security circulated a clumsy forgery against Brissot, Marat's was the only paper to print it (15 February 1793). That could merely mean that he was unscrupulous. He apparently told the Montagnard deputy, Bazire, that 'My hand would wither rather than write if I had been sure that the people would have done what I told them to do.'[24] Robespierre seems to have suspected something of the kind. According to Marat's account of their interview, when he said that his influence depended on his vehemence, Robespierre accused him of talking for effect. Marat replied that he had meant it when he advocated burning down the Tuileries and impaling the deputies. 'Robespierre listened to me in terror, went pale and remained silent for some time' (3 May 1792). Of course, if it was all a confidence trick, he would have been unlikely to confide in Robespierre or to let his readers into the secret. On the whole though, his behaviour in September 1792 suggests that it was Bazire who was taken in. Marat certainly lied, as when he told his readers about 'the establishment that the king of Spain proposed to me in 1785' (25 June 1790). He may or may not have believed the curriculum vitae that he invented for himself. He was careless about facts and self-contradictions and took liberties with the truth but it defies plausibility to believe that he was merely writing for effect. It does not matter very much, except with regard to his own reputation. To a considerable extent, the conclusions that Marat welcomed were ones to which more thoughtful and more honourable revolutionaries were inexorably driven. He was the Mephistopheles to their Faust.

[24] Dr. Cabanès, *Marat inconnu*. Paris, n.d., p.302n[1].

Chapter 11

Robespierre II

In the Constituent Assembly, from 1789 to 1791, Robiespierre was one of a tiny group of deputies who sat on the extreme left. Even when he had won a reputation as a democrat and become the idol of the radical press, his influence in the Assembly itself was very limited and almost all of his proposals were rejected. He did not become the leader of the Jacobins until the club split and most of its members deserted it, in the stormy period in the summer of 1791 that followed the king's flight. In this situation, he was enough of a realist to stick to practical issues and to try to shame the deputies into conforming to their own Declaration of the Rights of Man, which they had voted in the radical days of August 1789. He seems to have believed, like most of his contemporaries, that the revolution was behind him. France had become and would remain a constitutional monarchy and the most that a democrat could do was to make the new constitution as liberal as possible, to make the best of what was likely to prove only a moderately satisfactory job.

Robespierre's occasional references to Marat suggest that he was far from reciprocating the hero-worship of the *Ami du Peuple*. This may have been partly a matter of jealousy, since Robespierre aspired to the same title and both he and Marat insisted from the start that they were martyrs of the revolution. When Marat actually was murdered Robespierre, in an extraordinary speech, said that it was merely a matter of chance that Marat's death should have preceded his own, and tried to keep him out of the Pantheon.[1] Each was given to retailing the

---

[1] 14 July 1793. Unless otherwise indicated, all references in this chapter are to *Oeuvres des Maximilien Robespierre* (ed. M.Bouloiseau, J.Dautry, G.Lefebrvre and A.Soboul), Paris, 1950-67, vols VI-X.

story of his life and saw himself as the only man who understood
what the revolution was really about. There must have been
more to it than that, for Robespierre could be generous towards
possible rivals such as Pétion and Danton. He told Marat that
his extravagance discredited the policies of the *patriotes* and he
was probably irritated to find his own high principled reflections
reduced to screaming abuse and bloodthirsty slogans at Marat's
hands. He even insinuated at one point that Marat's excesses
might have been calculated to provoke moderates into
supporting the Girondins.[2] There was probably even more to it
than *that*. Marat was constantly reminding Robespierre of what
he would have preferred to forget or deny. They shared a good
many assumptions about the revolution that led Marat to
conclusions that Robespierre did not want to accept. Both agreed
that the initial victory had been won by force and not by consent.
Each was convinced that the king, the government and the
majority of the upper clergy and nobility were not reconciled to
the new order but hoped to overthrow it. Credulous and
suspicious, they believed the country to be infested with counter-
revolutionary plotting; since this had to be exposed, journalists
must be free to attack public men without any legal obligation to
substantiate their charges (11 May 1791). Robespierre, if he did
not borrow ideas from Marat, shared them. They wanted the
Assembly to meet in the presence of thousands of spectators;
they thought the survival of the revolution was due to the
beneficent intervention of Providence; they opposed the war on
much the same grounds and consoled themselves for their
apparent harshness with the thought that, as Marat put it,
'indulgence towards villains becomes barbarity towards the
people'. All this fitted easily enough into Marat's pessimistic
view of politics as an eternal struggle between rulers and their
victims. For Robespierre, however, the French revolution offered
a possible escape from the treadmill of history.

Throughout the whole course of the revolution his thinking
was dominated by the influence of Rousseau. Montesquieu may
have been always at the back of his mind but he rarely earned
more than a casual mention. Rousseau was invoked all the time,
occasionally by name but more often by some such epithet as

---

[2] *Lettres à ses commettans* (ed. G.Laurent), Paris, 1911, p.203.

'the virtuous philosopher of Geneva', 'the sublime and true friend of humanity', as though his very name were too sacred to be pronounced lightly. Robespierre quoted him, paraphrased him and saw politics in Rousseauist terms. This did not mean that he slavishly accepted anything that Rousseau had written, or pretended to be interpreting him when he twisted his meaning to serve his own purposes. Like all the revolutionaries, he disregarded Rousseau's assertion that the general will could not be represented, and was even prepared to argue for much of the time that the Assembly was the embodiment of popular sovereignty. Unlike Rousseau, he rejected the death penalty. Towards the end of his life he defeated a proposal to banish atheists with the sensible comment that 'that truth is better left in the writings of Rousseau' (15 May 1794).

Despite such reservations, Robespierre's attitude to the drafting of a constitution and the governing of France was based on the fundamentally Rousseauist principle that the law was, or ought to be, the expression of the general will. This was located in the Assembly, to the extent that the majority of the deputies had not been corrupted by the Court and the Ministers. From the start he took it for granted that there could be no honest disagreement about what *was* the general will. Politics was not a matter of arbitrating between competing interests; it was always a question of choosing between the general interest and sectional privilege. Those who opted for the latter knew perfectly well what they were doing: they chose evil because they lacked *vertu*. Rousseau would have agreed that, in any situation, the general will must exist, but he would have been less confident about its infallible identification, except by his semi-divine 'legislator'. It was perhaps not his fault if those who tried to put his theories into practice found that *la force des choses* was propelling them into this rôle.

What most people wanted was right, not because they were the majority, but because the nation consisted for the most part of humble people who wanted only the necessities of life, justice and tranquillity. 'The rich lay claim to everything, they want to encroach on everything, to dominate everything. The people's interest is the general interest; the interest of the rich is a particular interest' (March 1791, undated speech on the franchise). At first he was prepared to concede that the French, unlike the British, with their greater political experience, suffered from fickleness and weak *moeurs* (September 1789, undated speech on the veto). This was where the fact that Rousseau had distinguished between the general will and the will of all allowed revolutionary politicians to claim to know better than the people themselves what they really wanted. When the population of Avignon and the Comtat Venaissin was debating whether or not to reject Papal sovereignty and become part of France, Robespierre argued that those in the Comtat who had not voted for union must have been intimidated since 'The people of Avignon and the Comtat must have wanted liberty' (25 April 1791, 2 May 1791). This may not have occurred to the Pope.

Robespierre was therefore able to count heads when it suited his purpose and to disregard the result when it did not. Although he was one of a tiny minority in the Assembly he was, in fact, representative of the 'people' whose will was general in the sense that it was opposed only by the self-interest of the majority of the deputies. The fact that he was popular with sans-culotte militants and acclaimed in the radical press gave this point of view added plausibility. Like Rousseau, he opposed the survival of any corporate bodies that could interpose their sectional interests between the citizen and the state (7 April 1790, 9 June 1790). What Montesquieu would have seen as legitimate foci of obligation and useful counterpoises to the central government were for him merely obstacles to the expression of that single national will that was always the goal. Robespierre regarded the Church, and religion itself, as essentially social. 'All public institutions are social creations' (31 May 1790). Its rôle was therefore not, as Montesquieu had argued, to create an autonomous circle of rights and obligations, but to conform to the requirements and to reinforce the cohesion of the national community. His fellow-deputies stopped him from going on to recommend clerical marriage, but Brissot came to his support in the *Patriote Français*.

Robespierre's version of the origin of the social contract was a paraphrase of *Du contrat social*. Like Rousseau, he interpreted the collective well-being of a society in moral rather than economic terms. In this context he paid tribute to 'that sensitive and eloquent philosopher whose writings developed amongst us those principles of public morality which made us worthy to conceive the plan of regenerating our *patrie* (March 1791, speech on the franchise). This was of course the meaning of the revolution and for Robespierre, as for Rousseau, a society was judged by the extent to which its politics were determined by the general will and not by its constitutional arrangements. 'The progress of a revolution is not subject to the rules appropriate to the peaceful state of an established constitution' (23 August 1790). 'What would be a crime at other times becomes a praiseworthy action' (27 July 1789) – that was about respecting the secrecy of the mails. If Robespierre was referring merely to the need to win, when social conflict had become physical, what he was saying was unexceptionable enough, despite its somewhat sinister implications. On the whole, during the period of the Constituent Assembly, he was doing no more than that.

On several occasions he surprised his opponents and disconcerted his allies (who once shouted to him to go and sit on the right) by accepting the need for rules that applied impartially to both sides. His commitment to freedom of speech and of the press was absolute. He applied it in defence of Mirabeau's ultra-royalist brother (17 November 1789), to the Estates of Cambrésis (19 November 1789) and to clergymen who opposed the Church settlement (19 March 1791). He even – rather rashly as it turned out – invited his fellow-citizens to denounce him as a traitor if he ever complained of any libel against himself (2 May 1791). He opposed any kind of censorship in the theatre (13 January 1791). He defended the parliamentary immunity of deputies, in the case of the comte de Toulouse-Lautrec (25 June 1790) and insisted on the right of anyone who wanted, to leave the country (18 February 1791). In the debates on the reform of the law he maintained that detention on mere suspicion was permissible only until the suspect could be brought to trial. It was better to allow 100 guilty men to escape than to convict one who was innocent (13 March 1790). When it came to a trial, juries should not return a verdict of guilty unless the evidence was confirmed by their own inner conviction (4 January 1791). In general, the revolutionaries should be indulgent towards those who found it difficult to rid themselves of old prejudices (2 May 1791).

It would be easy, but almost certainly unjust, to write off all this as a tactical appeal to the law by someone who was not yet strong enough to disregard it. Robespierre's attitude corresponded to his lasting conviction of the way in which a constitutional government ought to operate. What changed was his opinion of whether or not France had emerged from a revolutionary period in which victory had to be won at virtually any price. In 1790 and 1791, he thought she had. By 1792 he was having serious doubts.

The turning-point was the argument about war and peace in the winter of 1791-2. Like Brissot, Robespierre had originally taken the view that it was only the counter-revolutionaries who were hoping for war (5 May 1790, 30 June 1790, 4 July 1790). When he returned to Paris in November 1791, after a stay in Arras, when the Constituent Assembly had finally dissolved itself, he briefly fell in with Brissot's new policy of provoking a war. Possibly influenced by Marat and Billaud-Varenne, he dropped this almost at once and became Brissot's principal opponent in the Jacobin Club. There was a certain amount of equivocation on both sides. When Brissot scandalised Robespierre by calling for an end to *défiance* with regard to the Ministers, he could hardly explain that one of the objects of the war policy was to instal his friends in office. Robespierre, for his part, had to come out in defence of a constitution in which he no longer believed. When he started a newspaper in the spring, he called it the *Défenseur de la constitution*. At first courteously, he cut to pieces Brissot's windy bombast: if the foreign powers were to be feared, war was a dangerous gamble; if – as Brissot cheerfully assured everyone – they were helpless, it was unnecessary. No one liked 'armed missionaries' and foreigners would not welcome liberation. In the society of the *ancien régime*, revolution was only possible when the power of the monarchy was challenged by the nobility. Seeing where this had led in France, the nobility in the rest of Europe was most unlikely to repeat the experiment (2 January 1791). This was Robespierre at his best: calm, lucid and statesmanlike. He was right, but he could offer only *défiance* where Brissot aspired to create a revolutionary government. Brissot's mistake was to confuse office with power and to start a war that he did not know how to win. When the calamities that Robespierre foresaw raised him at his rival's expense, it was Brissot's turn to warn against wars of liberation, when Robespierre wanted to overthrow all the crowned heads of Europe.

Robespierre maintained that France could be regenerated without war. On 10 February 1792 he explained the kind of ideological mobilisation that he had in mind. The first need was for 'education', not *un système régulier de pédagogie*, which it would require the genius of a Rousseau to devise and which would, in any case, be perverted by the government for its own purposes, but propaganda, in the form of patriotic fêtes, in imitation of those of the Greeks, and suitable plays. The theatres, which the Constituent Assembly had treated with an *immorale légéreté*, should be made to put on plays about Brutus, William Tell and Gracchus. Victory in war was essentially a matter of *vertu*: 'Only be yourselves', he told the Jacobins, 'be what the nation wants, and our enemies are no more.' Naturally, if the Assembly were to betray the nation, he 'would call on the pure and courageous minority to crush the imbecile and corrupt majority'.

When the Jacobins were torn apart by the question of war, Robespierre saw the division not as a question of party tactics but as a conflict between absolute good and total evil. His struggle with Brissot was one between 'probity and perfidy, virtue and vice' (23 April). Providence was on the side of the just. In an angry exchange with the Girondin, Guadet, he said that 'to invoke the name of providence and broadcast an idea of the eternal being who exercises a decisive influence on the fate of nations and seems to me to watch most particularly over the French revolution ... is not too speculative an idea, but a feeling of my heart, a feeling that is necessary for me'. Increasingly convinced of his own providential rôle, he tried the patience of the Jacobins with long accounts of his lifelong devotion to the cause. 'I realised [in 1789] that great moral and political truth announced by Jean-Jacques, that men only really love those who love them, that only the people are good, just and magnanimous and that corruption and tyranny are the exclusive appanage of those who despise them.' Angered by the attacks in Condorcet's *Chronique*, he accused the philosophes of having paid court to the great men of their time and persecuted Rousseau. As for Robespierre himself, 'Heaven ... is perhaps calling me to trace with my blood the route that must lead my country to happiness and liberty' (27 April). This was dangerous stuff. The source of much of it must lie in Robespierre's own temperament, but Rousseau provided both the example of a kindred spirit and a political philosophy that lent itself only too easily to Robespierre's inclinations.

Increasingly, he substituted a conception of legitimacy based on ends for one based on rules. Mutinies in the army were no problem since 'The people are just and, as a general rule, their anger, like that of heaven, strikes only the guilty'.[3] In the revolutionary sense, the troops had never violated military discipline since 1789.[4] 'All our quarrels are merely a struggle between private interests and the general interest, between cupidity and ambition and justice and humanity.' In such a case, it would be pedantic to allow the righteous to perish because of the constitution. Citizenship itself was conditional on acceptance of the general will. 'The duty of every man and citizen is therefore to contribute, to the best of his power, to this sublime enterprise, by sacrificing his particular interest to the general interest ... He must, so to speak, bring back to the common mass that portion of the public power and of the sovereignty of the people that he exercises, or else he must be excluded, for that very reason, from the social pact.' The problem posed by the question of regeneration was more apparent than real: 'When a people passes suddenly from servitude to liberty, it finds itself in a very crucial situation since its *moeurs* and habits are in contradiction to the principles of its new government.' Fortunately, 'The mass of the nation is good and worthy of liberty; its true wishes are always the oracle of justice and the expression of the general interest ... The people are not affected by the causes of moral degeneracy that are the undoing of what are known as the upper classes.'[5] This could take one a long way, especially since someone would have to decide what *were* the 'true' wishes of these moral paragons.

The situation in the summer of 1792 was in any case slipping beyond the means of constitutional resolution. With invasion threatening and an Assembly that suspected the king of hoping

[3] *Défenseur de la constitution* (ed. G.Laurent), Paris, 1939, 17-18 May.
[4] Ibid. 24-25 May.
[5] Ibid. 7 June.

for an allied occupation of Paris, but would take no action against him, the choice probably lay between defeat and insurrection. Robespierre was only putting this in theoretical terms when he said that the Assembly itself was subject to the general will and could no longer exist if it acted in defiance of that will (8 June). 'The main cause of our woes lies in both the executive and the legislature ... the state must be saved, by whatever means, and the only thing that is unconstitutional is what tends towards its ruin' (29 July). His own solution to this dilemma was to elect a sovereign Convention that would be a direct expression of the general will and would have the right to change the constitution. For reasons of politics rather than of logic, he would have prohibited the 'sovereign' people from re-electing men who had sat in either of the previous Assemblies. Since there was no prospect of the Legislative Assembly agreeing to its own demise, Robespierre's solution left the practical problem where it was before. It was solved by the insurrection of 10 August and the forcible overthrow of the monarchy.

For Robespierre, this was the real revolution, the beginning of a new age in the history of humanity. Although he had told his readers in May that monarchy and republic were only words, the essential thing being that the government should be responsive to the general will, he could not fail to greet the actual republic as that regime which Montesquieu had reluctantly given up as too good to be practicable, and Rousseau had made the basis of his ideal society. 'Thus has begun the finest revolution that has ever honoured humanity, or rather, the only one to have an object worthy of man: that of founding political society at last on the immortal principles of equality, justice and reason. Frenchmen, never forget that the destinies of the universe are in your hands.' The only choice now was between 'the most odious of all forms of slavery or perfect liberty'.[6]

For the first time in his career, Robespierre now found that power belonged to 'us' rather than to 'them'. He was only a member of the Paris municipal council, but had not the insurrection proved that the Commune was the vehicle of the general will and the discredited Assembly, awaiting its replacement by the Convention, merely a collection of

---

[6] Ibid. *c*20 August 1792.

caretakers? The attack on the Tuileries had been 'that great action by which the sovereign people recovered its liberty'. The Commune must therefore enjoy 'the plenitude of power appropriate to the sovereign' (12 August). This was exactly what Brissot had said, three years before, when he had been a member of a different Commune, after a different revolution. As the Commune's spokesman, Robespierre told the Assembly that the people needed a government worthy of it. 'The people are resting but they are not asleep ... You should not give them laws that are contrary to their unanimous will.' The Girondins were not the only deputies to think that the Commune was getting above itself, but the insurrection *had* saved the revolution when the Assembly had been unwilling to act. To anyone who saw politics in terms of a single national will, it was difficult to resist the Commune's claim to embody it.

On 1 September Robespierre read to the Commune an address to the Paris Sections that it had invited him to draft. This shows how his juggling with the concept of the 'people' allowed him to make the best of both worls. The members of the Commune were the first elected representatives to have been drawn from the people. This was true, if it meant that most of them – although not, of course, Robespierre himself – came from the lower social classes in Paris. They had forced the Assembly to vote what the people had been wanting since 1789. The legitimacy of this, from Robespierre's point of view, dependended on the 'people' meaning the mass of the population in the country as a whole. Only if the people in the first sense were credited with representing a monolithic general will, could they be assumed to speak for the people in the second sense. If one did make that assumption, it was reasonable to accuse journalists, who criticised the Commune, of being guilty of 'insolence'; they were, as a matter of fact, lucky to get away with that, and not to be accused of the ultimate crime of *lèze-nation*. The Commune was therefore justified in hauling up Brissot's editor, Girey-Dupré, because of 'the need to put an end to the excesses of hacks in the pay of a cabal of enemies of the people'. The Girondins, if they were not actually in league with the invaders, were certainly frightened of the new revolution 'which threatened to elevate the sovereignty of the people and the reign of the general will on the ruins of all the factions'.

Brissot and his allies were saying exactly the same thing. It *was* a straight fight between disinterested *patriotes* and factious men who thought only of their own interests, between those who embodied the general will and the enemies of regeneration and of the revolution. Freedom of the press meant the right to print what was 'true'. Brissot was scandalised by the attempt to interfere with his *Patriote Français*, but he would not have dreamed of tolerating a royalist newspaper. Perhaps that would have been asking rather a lot, with the *de facto* republic barely a month old. The point was that men brought up to think in Rousseauist terms were obsessed with the idea that the general will must be as unanimous as it was infallible. They naturally saw themselves and their policies as its embodiment and anything that opposed them as factious and evil. Historians have expended much ingenuity on explaining why the Girondins and Montagnards should have hated each other so bitterly. They have invented distinctions or treated as causes what were, in fact, consequences of the two groups turning in different directions in search of support. Something, no doubt, was due to personal ambition and more to insecurity: men subjected to the pressures of revolution are apt to sniff treason in every hint of disagreement. Perhaps, as the future divisions within the Montagnards would suggest, revolutionaries are a fissiparous species. When all such allowances have been made, it is difficult to resist the conviction that their adherence to a kind of political monotheism had something to do with conflicts that were more like religious wars than political rivalries.

For Robespierre now, revolutionary ends could legitimise any political means. The Commune was accused of dictating laws to the Assembly. What did that matter, provided that they were good laws? 'Merciful heaven, does the legislative body then contain men perverse enough to pretend that they have sometimes served the people despite themselves, and to make it a crime on our part not to have allowed them to consummate the ruin of the *patrie*?' The only answer, for a Rousseauist, was an argument about the location of the general will; it was all a matter of who was infallible. Robespierre ended his address with a threat: 'Remember that the courage and the energy of the people alone can preserve its liberty. As soon as it sleeps it is enchained; it is despised as soon as it is no longer feared, conquered as soon as it pardons its enemies.' This was the language of Marat. On the following day the prison massacres began and Robespierre tried to have Brissot and other Girondins arrested. On 3 September he distinguished between the 'real' will of the people and the actual expression of their preferences, when he persuaded the Paris electors to expel from their ranks anyone who had previously belonged to a club that the majority considered 'anti-civic'. Before the elections began, Robespierre had insisted that the choice of deputies must be ratified by the Paris Sections. On 18 September, when it had become clear that the Montagnard political machine had the situation well in hand, he moved to have this rescinded, and tried to have a secretary dismissed for objecting. In the provinces, the Girondins were managing elections in much the same way.[7]

From the beginning of the Convention, in September 1792, until the overthrow of the Girondins early in June 1793, Robespierre was more or less the leader of the opposition. In one sense this was a retreat from the precarious authority he had exercised as spokesman for the Paris Commune in August, but he was far from the lonely outsider he had been in the Constituent Assembly, and his political perspective changed in consequence. In October he began a new paper, *Lettres à ses commettans*, which gave him space to develop his views on a number of general issues.

In the first number he surveyed the current state of the revolution.[8] 'The soul of the republic is *vertu*.' The French people had got rid of their kings but they were left with the vices that centuries of royal government had implanted. The republicans were therefore dividing into the virtuous and the egoists. The latter would be reinforced by defeated royalists and the vicious of all political persuasions. The war between the only two remaining parties, 'that of the good and that of the bad citizens' would therefore become more bitter. The political nation, in other words, was now confined to those whom Robespierre considered good citizens. The basic political problem was to give

---

[7] On this subject, see Alison Patrick, *The men of the first French republic*, Johns Hopkins University Press, 1972, ch III.

[8] *Lettres à ses commettans*. The quotations in this section all come from this source.

the government enough strength to force individuals to conform to the general will, without allowing it to become oppressive. As 'the most eloquent of our *philosophes*' had put it, 'It would need gods to give laws to men' (*Du contrat social* 2.7). The problem, as Robespierre expressed it with unusual succinctness, was that 'To draft our political institutions we should need the *moeurs* that the institutions themselves would eventually produce'. He was not the only theorist to have no answer to that, and he was content to fall back on the argument that the main need was to protect the individual from the (Girondin) government.

On 23 November he looked again at the freedom of the press. He was rather preoccupied with the media and had made 'calumny' the subject of an address to the Jacobins on 28 October, in which he had referred to 'the ignorant multitude' and also described the Parisians as 'an immense people, enlightened and used to unravelling the thread of intrigues', which allowed him to win, whether they supported him or not. As a public figure himself, his views had evolved since 1791 when he had defended the right of journalists to libel men in office. Most of them were only too ready to sell themselves to the government, with the result that the 'ignorant and credulous countryman' was liable to regard as odious monsters even 'the citizens most devoted to the happiness of their country'. He asked his readers whether this sort of thing could be allowed to continue, and eventually answered his own question in the Jacobin Club on 8 May 1793: journalists who perverted public opinion had to be silenced.

In January 1793 he turned to education, opening his article with a paraphrase of the first sentence of *Emile*: 'Man is good as he emerges from the hands of nature ... if he is corrupted, this disorder must be attributed to the vices of social institutions.'[9] Despite this appeal to Rousseau, he reassured his readers that he was not going to hold up Sparta as an ideal – but only because the French, emerging from centuries of decadence, were not up to Spartan standards. He was to change his mind about that. Since any system of public education would be under Roland, the Girondin Minister of the Interior, Robespierre stressed the need for public opinion to be independent of government control

[9] *Lettres àses commettans*. II/2, c10 January 1973.

and argued against the state control of education.

In February 1793 he faced the awkward problem of militancy in the Paris Sections, over the question of food supplies, which confronted the Convention with petitioners who directed their abuse impartially against both Girondins and Montagnards. On the face of it, this was both a popular movement and a mass movement, an expression of the general will that was facing the wrong way. The problem, however, was more apparent than real. Although the intentions of the people were always pure, they were easily misled by intrigue. 'The mistakes of the people are few and transient, always the product of the fatality of circumstances or the crime of perverted individuals.' The Parisian deputies, in a circular that reads as though Robespierre drafted it, said they thought the rioters might have been aristocrats in disguise. By 6 April Robespierre was sure of it.

Everything that went wrong was due to the Enemy. 'To overthrow the Bastille, destroy the monarchy, tame tyrants and punish traitors: those are the exploits of the people of Paris; everything else is the work of its enemies.'[10] This was as true of the army as of food riots in Paris. 'With a French army, it is impossible for a general not to win' — unless, of course, he was not really trying.[11] By now Robespierre had forgotten his wise objections to Brissot's war policy and was confident that foreigners would welcome their liberation and victory prove easy if only the right domestic policies were followed.[12] Brissot would have agreed that it was all a matter of willing the right thing. Indeed, under the shock of the February food riots, it looked for a moment as though the two groups might agree on the same Enemy and they drew briefly together, until the Sectional movement subsided and it was safe to quarrel again.

In the Convention itself, this battle had been waged from the beginning and it was mainly the responsibility of the Girondins. When one of their sillier spokesmen, Louvet, accused Robespierre of having been aiming at dictatorship, he had no difficulty in disposing of the charges (5 November). Very reasonably, he replied to the accusation that the Commune had

[10] *Lettres à ses commettans*. II/9, 6 April 1793.
[11] Ibid. II/7, late February 1793.
[12] Ibid. pp.60, 244.

acted illegally, 'All those things were illegal, as illegal as the revolution, the fall of the throne and of the Bastille, as illegal as liberty itself ... Do you want a revolution without revolution?' He moved on to more dangerous ground when he argued that the magistrates would not have been justified in trying to stop the September massacres since they were a popular movement. On 10 April 1793 he was to describe the lynching of the prisoners at Orleans, in the previous September, as 'revolutionary justice'. In his paper, he wrote that measures amounting to cruelty and oppression, when used by despots, were acts of *bienfaisance universelle* when employed on behalf of the people.[13]

On 2 December he joined in a debate on the grain trade. His position with regard to social and economic questions had not altered much since 1789. He thought that all wealth was social in origin and therefore liable to regulation by the state (26 August 1789). Extreme inequality was not a necessary and incurable evil (speech of March 1791 on the franchise). Something could be done to mitigate it by regulating inheritance (5 April 1791). Any idea of redistributing land in such a way as to achieve complete equality was, however, 'a scheme equally dangerous, unjust and impracticable', since it would destroy individual incentives.[14] Provided that subsistence was assured, there were more important things to think about than degrees of prosperity, and the people should lift their thoughts above 'paltry merchandise'. It was, however, the duty of the state to allow the poor to discharge their civic duties, by paying them to attend electoral assemblies and to buy National Guard uniforms (5 December 1790). In the December speech he argued that what was necessary for men's subsistence belonged to society as a whole, only the surplus being private property. This could mean anything or almost nothing. What Robespierre presumably intended was that honest trading should be protected – he said there would be no objection to free trade if everyone was just and *vertueux* – but that the state must intervene to stop speculation and profiteering. This would be to the advantage of the propertied since it would reduce plunder and assault. He put this in Rousseauist terms: 'the greatest service that the legislator can render men is to force them to be

---

[13] Ibid. p.322.
[14] *Défenseur de la constitution*, p.117.

honest', but what it amounted to was no more than the traditional practice of the *ancien régime*.

Over the king's trial, Robespierre followed Saint-Just's lead, asserting that the question was not a judicial one at all. This made good sense, especially from a Rousseauist point of view. 'If Louis can be presumed innocent, what becomes of the revolution?' If the insurrection of 10 August was assumed to be an act of popular sovereignty, to question the king's guilt was to challenge the general will; if it was *not* an act of popular sovereignty, the consequences were even more embarrassing! Louis's guilt was axiomatic; his death was necessary because the unsettled state of the republic made clemency too dangerous. That was more open to argument. When it came to the question of a referendum, Robespierre, like Brissot, found that political tactics dictated an attitude that was difficult to square with ideology. He was not the man to be defeated by that. It would be useless to submit the question of the king's fate to the *assemblées primaires* since the 'people' would not have time to attend. (That would have applied to any election.) 'I feel that, by people we must understand the nation minus the previously privileged and the gentlemen (*honnêtes gens*).' They were presumably unpersons. The people themselves, so defined, often lacked 'finesse and eloquence' and were easily duped by scoundrels. In these circumstances, it was not surprising that '*Vertu* is always a minority in this world'. Since the minority was always right, at least at the end of 1792, it was entitled to 'make the voice of truth heard – or what it regards as truth'. This was not one of Robespierre's happier performances and he would not have appreciated having it quoted against him a year later.

During the spring of 1793 the Montagnards experienced a kind of political schizophrenia. They were gradually resigning themselves to the need for a Parisian coup d'état to get rid of the Girondins, while at the same time trying to draft an ideal constitution for the republic of their dreams. At first sight Robespierre's views about the constitution seem to indicate a reversal of that steady progression towards the dictatorship of the just that he had shown since 10 August. This was not so. Although he had not yet worked out its implications, he was already distinguishing between constitutional and revolutionary government. The constitution should consist of what ought to be.

Whether it would be safe to implement it was another matter. His proposed Declaration of the Rights of Man therefore put the emphasis on the protection of the individual against the state (24 April). Freedom of the press was an absolute right and any law that violated the Rights of Man was invalid. He was rather vague about the right of insurrection. 'No fraction of the people can exercise the power of the whole people.' On the other hand, the right of insurrection belonged 'to the people and to each fraction of the people'. That squared quite a few circles. Property was a social institution, taxation should be progressive, with those at subsistence level exempt. This was an advance on Brissot, who denounced progressive taxation as expropriation. When Robespierre addressed the Convention on the constitution itself, he began with another paraphrase of Rousseau: 'Man is born for happiness and liberty and everywhere he is wretched and enslaved' (10 May). When it came to preventing governments from abusing their powers, he rejected Montesquieu (a balance of powers), Marat (a tribunate) and Rousseau (direct democracy). He himself favoured as much decentralisation as possible ('give back to the liberty of the individual whatever does not naturally belong to public authority') and frequent elections. Once again he shied away from the insoluble problem of how a people corrupted by 'despotism' could be induced to will the means of its own regeneration, with the rather lame argument that the *patrie* must be saved by those to whom liberty and their country were dear. Apart from some Brissotin remarks (1792 vintage) on the duty of every nation to fight tyrants who oppressed their peoples, Robespierre's constitutional aspirations were admirable enough. The question was whether or not the means he now saw as necessary for their implementation would not make their attainment impossible.

While Dr Jekyll was thinking of a golden future, Mr Hyde was trying to dispose of the Girondins. He told the Convention on April 10 that the republic was for the people only. As always, this was an abstraction that did not correspond to any specific social class. It consisted of 'men of all ranks who have pure and lofty souls, philosophers who are friends of humanity, sans-culottes'. The people – and here he was presumably thinking of the sans-culottes rather than the pure and lofty souls – were exploited by the ambitious who used popular societies in order to win power and then turned against them when they had got where they wanted to be. There was some truth in this, and Robespierre could not have foreseen what he himself would be saying about popular societies before the end of the year. On 8 May he drew some practical conclusions. Conspirators exploited the constitution and the Rights of Man for their own purposes. Profiteering merchants, for example, were not entitled to the protection of the law. 'Are solicitors' clerks so interesting then?' On the same night he spelled things out rather more explicitly for the Jacobins. All 'rebels against humanity and the people' must be exterminated. Enemies of the people were 'corrupt men who put their own interest before the general interest'. All the corrupt were in league with the foreign enemy. As always, there were only two parties, 'that of the corrupt and that of the virtuous' and 'the sans-culottes are always motivated by love of humanity.' It naturally followed that aristocrats and moderates should be kept out of the Sections. Democracy was only for the *vertueux* and he knew how to separate the sheep from the goats. Rousseau might not have been happy about all this, but it was a logical consequence of seeing politics in terms of moral regeneration by a collective will.

It was apparently during the crisis of 31 May-2 June – 'the present insurrection' – that Robespierre jotted down some reflections on the situation. *'We need a single will,* ONE WILL *(Il fait une volonté,* UNE). It must be either republican or royalist. For it to be republican, we need republican Ministers, republican newspapers, republican deputies, a republican constitution ... The dangers at home come from the bourgeois;* TO DEFEAT THE BOURGEOIS *we must* RALLY THE PEOPLE ... *The people must ally with the Convention and the Convention must* MAKE USE OF THE PEOPLE (SE SERVIR DU PEUPLE)'.[15] This does not necessarily imply that the 'people' were to get what they thought they wanted. This became apparent within a fortnight of the expulsion of the Girondin leaders from the Convention, when, in a debate on the constitution, Robespierre opposed the right of the *assemblées primaires* to meet at will, since they might disagree with the

---

[15] E.B.Courtois, *Rapport fait au nom de la commission chargé de l'examen des papiers trouvés chez Robespierre et ses complices,* Paris, an III, p.181.

established government and 'overthrow national sovereignty'. The rich would prolong the meetings until the poor went home, and then pass whatever motions they liked. Anything of the sort would therefore be *'très-peu populaire par son excès de démocratie même'* (14 June). Robespierre had a point, but his argument applied to elections of any kind. That night he warned the Jacobins against *défiance universelle*, no doubt forgetting how shocked he had been when Brissot, in his time a great preacher of *défiance*, had also suggested that it had outlived its usefulness. Robespierre was not ambitious in the sense of wanting office for himself – which was probably true of Brissot as well. Throughout June and July he urged the Montagnards to have confidence in the Committee of Public Safety, and he was probably sincere when he said that he himself only joined it reluctantly towards the end of July. He was personally disinterested, but he was the victim of an ideology that turned the revolution into a Second Coming (actually, of course, a *First* Coming) and all persistent opponents into agents of Antichrist.

There was a brief alarm at the end of June when Jacques Roux once more mobilised the Parisian sans-culottes to put pressure on the Convention. Instinctively, Robespierre moved towards the centre: 'Those who preach against the Montagne in the Convention are the only enemies of the people.' A concerted Montagnard offensive disposed of Roux, who was in gaol by the end of the summer. Robespierre now saw the general will as located within the purged Convention and the revolutionary government. He showed considerable patience and understanding, in the Jacobin Club, in protecting Montagnards against each other, criticising their policies but never impugning their motives. When Hébert began denouncing those he called moderates, Robespierre came to their support while making it clear that he regarded Hébert as a good revolutionary. In an uncertain world, he put his trust in what could be called the Montagnard Establishment and reserved his suspicion for the *patriotes* of 10 August, and even more for those of 31 May. This did not imply any general policy of national reconciliation; quite the reverse. He told the Jacobins on 12 August, 'We have been too indulgent towards traitors'. He attacked the revolutionary tribunal for hesitating to convict general Kilmain, even though the Committee of Public Safety had told it that he was guilty

(11 August). He demanded the trial, by which he meant the execution, of general Custine and of the leading Girondins (12 August). On 24 October he argued that either documentary proof or the feelings of the jury was sufficient for conviction; in 1791 he had said that either was ground for acquittal, but then he had not been thinking of political cases.

This went with a growing suspicion of what purported to be popular movements. He had no hesitation, even though he failed to carry the Jacobins with him on this occasion, in denouncing a demonstration about wages as counter-revolutionary (4 September). When sans-culotte militants petitioned against the restriction of Section meetings to two days a week, he maintained that 'The people did not dictate the petition' (17 September). When the Sections evaded the restriction by setting up popular societies which met on the other five nights, he denounced this as intrigue. On 26 December he attacked the 'so-called popular societies', claiming, without producing any evidence, that the *patriotes* did not attend them and even when they did they were too ignorant to see through intrigues: 'The people are not there.' It may well have been true that the movement had been captured by his political rivals but, except to Robespierre, that did not amount to quite the same thing. In the case of the Jacobins – the most socially exclusive of all the political clubs – 'the situation is different: the people are there.' Logically enough, in view of this rather personal view of who was what, he concluded, 'I am better placed than anyone else to judge and make pronouncements about individuals'. He had, in fact, repeated Brissot's evolution of the previous year: the Convention, now that it had been purged of the Girondins, was pure and the people were always right; what looked like popular movements were actually the instruments of faction; the people, despite their *vertu*, or perhaps because of it, were so gullible.

At the same time, Robespierre became somewhat hysterical about foreign plots. He told the Jacobins on 11 August that the 'English faction' had hitherto dominated the revolution. He elaborated on this on 17 November, in the first of the political speeches that he made on behalf of the Committee of Public Safety. His diplomatic *tour d'horizon* was reminiscent of Brissot in one of his more irresponsible moods. Necker, Orleans, Lafayette, Lameth, Dumouriez, Custine and Brissot had all been

British agents and the Girondins had only started the war in order to lose it. 'Let liberty perish in France and the whole of nature will be covered with a funeral pall and human reason driven back to abysses of ignorance and barbarism.' French defeat would mean universal tyranny and a return to the Dark Ages. Despite the fiendish plots of the Enemy, who had even succeeded in alienating the Turks, 'France's useful and faithful ally' (and Montesquieu's quintessence of despotism), there was, however, nothing to worry about. The allies were desperate and if only the peoples of Europe knew what the war was about, they would overthrow their tyrants. The Enemy's only remaining hope was to set the revolutionaries against each other – which reinforced the need to keep the Montagnards united and to exterminate those who were trying to divide them.

This was more easily said than done. He had meant it, when he told the Convention on 25 September, 'I promise never to divide the *patriotes*, but that does not include those who merely wear the mask'. When some of the revolutionaries launched an attack on religion in November, Robespierre was probably right in sniffing political motives, but not necessarily in seeing dechristianisation as a foreign intrigue. But by now 'The foreign courts are the real authors of all our troubles'. Religion was only a pretext: the revolt of the Vendée had not been due to religious feeling but to the treason of previous governments. The Enemy was supporting atheism because it was aristocratic. 'The idea of a great being who watches over oppressed innocence is *toute populaire*' (17 November). Robespierre was right to see the new movement as irresponsible political opportunism, but he could not hope to contain it if he called it treason. His own deepest feelings were outraged and the kind of emotional deism that moved him most was one of the most salient elements of the Rousseauist legacy.

Despite the fact that the Committee of Public Safety was now inspired by the general will, Robespierre had to admit that things were not going well and the millennium seemed as far away as ever. There were grounds for his belief that the British Government was trying to stir up trouble in the Jacobins. He did his best to discriminate between the trouble-makers and those they were misleading, but since he could not recognise the legitimacy of any kind of political opposition, sooner or later he was bound to damn all disagreement as counter-revolutionary. He began by having a very dubious quartet of political adventurers, Proli, Desfieux, Dubuisson and Pereira, expelled from the Jacobins, pointing out that, besides being active in dechristianisation, they had been busy founding popular societies and had supported the *républicaines révolutionnaires*, a feminist group that the Jacobins had proscribed. With Hébert, he persuaded the Jacobins to purge their members. On 12 December this led to the expulsion from the club of two deputies, Duhem and Clootz, the latter 'a foreigner who wants to be more democratic than the French'. Robespierre was both an intelligent man and an experienced politician and he could see himself being dragged down a road where he did not want to go. Although he suggested that Proli & Co. were foreign agents, he did not propose their arrest, but was content to have them thrown out of the club. He defended Montagnard Old Boys, such as Desmoulins (20 December) and Philippeaux (23 December), even when they made savage criticisms of the government. He was helpless in the face of the bitter feud that developed between those who wanted to intensify the Terror, and perhaps organise a 'third revolution' to their own advantage, and those who hoped for a quick return to constitutional government. Each side was led by veterans whom he trusted. Believing them to be the unconscious tools of foreign agents he defended them against each other's attacks and tried to divert the Jacobins from the personal feuds they obviously enjoyed, into an examination of the crimes of the British government. Though heinous, these were not inexhaustible, and the members were soon at each other's throats again. Robespierre was in an impasse.

With his political world beginning to disintegrate, he tried, in two theoretical speeches, to define the basis of the new revolutionary order. On Christmas Day 1793 he told the Convention that it was not to be found in books. He distinguished between constitutional government, which was mainly concerned with civil liberty, and revolutionary goverment, the means by which the former could be established. Revolutionary government was a state of war in which public liberty took precedence over civil rights. Those who wanted to observe the constitutional rules in time of revolution were actually working for 'the resurrection of tyranny and the death of the *patrie*'.

Revolutionary government owed protection to all good citizens and 'death to the enemies of the people'. If there seemed no end to the revolutionary phase, this was because of faction. Only by the destruction of the factious could the way be opened to a free and happy future. The two factions that appeared to be fighting each other were actually part of the same counter-revolutionary movement, directed by the foreign enemy, and the rot had now reached the Convention itself. His audience must have been expecting him to conclude with the demand for a purge, but all he asked for was the speedy judgment of generals and foreigners.

On 5 February he tried again. The progress of the revolution had hitherto been instinctive. Now, for the first time, he was providing it with 'an exact theory and precise rules of conduct'. In a long and moving passage he defined the goal: 'We want an order of things where all base and cruel passions are bound up and all the benevolent and generous passions are aroused by the laws ... In our country, we want to substitute morality for egoism, probity for honour [in the aristocratic sense of honour], principles for habits, duty for social convention, the empire of reason for the tyranny of fashion ... ' There was a tragic dimension to Robespierre. He pursued his Grail with disinterested passion by means that destroyed any prospect of its attainment. The legislator must reinforce the principle of democratic government, which was *vertu*. This came naturally to the people but united all the vicious and corrupt against them and their government. 'It is as though the two opposing spirits that have been contending for control of nature are fighting, in this great epoch of human history, to establish irreversibly the history of the world, and France is the theatre of this awesome combat.' Popular government in time of revolution must therefore rest on a combination of *vertu* and terror: 'One leads the people by reason and the enemies of the people by terror.' This was not a bad anticipation of the 'democratic dictatorship of the proletariat'. At this point the ghost of Montesquieu, like Mozart's Commendatore, appeared to give him a last warning. 'It has been said that terror is the mainspring of despotic government.' It had indeed, in *De l'esprit des lois*, but Robespierre brushed it aside. Revolutionary government was 'the despotism of liberty against tyranny', whatever that meant. 'In a republic the only citizens are the republicans.'

Robespierre's definition was becoming more restrictive all the time and it now excluded all moderates: 'Whoever does not hate crime cannot love *vertu*.' He became gloomier: the government had recently been finding the going harder, all its activities impeded by a hidden malevolence. There was no conclusion, no call for action, either because he could not bring himself to propose any or because his colleagues on the committee would not accept it. In less than a week he had taken to his bed and he was to stay there for over a month.

On one or two previous occasions he had been afflicted by some kind of nervous disorder when he had seen crises approaching, but never for more than a few days. It is a reasonable conjecture that he could not bear to face the consequences of his failure to contain the opposition by political means. On the day he returned to duty, the governing committees decided to destroy Hébert and the radicals. From now onwards it was all downhill. Once Hébert had gone, despite Robespierre's vehement protest, he had to accept the proscription of the moderate leaders, his friends Danton and Desmoulins. One is always baffled by the elasticity of his principles and driven to wonder how far they amounted to anything more than expediency in fancy dress, but never more so than on this occasion. Having failed to save Danton, he provided Saint-Just with the 'evidence' for his impeachment and, more reluctantly, that of Desmoulins too. When the Convention looked like rebelling, it was Robespierre who had to save the committees by forcing through the purges that he had opposed, denouncing Danton as a 'long-rotten idol' and silencing Danton's friends with 'Whoever trembles at the present time is guilty'. Brissot had said that too, and lived to regret it. The nervous wear and tear this must have imposed on him can hardly be imagined.

All that was left to him was *vertu* and he saw now that it could not be gathered wild amongst the people, but had to be cultivated. Already in the previous August he had presented to the Convention an education bill drafted by the murdered deputy, Lepeletier, which was to provide comprehensive boarding schools for both boys and girls, in which 'the raw material ... never leaves the mould'. These were to be Spartan in every sense of the word and were intended to create 'a renewed race, strong, hard-working, orderly, disciplined, distinct from our own aged race'. The *comité d'instruction publique* had sabotaged the scheme by refusing to make it compulsory, and although the Convention had voted it, nothing had been done about it.

Robespierre now turned to religion in a speech on 7 May, which committed the country to the worship of the Supreme Being. This was something very close to his heart, and it was the last time that he sounded cheerful or optimistic about the future. 'The whole physical world has changed [because of technology]. Everything must change in the moral and political world.' The republic was not a natural regime but depended on men overcoming their passions. The objective of all social institutions was to direct them along the right road. Human authority alone was insufficient for this and needed to be reinforced by religious sentiment. He attacked the philosophes as the pusillanimous advocates of mere intelligence, who had persecuted the one man who had shown himself worthy to be 'the teacher of the human race'. Robespierre was now more of a Rousseauist then ever. His programme of religious fêtes was inspired by the penultimate chapter of *Du contrat social* and by the *Lettre à d'Alembert*. Sparta, which he had rejected as recently as 5 February, was now the goal. It had 'shone like a flash of lightning in the immense darkness'. But France was bringing it back to life again: 'O French women ... what have you to envy in the women of Sparta?' When he presided over the inaugural fête on 8 June he called it the greatest day since the creation of the universe. As he walked at the head of the procession, behind him he could hear his colleagues' mockery.

After that everything was an anticlimax. By the end of the month the Furies were back and they were not to leave him again. He had had his black moments before: at some time in the late summer he had jotted down and crossed out, 'When will the people be enlightened? When it has bread, and the rich and the government stop hiring perfidious pens and tongues to deceive it. When their interest is fused with that of the people. When will their interest be fused with that of the people? NEVER.'[16] In the past he had always been able to persuade himself that things would turn out well in the end. It was not so now. On 26 May he ·

---

[16] Courtois, op.cit. pp.180-1.

told the Convention that everything had still to be done, laws to be made, the government consolidated and *moeurs* to be regenerated. There were now two 'peoples' in France, the one 'pure, simple and thirsting for justice', the other composed of 'crafty and babbling charlatans' who interposed themselves between the real people and its representatives. When mere self-preservation drove some of the deputies to challenge the savage law of the 22 *prairial* (10 June), proposed by his friend Couthon, which turned revolutionary 'justice' into a simple instrument of murder, Robespierre came to Couthon's support. 'It is not natural that a kind of coalition should be springing up against a government that is devoting itself to the salvation of the *patrie*.' As if *patriotes*, before a *patriote* jury, needed witnesses to prove their innocence! Two days later he said that when *moeurs* had become purer the Committee of Public Safety would be blamed for its laxity. By implication at least, he defended the government's decision that no British or Hanoverian prisoners would be taken.

His ferocity was a sign of desperation. The ranks of the just were thinning all the time. As late as 12 June the Montagnards were still pure but by 26 June he was attacking 'men who call themselves representatives of the people and whom I don't regard as such'. The Committee of Public Safety was the victim of a new conspiracy so vast that one man could not expose all its ramifications – but it did not intend to prosecute any of the guilty and would merely disregard them. On 1 July he told the Jacobins that they would shudder if they knew in what quarters foreign libels against him were being repeated. In other words, the rot had spread from the Convention to the government itself. He did not publicise the fact that he was now boycotting the committee's meetings. On 9 July he admitted that few men loved *vertu* for its own sake – which implied that even the people were unreliable. The goal was as far away as ever, and military victory merely bred a false sense of security. He still insisted that he had no intention of harming any of the guilty. By now it was impossible for any of those who listened to his rambling laments to have any idea of what was going on. When an over-enthusiastic supporter proposed that the Jacobins should hold a special meeting at which Robespierre and Couthon could tell the club all about the plots, they apparently froze him into terrified silence (24 July).

Robespierre must have been going through some kind of private hell, and the most obvious explanation of all this unpunished treason was that he wanted another 'final' purge and his colleagues would not agree. According to Carnot's son, his father persuaded the Committee of Public Safety, after the action against Danton had almost misfired, that they should never risk arresting another deputy.[17] If this were the explanation, however, one would have expected some of Robespierre's colleagues to have quoted it in their defence when they in turn were accused of terrorism. Perhaps Robespierre, like Rousseau himself, had come to inhabit a twilight world, surrounded by invisible enemies so numerous that he did not even know who they were.

On 26 July he took the offensive in the Convention. If the numerous repetitions in the surviving versions of his speech are not printers' mistakes, it was quite extraordinarily incoherent, a rag-bag of contradictions and things that he had said before. Although the revolution was a struggle between virtue and vice, all the trouble was due to faction and the government had not been repressive enough, he was not going to accuse any of the guilty. 'If there are privileged conspirators, inviolable enemies of the republic, I consent to maintain an eternal silence about what concerns them.' That was presumably meant to be conciliatory. Everything was going wrong: 'Public affairs are once more taking a perfidious and alarming turn.' Everyone was trying to blame him, but he did not dare to name those responsible, 'at this time and in this place'. He had a last moment of optimism when he digressed to evoke the fête in honour of the Supreme Being. Then he returned to the plotters, sometimes denounced as extremists, sometimes as aiming at *une extrême indulgence*. In the middle he produced his *testament redoutable aux oppresseurs du peuple*, which apparently consisted of nothing more than *la vérité terrible ou la mort*. Then he went back to his circuitous diatribe, occasionally naming enemies but more often sticking to allusion and insinuation. 'Let the reins of revolution escape for one moment and you will see military despotism take over ... A century of civil war and calamity will afflict our country.' (That

---

[17] *Mémoires sur Carnot par son fils*, Paris, 1861, p.369.

had been a favourite theme of Marat's.) He was still imprisoned in the old dichotomy: 'If justice does not hold absolute sway in the republic ... liberty is merely a vain name.' It was a wild speech that led nowhere and arrived at no conclusion. Perhaps the key to it lay in one sentence: 'My reason, but not my heart, is on the point of doubting that virtuous republic whose plan I had traced out for myself.' The goal remained the same but France was not going to attain it. All the heroism, the sacrifices and the bloodshed had served no purpose. If he fell, everything would fall with him. Even then he did not think he had been wrong. The others had proved unworthy. The general will was still the only hope, even if he had come to realise that it was his own.

Chapter 12

Saint-Just

Saint-Just was born in 1767, which meant that Marat was old enough to have been his father. He was the only man in this book whose intellectual apprenticeship overlapped the revolutionary crisis. Like the others he came from a middle-class background, although his father was a cavalry officer who had been decorated with the Cross of Saint Louis. When he died, Saint-Just was only ten. His wife, a formidable woman, came from a merchant family.[1] In 1786, when Saint-Just was away in Paris, she helped to marry off a girl he loved and intended to marry himself. Some months later he took some of his own or the family's silver and went into hiding in Paris. His mother then had him tracked down and locked up for six months. It may be purely coincidental that Saint-Just, Brissot and Robespierre all lacked the support of affectionate parents and that Marat left home when he was only 16.

Saint-Just's first work of any consequence was *Organt*, a long mock-heroic poem, written between the ages of 16 and 20 and

[1] There is no satisfactory biography of Saint-Just, although there is an excellent account of his service with the armies in J.P.Gross, *Saint-Just, sa politique et ses missions*. For his career as a whole one can consult E.N.Curtis, *Saint-Just colleague of Robespierre*, and A.Ollivier, *Saint-Just ou la force des choses*. Important new material on his early life is to be found in M.A.Charmelot, *Saint-Just ou le chevalier Organt*. Mme. Charmelot does not appear to have published the full biography that she promised in this sketch. A.Liénard, in *Saint-Just, théorie politique*, provides a very useful edition of his more important theoretical writings, which are discussed by M.Abensour in 'La philosophie politique de Saint-Just: problématique et cadres sociaux', *Annales historiques de la Révolution française*, 1966. C.Manceron relates the story of his youth, in characteristic style, in *Les hommes de la liberté*, vol.IV, *La révolution qui lève*, pp.319-52.

published in 1789. He thought well enough of it to bring out a second edition soon after his election to the Convention. It consists of an ambitious and often entertaining account of the adventures of some of Charlemagne's paladins, after France had been taken over by Folly. Attempts have been made to explain it as a political allegory. Mme Charmelot, on the other hand, has made out a case for its being autobiographical. Her argument would carry more conviction if she had not identified within it references not merely to the present but to the future. It does contain one ironical, if accidental foretaste of the future, in the passage where its author mocked

> Ces conquérants, sous les noms imposteurs
> De liberté, de soutiens, de vengeurs,
> A l'oeil surpris, découvriraient peut-être
> Un scélérat, honteux de le paraître.

This is an astonishing anticipation of the sixth verse of the Marseillaise:

> Amour sacré de la patrie
> Conduis, soutiens nos bras vengeurs,
> Liberté, liberté chérie,
> Combats avec tes défenseurs.

More to the point is the fact that *Organt* was a thoroughly Voltairean poem, and naughty enough in places to scandalise some of Saint-Just's more pious hagiographers. It is also a cut above the literary efforts of Marat and Robespierre. As befitted the genre, it was satirical about everything: religion, human nature and politics, and it abounded in adolescent cynicism:

> Homme est un mot qui ne caractérise
> Qu'un animal, ainsi qu'ours ou lion,
> Son naturel est erreur et sottise,
> Malignité, superbe, ambition ...

Its aspiration and temper were in striking contrast to the literary sentimentalities of Mercier, Marat and Robespierre, and it was wholly out of keeping with what Saint-Just was to become.

Despite his youth, he played an active part in local politics after 1789 and was even made a lieutenant-colonel in the

National Guard, in which capacity he attended the Fête de la Fédération in Paris on 14 July 1790. By that time he was already writing to Desmoulins on familiar terms and in August 1790 he sent a rather more ceremonious letter to Robespierre, asking for his support in a local dispute about the siting of a market: 'You whom I know, like God, only through his miracles ... '[2] Maximilien must have liked that; he certainly kept the letter. Saint-Just hoped for election to the Legislative Assembly but was excluded on grounds of age.

In 1791 he published his first theoretical work, *Esprit de la révolution et de la constitution de France*.[3] Everything about this, beginning with the title, is reminiscent of Montesquieu, who was frequently invoked and always with approval. The succession of short chapters with titles like 'Of the nature of the French constitution', 'Of the principles of the French constitution', 'On the relationship between nature and the principles of the constitution', betrays his debt to *De l'esprit des lois*. It was the work of a rather self-consciously clever young man with a weakness for epigrammatic pseudo-profundities: 'Nothing is sacred except what is good ... only truth is absolute.' 'Nowadays only trade can make a nation prosperous but luxury poisons it.' Saint-Just's description of the state of France before 1789 combined the exaggeration of Marat with an attempt at the style of Tacitus. Like Marat, he thought that Necker had been trying to starve France. The insurrection of July 1789 was a slave revolt by a corrupted people, which accounted for the atrocities perpetrated by the mob. The Assembly however – and here he parted company from Marat with a vengeance – skilfully played off the factions against each other in order to bring them under its control.

His evaluation of what had happened since 1789 was very much in the Montesquieu mould. The legislators of classical times had done everything for the republic, whereas the French had done everything for man. 'The rights of man would have destroyed Athens or Sparta. They knew only their beloved *patrie*

---

[2] *Oevres complètes de Saint-Just* (ed. C.Vellay), 2v., Paris, 1908, I/220-1; E.B.Courtois, *Rapport fait au nom de la commission chargé de l'examen des papiers de Robespierre et complices*, Paris, an III, p.122.

[3] Text in Vellay and Liénart, op.cit. and A.Soboul, 'Un manuscrit inédit de Saint-Just', *Annales historiques de la Révolution française*, 1951.

there and subordinated themselves to it. The rights of man strengthen France; here the *patrie* subordinates itself to its children.' France had a mixed constitution, which was the best kind. 'In a mixed government, all incoherence is harmony, all uniformity is disorder.' Montesquieu would have seen the point, though he might have thought that this was going rather too far. The democratic element was based on *une liberté modérée*, the aristocratic on equality of rights and the monarchical on justice. If this was not the best of all possible worlds it was not far off it. Saint-Just approved of the secret ballot and of the disfranchisement of 'passive' citizens, since universal suffrage would have made the constitution 'popular and anarchic'. He was tempted by the idea of economic equality and abandoned it only with regret. 'What is the point of recalling a moral order of no more use to men, unless their corruption brings them back to nature?' Although he approved of private property – the only means of attaching selfish men to their country – he was violently hostile to 'feudalism' and only resigned himself to the retention of seigneurial land dues because of the need to go cautiously. He approved of trade, though he favoured taxing consumption in order to discourage luxury. This was orthodox, middle-of-the-road revolutionary doctrine. He praised almost everyone: Marat (full of good sense, although too anxious), Mercier (for his strength of character), Robespierre, the Assembly, for disregarding the cries of the multitude who were always clamouring for those in office to render their accounts, and demanding the dismissal of Ministers. This was having one's cake and eating it, with a vengeance.

There were occasional passages of a more extreme and original nature, always in the direction of libertarianism. 'All crime is due to the corruption of the laws.' 'When crime increases, one must change the laws.' A special court to try crimes against the state would be intolerable, except during the crisis of a revolution. To be more precise, such ideas could appear libertarian, but they were capable of a different interpretation since they involved regarding the state as a moral entity. 'Indifference towards the *patrie* and love of self is the source of all evil.' Liberty was not about happiness but about *vertu*. 'When *vertu* is so much the spirit of a constitution as to form the national character, when everything is *patrie* and religion, people are ignorant of evil and are no more aware of what constitutes good than an ingenuous virgin of her innocence. As laws grow rusty, people reward good and punish evil. As corruption intensifies, so do rewards and penalties. Soon one has triumphal marches and breakings on the wheel; *vertu* loses its taste and vice its sensitivity.' The sentiment was generous enough, but it was all a matter of whether or not one tried to enforce *vertu* by Act of Parliament.

As Saint-Just's attention shifted from the balanced constitution to the state as moral agent, quotations from Montesquieu tended to give way to references to Rousseau, generally of a fairly critical kind. He was praised for his opposition to standing armies but condemned for saying that Christianity was not a social religion. When he wrote about liberty, 'sublime though he was, he was generally thinking of men's pride and not of bringing them back to simplicity by way of *vertu*'. This seems rather hard on Rousseau. When he praised the liberty of Rome, he forgot that war brought tyranny and the rest of the universe was in chains. 'Whatever veneration the authority of Jean-Jacques Rousseau imposes on me, you are unpardonable, O great man, for having justified the death penalty.' This did not prevent Saint-Just from advocating it himself, in his conclusion, for those who took up arms against the general will.

Like Brissot, he included Montesquieu and Rousseau – and no other eighteenth-century French writers – in a list of men deserving statues, but he does not seem to have had a very clear idea of where they differed on the issue of sovereignty. Saint-Just said that rogues were no part of the sovereign people, which was to become the standard argument of the revolutionaries for proscribing their opponents. What he seems to have meant was that everyone was accountable to absolute moral standards that transcended the interests of a particular society. 'Every will, even a sovereign will, that is inclined towards perversion, is nul. Rousseau did not exhaust the subject when he described the will as incommunicable, imprescriptible, eternal. It must also be just and reasonable. It is no less criminal for the sovereign to be tyrannised by himself than by someone else ... every individual would be part of the [collective] tyranny and servitude.' Both in theory and in practice, Saint-Just was more of a moderate and less of a Rousseauist than Brissot, Marat or Robespierre in 1791. From where he lived in the provinces, the revolution probably appeared as a beneficent entity, and he had not yet had an inside view of Parisian politics or been exposed to the temptations of power.

It was probably during the following year that he wrote, but did not complete or publish, *De la nature*.[4] The fact that the unwritten section dealt with the monarchy could imply that he was interrupted by the insurrection of 10 August 1792 and his own election to the Convention. This was a very different work from the previous one. Although its form was still reminiscent of *De l'esprit des lois*, its content was wholly original and owed virtually nothing to Montesquieu and not much to Rousseau. Saint-Just was never to abandon the ideas he now put forward, although they took on a very different significance during the Terror.

Like Rousseau, he started from the assumption that man was naturally good, but for Saint-Just he was a social animal. 'Natural' society was therefore a harmonious and self-regulating business that required no constraint. One is reminded of Blake. Political relationships, which implied rules, sanctions and an ultimate resort to force, were necessary only between different societies. In practice, they were imported within particular societies, partly because political theorists had wrongly inferred from the example of savage societies that man was a Hobbesian animal. Legislators had therefore striven to civilise and discipline him by imposing rules and it was this very process that had made the rules and penalties both necessary and insufficient. Saint-Just therefore distinguished between a 'social state', which was one of natural and unconstrained co-operation, and a 'civil state' of imposed political order. In other words, he shared Rousseau's conviction that contemporary political institutions were a denial of men's true nature, but vehemently rejected his deduction that the way back was by Spartan discipline and by forcing men to be free. He would have nothing to do with Rousseau's insistence on the need for vigorous

---

[4] Slightly different versions of the text, which is not easy to read, are to be found in Liénart, op. cit. and A. Soboul, 'Un manuscrit inédit de Saint-Just', *Annales historiques de la Révolution française*, 1951.

government. 'He strangles liberty with his own hands. The more safeguards he establishes against despotism, the more weapons he forges for tyranny.' For Saint-Just, on the other hand, 'If you base your society on laws of constraint, all its relationships will need coercion. If you found it on nature, these relationships will arise out of each other.' This applied to every kind of relationship, including religious and commercial ones, which had been perverted by being conceived in terms of the state rather than as natural activities arising within a society.

Saint-Just distinguished between property, which was what a man needed to live a full life, and possession, which was what he happened to own.[5] A natural society was assumed to be egalitarian, in the sense of 'to each according to his needs'. Crime was a consequence, rather than a cause of repressive laws. 'Crime is born of force; it is not in men's hearts.' The way to suppress crime was therefore to abolish punishment. 'No one on earth should command; all power is illegitimate.' Not surprisingly, he thought Rousseau's beloved Romans 'the most corrupt people on earth'. Saint-Just denied that what he was advocating amounted to anarchy, but he seems to have interpreted the word as meaning 'disorder' ; what he was preaching certainly looked very much like anarchism.

All previous revolutions had been disastrous – 'full of crimes and catastrophes' – because they had been rooted in the false conception of society as political. A new revolution based on good laws and skilfully conducted by men intent on restoring the natural order, would 'change the face of the world without upheaval'. Once again he wrestled with the slippery problem of the general will. 'Laws are natural relationships between things and not relative relationships or the effect of the general will. Rousseau, when speaking of laws, says they can only express the general will and ends by acknowledging the need for a legislator. A legislator might express the will of nature and not the general will. Moreover that will can be mistaken and the social body must not be oppressed by itself any more than by someone else.' This is far from clear. Since he seemed to think – to judge from what he said at a later date – that Rousseau imagined the general

---

[5] This definition of property had also been that of Brissot, in an early work, *Recherches philosophiques sur le droit de propriété considéré dans la nature,* n.p., 1780. Neither of them gave much thought to its implications.

will to be no more than a majority, when everyone voted for what he thought would suit him best, Saint-Just may have been making Rousseau's own point: that the right solution was to give people what was good for them, rather than what they wanted. On the whole, it looks rather more likely that he was arguing that people should be allowed to go their own ways.

When he glanced at the practical implications of restoring 'natural' society, he certainly drew closer to Rousseau, assuming the need for rules that might have struck some of his ideal citizens as state interference with the exercise of their natural rights. Inheritance was reserved for direct descendents, in whose default property reverted to the state. Anyone owning more than the permitted maximum of land was required to sell the surplus. Anyone with less than the required minimum would be banished, as would anyone who refused to marry, 'for every member of the city ought to be bound to it'. Special laws would be required to attach merchants to the public interest, since they had no stake in the country. If one assumes that he had tried to throw Rousseau out by the front door, he seemed to be creeping in at the back.

In July 1792 Saint-Just wrote an odd letter to his friend Daubigny in Paris.[6] 'I am excited by a republican fever that is eating me away ... I feel I have what is needed to make my mark in this century ... I will put up with everything, but I will proclaim the truth. You are all cowards who have not appreciated me. My star will rise though and perhaps eclipse yours ... O God, has Brutus to languish forgotten, far from Rome! Nevertheless, my mind is made up: if Brutus does not kill the others he will kill himself.' It was rather strange that a man who thought the Romans the most corrupt people on earth should have been so keen on playing Brutus.

Brutus got his chance at last, when he was elected to the Convention, despite some argument about his age. He joined the Jacobin Club, where he made his first two speeches on 22 October and 4 November. These managed to combine a plea for mild government – 'What a government is this that plants the tree of liberty on the scaffold?' – with the suggestion that the

---

[6] Vellay, op.cit. I/349. Unless otherwise indicated, the speeches in the rest of this chapter are to be found in Vellay.

Girondins were crypto-royalists and an invitation to members of
the club to denounce traitors. He possibly came to regard this as
a false start; from then onwards he rarely addressed the club and
never intervened in the faction fight in the Convention, treating
his opponents' arguments courteously and never impugning their
motives, until the entire political situation was changed by the
coup d'état of 31 May-2 June. He confined his speeches in the
Assembly to major issues, always looking for the question of
principle behind a specific issue and trying to find a 'republican'
solution. The result was that he very quickly acquired a
reputation as an epigrammatic orator and an original thinker,
winning the praise of men as dissimilar as Brissot and Marat.

On 13 November he cut through the embarrassed arguments
about the legality of putting the king on trial, with the blunt
assertion that Louis XVI was already condemned. Monarchy was
illegitimate because it was contrary to nature: 'One cannot reign
innocently.' Even if the people were to want a king, nature ruled
that they must not have one. Louis XVI was therefore no part of
French society. As a foreigner, he could not be tried in a French
court. As a man who had made war on the French people, he had
simply to be executed. It was not the only way of looking at the
problem but it was at least more honest than the attempt of
many deputies – both the regicides and their opponents – to
disguise expediency under a cloak of principle. An Assembly of
republicans was likely to agree that monarchy was unnatural.
When it came to other issues, they were not going to find 'nature'
any less ambiguous than the general will.

On 19 November Saint-Just intervened again, on the question
of the grain trade and price controls. In contrast to the plodding
Robespierre, one is struck by the way in which he tried to bring
everything within the unifying perspective of a general theory.
He was impatient with those who could see no further than the
sterile argument between free traders and their opponents. What
was at issue was the whole economic policy of the republic. The
prevailing distress had two main causes: the inflation of the
money supply by the over-issue of *assignats* and the collapse of
the luxury trades as a result of inflation. Not merely were there
too many *assignats*; unlike gold, they were unattractive to
hoarders. Farmers were therefore less interested in producing for
the market. In the past, the wealthy had maintained the towns,

and especially Paris, by their consumption of luxuries. The problem now was to discover whether or not ordinary people could live by 'the simple correlation of their individual needs'. The whole question was complicated by the fact that the entire population had been corrupted by centuries of unnatural government: 'Everyone wants the republic; no one wants poverty and *vertu*.' This very fact provided a clue to the answer: 'The people's virtues and vices are your work ... at a stroke you can give them a *patrie* and then the poor will forget their licence and the rich remember their hearts.' What was needed was not to enforce free trade by laws and armed escorts, but to create conditions that would lead everyone to want trade to be free. Trade itself, even luxury trade, was a necessity. 'In your republic you need luxury, or repressive laws against the farmer that would destroy the republic.' One had to legislate for people as they were. 'If you want to give this great people republican laws and bind its happiness to its liberty, you must take it as it is.' His solution was an economic programme that included reducing the money supply, accelerating the sale of *émigré* estates, collecting as much taxation as possible in kind and exploiting the conquered territories – he shared some of Rousseau's indifference towards what happened to foreigners.

It was an extremely impressive performance. Despite his remark that Adam Smith and Montesquieu had no relevance to the particular situation in which France found herself, he was closer to them in spirit than to the *dirigiste* Rousseau. He did not, however, explain how one could reduce the money supply without ending the war, and when he got away from strictly economic issues, there was a certain ambiguity about his principles. On the one hand, he favoured taking people as they were and providing them with incentives to which they would 'naturally' respond. At the same time, he was beginning to think in terms of regenerating them by legislation. 'The extraordinary thing about this revolution is that a republic has been built from vices. Let us make one out of virtues; the thing is not impossible.' *Moeurs* in the widest sense could only be changed over a period of time but 'there are political *moeurs* that a people adopt the moment they are given laws'. When he wrote *De la nature*, whatever was political was enforced and unnatural. That was a point of view that had not survived his own introduction to the political process.

He moved further along this road on 28 January 1793, in a speech on the reorganisation of the War Office. In a monarchy, unity was assured by the ambition of the king's servants. A republic had to find some substitute for this and reliance on 'the principles and ideas of liberty' was not enough. 'It is necessary that there should be only one will in the state.' (Robespierre often picked up ideas from his colleagues and he may have had this in mind when he wrote, four months later, '*Il faut une volonté, UNE*'.) 'Happiness and individual interest are a violation of the social order when they are not a part of the public interest and of public happiness.' In other words, his emphasis was shifting from the community as an aggregation of individual preferences, to society as the arbiter of what was individually permissible. That he was not altogether happy about the direction in which he was moving was suggested by a speech on the reorganisation of the army on 12 February. Emphasising the republican spirit, rather than numbers or discipline, he argued for the election of officers, up to regimental level, on the ground that 'if you want to found a republic, take as little power as possible from the people and make it exercise those functions that it can perform'. He even objected to the use of 'command' as a noun, since 'the only true command is that of the general will and the law'. It was noticeable that, whatever the point he was making, he was now talking in terms of the general will, a concept that he had challenged in his theoretical works. His remark that 'One can only make a republic by means of frugality and *vertu*' was also a good deal more Rousseauist than the economic policy he had put forward in the autumn.

Like Robespierre, Saint-Just set out his ideas about the shape of the new constitution, and even proposed a complete draft of his own (24 April 1793). As in Robespierre's case, he took this as an invitation to think in terms of the ideal society of the future. This took him back to *De la nature*. 'Nothing is orderly except that which moves by its own volition and obeys its own harmony ... Laws only repel evil: innocence and *vertu* go their own ways about the earth.' 'The social order precedes the political order ... Men in the same society naturally live in peace; war exists only between peoples, or rather, between those who dominate them.' In view of the situation within the Convention, it took a certain amount of optimism to say that, in April 1793. 'When a

revolution suddenly changes a people and one takes it as it is and
tries to reform it, one has to give way to its weaknesses and show
discretion in submitting it to the genius of the institution. One
must not make it fit the laws, but rather make the laws fit the
people.'

This was all very well as far as it went, but it did not go as far
as it had done in the previous year. He repeated his old argument
that Rousseau had not allowed for the general will being
mistaken, but this time he made it clear that he had not
understood Rousseau's meaning, when he assumed that the
general will was an expression of the majority of particular
interests. 'The material will of the people ... its objective is to
sanctify the objective interests of the majority.' Since everyone's
will was determined by his interests, the will of the majority
must 'necessarily' embody the interests of the majority. This did
not get anyone very far. Although he did not suspect it, Saint-
Just was actually following Rousseau when he rejected it as
unsatisfactory and inadequate. 'There are few men who do not
have a secret penchant for wealth. The calculations of ambition
are impenetrable. Break, O break all the roads that lead to
crime.' Earlier in his speech he had plagiarised Rousseau to the
effect that 'It is for him [the legislator] to make men what he
wants them to be'. In his article in the Encyclopaedia, Rousseau
had said 'what he needs them to be'. Where Saint-Just still
differed from Rousseau was in the belief, which he held to the
end of his life, that whatever social conditioning might be
applied to the nation as a whole, the innocent and virtuous were
still being allowed to go their ways in peace. This, however,
became increasingly meaningless as he insisted on making all
the right ways compulsory. By now his general approach to
politics was essentially Rousseauist, and it was logical for his
draft constitution to include the death penalty for murder,
military training for the young and compulsory service for all in
time of war.

When on 15 May, he spoke about the division of the country for
local government purposes, it was entirely in terms of the general
will. The nation must be considered as an indivisible group of
people, rather than as an agglomeration of territories, each of
which might claim the right to secede. In order to weaken local
loyalties, he favoured abolishing the Departments as centres of
local government. His intention may have been, as he said, to

strengthen the general will vis-à-vis the government; when something similar was tried later in the year, its effect was to centralise government and concentrate power in the hands of the Assembly and its committees. Rousseau would have approved but it did not make life any easier for the innocent who only wanted to go their ways in peace.

On 30 May Saint-Just was added to the Committee of Public Safety, to help with the drafting of the constitution. His first report to the Convention on behalf of the committee was concerned with quite a different matter: what to do about those Girondins who had been arrested, some of whom had escaped to the provinces where they were trying to organise a march on Paris. The first draft of his speech was read to his colleagues on 24 June and the final version was not presented to the Convention for another fortnight, which suggests that it was subject to a good deal of argument and perhaps alteration. It would therefore be rash to see it as necessarily a statement of Saint-Just's personal opinion, although he would not have agreed to present it if he had not been broadly in agreement with its conclusions. He began by representing the Parisian coup d'état of 2 June as a *Girondin* plot that had resulted in the arrest of those whom public opinion had denounced to the Assembly, which was one way of looking at it. He repeated the standard Montagnard charges against the Girondins, individually and collectively: 'All the vices hunted each other out and joined forces, while the poor remained alone, a prey to deformity, indigence and *vertu*.' He always had a weakness for an arresting phrase, though they generally meant rather more than that one. In any case, what was at issue was not a question of political judgement but of who had custody of the general will. Saint-Just's conclusion was as moderate as circumstances permitted. The majority of those arrested had merely been misled, 'and which of us can flatter himself that he never is?'. For a Montagnard, this was a rare and dangerous admission: it would not be long before being misled about the location of the general will was an infallible sign of both moral turpitude and counter-revolutionary politics. 'Error must not be confounded with crime and you hate severity.' He asked for the outlawry of the nine who were trying to raise the provinces and the trial of five of those who had remained in Paris. The remainder – who, perhaps by an oversight, included Brissot – should be allowed to resume their seats in the Assembly.

He did not address the Convention again until 10 October, in sharp contrast to Robespierre, who talked all the time, either in the Assembly or the Jacobin Club. The Committee of Public Safety had come under pressure from Hébert and the radicals who now controlled the Paris Commune. They wanted to implement at least that part of the new constitution that related to the election of Ministers – it was said that Hébert had his eye on the Interior. To head this off, the committee decided to get the Convention to vote that government should remain 'revolutionary' for the duration of the war. This was just the kind of subject that Saint-Just enjoyed. His attitude had hardened since the spring and was now much closer to that of Robespierre. 'The republic will only be established when the will of the sovereign represses that of the royalist minority and rules over it by right of conquest.' It was the business of Louis XVI all over again: monarchists of every kind were to be treated as foreigners. This time he went further: 'We can hope for no prosperity so long as the last enemy of liberty still breathes. You must punish not merely the traitors, but even those who are merely indifferent ... Since the French people have made known their will, everything opposed to them is outside the sovereign and whatever is outside the sovereign is enemy.' He even made use of Marat's old argument that France would already have been a land of peace and natural justice if only there had not been too much indulgence in the past. In these circumstances the constitution could not be brought into force since it lacked the 'violence' that was needed to deal with counter-revolutionaries.

He was able to play on the fact that the Committee of Public Safety was nominally no more than a committee of the legislature, in order to reaffirm his old belief that 'the people's only dangerous enemy is its government', by which he meant the civil and military administration. With this went a Robespierrist idealisation of the 'people' as a convenient abstraction. 'Those who desire only what they need are patient; those who want superfluities are cruel. Hence the sufferings of the people whose *vertu* is powerless against the activity of its enemies.' Like Robespierre, he wanted 'a government which, mild and moderate towards the people, will be terrible towards itself'.

Ultimately, the solution could only come from 'institutions and military laws in accordance with the system of the republic that is to be founded'. This was more than an enabling act to give the Committee of Public Safety the powers it needed to deal with a temporary emergency. It implied a long-term programme, if the object of 'revolutionary' government was to create the conditions in which the republic would be able to perpetuate itself.

He still had one foot on the ground. When Robespierre had already come to see all opposition as part of one vast foreign plot, Saint-Just insisted, in a sensible speech on the need to intern British civilians, that foreigners, the corrupt and those impatient to win power and fame or to profit from the revolution, constituted separate threats to the republic (16 October 1793). For most of the next three months he was away at the front, where he seems to have been an active and intelligent commissar, much less addicted to wholesale terrorism than some of his colleagues.

On 26 February 1794 he delivered another report on behalf of the committee, on the treatment of interned suspects, whose numbers may by this time have run into scores of thousands. Whatever the Committee of Public Safety may have intended, his argument, and notably his attack on moderates, was very much his own. His general thesis and occasionally his language were reminiscent of Robespierre's speeches of 25 December and 5 February, which he had probably read. He had been away from Paris when they were delivered. He began by saying that the internment of the suspects was not a judicial measure but a political one, to safeguard 'the people and the government'. 'We must be just all the same, but in terms of the public interest and not of private interests.' This was Robespierre's argument. It was significant that Saint-Just had stopped pretending that the Committee of Public Safety was not the government, and he was beginning to locate the general will within the committee rather than the Convention. 'A revolution has taken place within the government; it has not yet penetrated civil society.' It was therefore the duty of the regenerated government to bring the people up to its own level, by means of republican institutions. 'In a republic, besides the government, there are institutions, either to repress *moeurs* or to arrest the corruption of laws and men.' An individualist conception of the republic would be fatal to liberty. 'A society whose political relationships are not natural ones must make the greatest efforts to purify itself if it wants to sustain itself.' This was not going to appeal to those whose *moeurs* were to be *comprimées*. As in the previous autumn, everything was either black or white. 'What constitutes a republic is the total destruction of whatever is opposed to it.' 'In a republic, which can only be based on inflexibility, the expression of pity for crime is a striking sign of treason.' Since 'monarchy is not a king, it is crime; the republic is not a senate, it is *vertu*' it followed that 'whoever spares crime wants to restore the monarchy and to immolate liberty'.

Like Robespierre, Saint-Just allowed himself a brief glance at the future that was to make all the killing worth while. 'We want to establish an order of things such that a universal tendency towards the good is established.' It was characteristic of the two men that Robespierre had lingered over his vision of the ideal society. Saint-Just gave it half a sentence, followed by 'and such that the factions find themselves suddenly hurled on to the scaffold'. Unlike Robespierre, he praised Marat and once again used Marat's argument that if all the royalists had been arrested in time, there would have been no civil war; earlier indulgence had cost the lives of 200,000 men in the Vendée and its continuance would mean 30 years of civil war. Whereas Robespierre only reluctantly came to accept that regeneration meant the Terror, Saint-Just, who had at least appeared to start from much more libertarian premises, had fewer inhibitions about coming to the same conclusion. He was already justifying the Terror as necessary for regeneration, whereas Robespierre was still thinking of it as a short-term measure, to destroy political opposition.

The last part of his speech seemed to surprise him as much as it must have startled his audience. 'Force of circumstances is perhaps leading us to conclusions about which we had never thought ...' The revolution was a war of the just against the unjust. Wealth implied power to control men's lives. Therefore, 'The revolution leads us to recognise the principle that the man who has shown himself to be the enemy of his country cannot be a proprietor in it'. This has aroused so much enthusiasm from those who see the expropriation of anyone as a step in the right direction, that it is worth pointing out that Saint-Just did not intend it as class legislation. He continued, 'The property of *patriotes* is sacred, but the goods of conspirators are there for all the wretched'. Permissible wealth was a function of republican morality. He did say, in his old vein, 'The unfortunate are the powers of the earth, entitled to speak as masters to governments who neglect them'. This probably made him feel better but it meant virtually nothing. So long as he was a member of the government, it would have the last say on whether or not it was neglecting them and anyone who challenged its verdict would be liable to some forcible regeneration. In actual fact, the poor were not going to get any of the 'goods of the conspirators' and when two of the *commissions populaires* that were to examine the cases of the internees were created, they sent almost everyone before the revolutionary tribunal. Whether or not Saint-Just intended his measures to be primarily repressive, that was their effect.

By now he was becoming the government's spokesman whenever the Convention had to be persuaded to vote a purge. On 13 March he delivered an attack on the agents of the foreign enemy. When they were arrested that night, these turned out to be Hébert and his allies. Saint-Just now spoke of a 'natural compact between governments and peoples', which was very different from the case he had argued in *De la nature*. Since the government relied on the justice and *vertu* of the people, the most heinous of all crimes was to corrupt public opinion, which was Rousseauese for criticising the government. 'Let the people demand liberty when it is oppressed ... but when liberty triumphs and tyranny expires, it is cowardice and criminal hypocrisy to forget the general good and destroy the *patrie* in pursuit of a particular good.' One wonders if there has ever been a government that was not convinced that it stood for the general good. Saint-Just praised Marat yet again and joined Robespierre in lamenting that the popular societies had been taken over by the ambitious. 'Everyone wants to govern and no one wants to be a citizen.' This was scarcely surprising since the rewards of mere citizenship were somewhat meagre: 'We offer you the happiness of Athens and Sparta in its finest days.' The inhabitants of the Corrèze won special commendation for their ability to survive on a diet of chestnuts.

On 31 March it was Danton's turn. Saint-Just began by

saying, quite rightly, 'There is something terrible about the *amour sacré de la patrie*. It is so exclusive that it immolates everything without pity, without fear, without respect of persons, to the public interest.' In a sense, this was a joint performance since Robespierre, although he disapproved of the decision to destroy Danton, had provided Saint-Just with the 'evidence' necessary to do so. It was to be the last purge. 'After this, there will be only *patriotes* left.' The Convention was treated to the full scenario: this was the final remnant of the British plot that had been going strong since 1789 and had been responsible for inflation, colonial unrest, the destruction of French overseas trade, interference with the grain trade, federalism, the civil war in the Vendée and Marat's murder. Referring to the fact that some of the accused had been apprehensive about what was in store for them, he came out with the old argument of Brissot and Robespierre: 'Does the innocent man talk of defending himself? Has he premonitions of terror before anyone talks about him?' In 1794 he certainly had, if he had any sense; all the more so since the first indication that anyone was talking about him might be an arrest warrant.

In a private speech to the Committee of Public Safety on 2 April, on trade and the neutrals, he told his colleagues that 'Republics are the asylum of truth ... it must reign in France, but its sanctuary is here.' The general will, in other words, for him as for Robespierre, was now located within the government. Two days later he lied to the Convention about an alleged revolt by Danton and his fellow-accused, during their trial, and produced evidence of yet another plot, to rescue them. He did not tell his colleagues that it came from a professional informer. The ways of republican *vertu* could sometimes be rather strange, but he had been insisting for some time that republicans were entitled to use in a good cause the weapons that their enemies employed against them in a bad one.

On 15 April he returned to what was now almost his only theme: conspiracy and regeneration. Predictably enough, the execution of the Dantonists had not, after all, disposed of all the wicked. The evil that men did lived after them: 'It is not enough, citizens, to have destroyed the factions; we have still to repair the damage they did to the *patrie*.' The vast foreign plot was extended to include Necker, the first man to try to starve the people. That had been an invention of Marat's, and it was wholly appropriate that Saint-Just's picture of the ideal revolutionary should have been followed immediately by a tribute to Marat, 'gentle at home, the only men he terrified were traitors'. Robespierre is unlikely to have appreciated that. Saint-Just borrowed from Marat the curious idea that the best way to restore abundance was 'to track down, throughout the whole breadth of the country, the instruments and accomplices of the factions'. In the teeth of the evidence he insisted that the courts, by which he presumably meant the revolutionary tribunals, were becoming slack. All those who 'depreciated' the republic must be treated as enemies. The difference between a free state and tyranny was not in the methods they used but in the fact that the former employed them against the minority. (Since the government was by now replacing the elected officials it purged by its own nominees, the majority did not, in practice, have much of a chance to say what it wanted.) If the Romans could have returned, they would have been proud of the French revolution. With this went the inevitable pious platitudes about the 'people' being just and the 'government' (which now presumably did not mean the Committee of Public Safety) being unjust. As usual, he emphasised the need for republican institutions to 'create a public conscience'. He contrasted this with the *esprit public*, which was a purely cerebral business. Saint-Just concluded with proposals, which the Convention knew better than to challenge, for an intensification of repression. All conspirators were henceforth to be tried in Paris, where the public prosecutor, Fouquier-Tinville, knew what was expected of him. Foreigners and former nobles were to be excluded from public meetings. Everyone was encouraged to denounce theft, anti-civic talk and oppression, which should have given the denouncers plenty of scope. Anyone under 60, without employment, who grumbled about the revolution, was to be deported to Cayenne.

All the time he was jotting down ideas for the 'republican institutions' that were to provide the means of escape from the infernal cycle of repression. He never had time to assemble these systematically, and all that survives is a jumble of unco-ordinated notes.[7] In one place he referred to these as part of a

[7] The most reliable text is perhaps that in Liénart, op.cit.

book; elsewhere he used expressions like 'It is for you, legislators ... ', which suggests that parts were drafts for a speech.
Statements of principle alternated with detailed proposals for
legislation, ideas from *De la nature* rubbed shoulders with notes
for his final speech in defence of Robespierre. It would be absurd
to expect the result to provide any kind of systematic
programme, but it does suggest the nature of the road along
which he had travelled.

A long introductory passage repeated his old belief in leaving
as much as possible to men's natural goodness. State
interference with people's private lives should be restricted to a
minimum. Society came before government and the social
contract was merely a means by which some people oppressed
others. In the distant future, social relationships would prevail
between peoples and all men would live as brothers. All of this
was completely vitiated by his assertion that the object of
politics was 'to substitute the public interest for all other
interests, to make nature and innocence the passion of all hearts
and to create a *patrie*. It was a strange 'nature' that had to be
imposed by politicians. This was the cue for the kind of day-
dreaming in which Rousseau too had loved to indulge, a picture
of a future society that was Spartan in every sense of the word.
'Children belong to their mother up to the age of five, if she has
breast-fed them, and then to the republic for the rest of their
lives.' From 5 to 10 they would be taught to read, write and
swim. 'The education of children from 10 to 16 is military and
agricultural.' From 16 to 20 they would be taught a trade. Taken
from home at 5, they would not be allowed to return until they
were 21. After that they would do four years service in the
militia. While at school they would live rough and be allowed no
meat until they were 16. Adults would have to put up with three
meatless days in ten, presumably to teach them the virtues of
self-denial. This 'independent' private life was, in fact, one of
suffocating orthodoxy. After 60 years of blameless life, the elders
were to be given white scarves and allowed to censure the private
lives of civil servants and those under 21. Social control implied
the kind of sanctions that would have been guaranteed to turn
every village into a little Vendée. Banishment was prescribed for
those who deceived girls, said they did not believe in friendship,
were friends of men who committed crimes, had no friends
themselves, were convicted of ingratitude or refused to justify

their quarrels with others. Women who hung around army camps were to be put to death. On the first of *floréal* every year a rich and virtuous young man would be required to take a wife from among the virtuous virgins, which might have suited the rich young man better than the virgin of his choice. This was reducing republicanism to the level of Cinderella. Saint-Just's indifference to the actual feelings of real people appeared in his extraordinary proposal to carry on transporting African negroes to the French colonies, where they were to be liberated and set up as farmers. The Convention had already voted to abolish slavery but, according to Robespierre, that had been a scheme of Danton's to ruin the French colonies.

The economic foundations of the Brave New World were somewhat obscure. In the best Rousseauist tradition, Saint-Just maintained that most republics had failed in the past because of economic inequality. He had now come round to the view that only farmers made good citizens. Everyone should therefore live off his own land and cultivate domestic industry merely for little luxuries. 'If everyone works there will be less need for money and no vice.' His economic thinking had reverted to primitivism. He was as opposed as ever to a general redistribution of land and repeated the idea he had first advanced in *De la nature* that there should be an upper limit to the land a man could hold, in order to make more available for the poor. He did not explain how they were to pay for it. Large landowners would be allowed to sell their surplus acres, in the hope that this would encourage them to go into trade. This would have diverted labour from agriculture to commerce, unless Saint-Just intended that they should set up as small shopkeepers. Provided that he did not exceed the permitted landholding, anyone could do whatever he liked with his wealth, so long as he did not interfere with others.

The point was not that he contradicted himself. That was only to be expected from an undigested collection of notes. The whole scheme was Mercier's year 2440 turned nightmare. Its social provisions were intolerable, when they were not unintentionally funny, and its economic foundation was infantile when compared with what Saint-Just himself had been saying in the autumn of 1792. The *force des choses* had led him to the Never-Never-Land of Rousseau's dreams.

He was away at the front during almost the whole of May and June, as efficient in action as he was utopian in theory. As the quarrel within the Committee of Public Safety came to a head in July, his colleagues seemed to think that he was not irrevocably committed to Robespierre and they entrusted him with a report that was to announce to the Convention the unity of the revolutionary government. Robespierre broke the precarious truce with his denunciation of 26 July, and on the following day Saint-Just tried to come to his rescue with a speech that was howled down before he had completed more than a sentence or two. This is unlikely to have made much difference. Although more coherent than Robespierre, he was trapped in the same dilemma. He admitted that the members of the committee were not divided over matters of policy. He could scarcely say, in so many words, that he, Robespierre and the faithful Couthon were the only *patriotes* left, but his real complaint about the others was that they had gone over to the Enemy. The result was a self-contradictory argument that could not have convinced anyone. The only answer to faction was, as always, republican institutions. Given such institutions, 'those whose arrogant pretentions I am accusing would perhaps be *vertueux* and would not have entertained evil thoughts'. The colleagues in question were hardly likely to have welcomed Saint-Just as their moral tutor. As it was, 'They have plotted the destruction of the best of men, so that they themselves could rule in peace'. 'In my eyes they stand accused of dangerous designs against the *patrie*.' There had been a plot to usurp power by destroying some members of the committee, dispersing the rest, suppressing the revolutionary tribunal and depriving Paris of its magistrates. This sounded rather serious. On the other hand, 'Perhaps it is not long since they left the beaten track of *vertu*'. There was really nothing wrong with them, except that they were too ambitious. 'I am not drawing any conclusions against those whom I have named. I want them to justify themselves and for us all to become more judicious.' If one could play around with *vertu* like this, it was difficult to take it very seriously – or to believe that Robespierre and Saint-Just, if they had been given another chance, would not have had another go.

Early in the morning of 28 July, Robespierre, Saint-Just and a handful of the faithful sat in a back room at the Hôtel de Ville. The Commune had called for an insurrection in their support and they had been outlawed by the Convention. Outside, the National Guards mobilised by the Commune had drifted away and they were quite alone. Couthon proposed drafting a proclamation to the armies. 'In whose name?' asked Robespierre. 'In the name of the Convention. [He really meant the name of the general will] Is it not where we are?' Robespierre preferred the name of the French people.[8] It was the end of the road.

[8] P.Sainte-Claire Deville, *La Commune de l'an II*, Paris, 1946, p.289.

Epilogue

By the summer of 1794 all the men whose careers have formed the subject of this book had died violently, with the exception of Mercier, and he was in gaol. After his release and brief return to politics, he tried to stage a literary come-back with *Le Nouveau Paris*, which he published in 1798, in six volumes. He had never been much of a man for consistency, and when he tried to sum up the revolution it was all too much for him. In his introduction he faced the question of whether it had been basically a matter of will or circumstance and decided that it was wholly both. 'It is quite simply the maturity of things and events. People bring in plenty of moral and rational elements but its causes were always determined by purely physical actions.' Just one page later, 'The word "Liberty", if pronounced loudly enough, has always made the people free. It depends only on the French, and above all on the Parisians formally willing independence and prosperity.' Whatever it was, he deserved his share of the credit for it. From the first moment of his literary career, he had been 'the herald, the friend and the collaborator in the great work of regeneration undertaken for the public happiness, that has already been brought to fruition in France, Holland, Switzerland, Italy and Egypt'. By the time he reached volume V, things looked rather different. In a section with the title 'Why I am a moderate', he explained that people like himself had merely been swept along by the revolution 'for no upright man could believe himself called upon to contribute to a revolution that was bound to create an infinite number of unfortunates'.

It had been a remarkable achievement all the same: 'The French have done more in three years than that justly famous people [the Greeks] accomplished in three centuries.' At least, if it *had* been a disaster, there was no going back. Women and bourgeois thought that if they could restore the *ancien régime* it would bring back the good old days, with bread at 2 sous, café-au-lait at 6 and meat at 8. On the contrary, 'the only thing to fear now is the cruel, the inevitable vengeance of the royalists, who would be worse than the Robespierristes if they returned as conquerors'. It was really all very complicated. Industry led to luxury and that multiplied poverty. On the other hand, if there were no industry everyone would be equally wretched. He was looking for the *juste milieu* but was not very confident of finding it.

He was not sure whether one ought to speak of regeneration or degeneration. 'They wanted to make entirely new men of us and they made us practically nothing but savages ... In order to proscribe superstition they destroyed all religious feeling; that was no way to regenerate the world.' At least, more breast-feeding and milder parental discipline would have a good effect on the children. 'They will be better than us because they have had a happier childhood.' One had to admit though, that 'by profaning language we have lost some of our virtues; what is most deplorable is to encounter everywhere troops of lawless and shameless children who swear, blaspheme and scandalise chaste and pious ears.' That was what came of the freedom of the press: he was particularly shocked by Sade's *Justine*. 'When a revolution does not bring out virtues it throws up vices and that is what has happened to our youth.' He was turning towards religion, although he was not sure which, and he had no use for either dechristianisation or the worship of the Supreme Being. Robespierre had missed his opportunity: he should have taken a Bible to the *Fête de l'Etre Suprême* and declared France Protestant. 'It is time that men began to love each other; then it would not be necessary to force them to swear allegiance to the laws of their own country and universal peace would reign on earth.' One of the things that made capitalists so nasty, however, was the fact that they had no country, and exile was too good for men like Billaud-Varenne and Collot d'Herbois.

The revolution had led him to have second thoughts about the Enlightenment and to see men like Voltaire and Helvétius in a different light. A proposal to put Descartes's remains in the Pantheon made him try to sort out his ideas. Descartes had started the atheistical trend. After that 'Locke and Condillac came to poison us with their crude reasoning about human understanding ... they did not feel that intimate liaison between men and the universal harmony ... Morality and will are everything and control everything and the moral instinct is always independent of physical organs.' Rousseau had been right, and in a line of succession that went back to Socrates, Plato and Marcus Aurelius. 'Struck by the profane immorality of the generation, we have seen, perhaps for the first time, a combination of the impetuous passions of savages and the depravation of civilised man. I have often said to myself, "What are the principles that, badly perceived or badly understood, have scoundrelised (*scélératisé*) so many heads?" It seemed to me that it was the attack on the spirituality of man that had given birth to that infernal spirit that has provoked so many scenes of carnage and grief ... Audacious materialists had prepared the reign of those guilty philosophers who want to explain everything in terms of the corporal senses and reduce everything to purely physical causes.' He would have been shocked if someone had told him that that was very much how Robespierre had felt. It was all Descartes's fault, although some of the blame must go to Voltaire, 'that great corrupter who flattered all the kings, all the great men and all the vices of his century'. *Candide* was a wretched production that cast doubt on the wisdom of Providence. An amalgam of the ideas of Rousseau, Voltaire, Helvétius, Boulanger and Diderot 'had formed a kind of paste ... that ordinary minds could not digest'. He seemed to have forgotten all about Montesquieu.

One thing that had survived the shipwreck of so much else was the conviction that, from start to finish, the British had been behind the lot. They had been responsible for the *Amis des Noirs*, which was why Mercier had refused to join (he had forgotten that he had been an enthusiastic Anglophil at the time). They had had their way when a slave revolt destroyed the prosperity of Saint Domingue. Brissot (despite the fact that he had founded the *Amis des Noirs*) had seen through them, and he had been right to campaign for offensive war. That was presumably why the British used their Montagnard agents to destroy Brissot and the Girondins. Like Robespierre, Mercier was convinced that everyone of whom he disapproved was in British pay; at one point he even seems to have included Louis

XVI, which was going rather far. The conclusion was irrefutable: 'War, war to the death against the English!'

In the end there was not much left for him to cling to except jingoism. 'Our victorious armies are reviving the Roman republic ... It is the French who are re-creating consuls; they regenerate the peoples who want to be their friends.' There was no need to teach people foreign languages: French had been the language of Europe even before it became the tongue of republicanism. With jingoism went the cult of the military leader: 'The bourgeois stoops to whisper in your ear, *Bonaparte is going to cross the Rubicon and imitate Caesar.*' 'The French are going to learn from him to be grave and respect their magistrates and their representatives ... Let all the republicans model themselves on Bonaparte.' He got that one right at least: they were soon going to have no choice.

Appendix

A comparison between the opinions of Brissot and Robespierre

On the philosophes

Brissot Aristipes modernes, qui vont ramper dans les antichambres des grands (*De la vérité*).

Robespierre Ils étaient fiers dans leurs écrits et rampants dans les antichambres (17 May 1794).

On the nature of the revolution

– an ideological war

Brissot La guerre du genre humain contre ses oppresseurs (23 April 1792).

Robespierre La guerre da la liberté contre ses ennemis (25 December 1793).

– no historical precedents

Brissot Existe-t-il dans l'histoire ancienne une révolution semblable à la nôtre? (30 December 1791).

Robespierre [the French constitution] est infiniment supérieure ... à celle des peuples de l'antiquité la plus réculée (15 April 1793).

– essentially moral

Brissot Qui n'a pas de moeurs privées n'a jamais sincèrement des moeurs publiques (17 May 1791).

Robespierre Ce qui est immoral est impolitique, ce qui est corrupteur est contre-révolutionnaire (5 February 1794).

Brissot Conquérir la liberté n'est rien; la savoir conserver est tout; or, on ne peut la conserver sans moeurs (24 September 1790).

Robespierre Vous avez chassé les rois; mais avez-vous chassé les vices que leur funeste domination a enfanté parmi vous? (19 October 1792).

– France ahead of Europe

Brissot Ce peuple qui, en deux ans, a déjà franchi presqu'un siècle (30 December 1791).

Robespierre Le peuple Français semble avoir devancé de deux mille ans le reste de l'espèce humaine (7 May 1794).

On social questions

– the nature of property

Brissot La propriété individuelle est fondée sur l'intêrét social ... l'état a droit d'en réclamer une portion pour la protection qu'il m'accorde (*Lettre à Joseph II*, 1785).

Robespierre La propriété est le droit qu'a chaque citoyen de jouir et de disposer de la portion de biens qui lui est garantie par la loi (24 April 1793).

– class war

Brissot Ce n'est plus contre le despotisme des rois, ou même des Ministres, qu'il faut maintenant se précautionner, c'est contre la préjugé en faveur des richesses (5 June 1790).

Robespierre Les dangers intérieurs viennent des bourgeois (*Carnet*).

On the people

– its sovereignty

Brissot Le peuple ne dépend que de lui-même dans l'exercice de sa souveraineté (13 August 1792).

Robespierre La force du peuple est en lui-même (June 1798).

– the custodian of the revolution

Brissot L'Assemblée Nationale n'a besoin que de s'élever à la hauteur des sentiments du peuple (29 June 1792).

Robespierre Il faut au peuple un gouvernement digne de lui (15 August 1792).

Brissot Le peuple peut se sauver sans ses représentants, et même malgré ses représentants, mais ses représentants ne peuvent le sauver ni malgré lui ni sans lui (27 July 1792).

Robespierre Il faut que l'Etat et la liberté soient sauvés; s'ils ne le sont pas par les représentants, il le faut bien qu'ils le soient par la nation (10 June 1791).

– has more sense than the educated
Brissot L'instinct du peuple vaut mieux que toute votre dialectique (10 May 1791).
Robespierre Les hommes de lettres se sont déshonorés dans cette révolution, et à la honte éternelle de l'esprit, la raison du peuple en a fait seule tous les frais (7 May 1794).

– rarely mistaken
Brissot Les égarements du peuple ne sauraient être longs (19 April 1792).
Robespierre Les erreurs du peuple sont rares, passagères (15-20 February 1793).

– slandered by its enemies
Brissot Les ennemis du peuple ne cessent du lui prêter une grande tendance vers les séditions (28 September 1791).
Robespierre Observez ce penchant éternel de lier l'idée de sédition et de brigandage à celle du peuple et de pauvreté (19 October 1792).

– self-identification with
Brissot Un démocrate ... ne dit pas *J'aime le peuple* ... Il est trop identifié avec le peuple pour le placer ainsi hors de lui (3 December 1790).
Robespierre Je ne suis ni le courtisan, ni le modérateur, ni le tribun, ni le défenseur du peuple; je suis peuple moi-même (27 April 1792).

On the special rôle of Paris

– municipal sovereignty
Brissot Le pouvoir législatif n'a aucun droit de se mêler des règlements de la municipalité (18 August 1789).
Robespierre Il faut que ceux qu'il [the people] a choisi lui-même pour ses magistrats, aient toute la plénitude du pouvoir qui convient au souverain (12 August 1792).

– guardian of the revolution
Brissot On entend dire partout que Paris a une trop grande

influence sur l'Assemblé Nationale ... C'est une ruse de nos ennemis (28 August 1789).

Robespierre [The Parisians] doivent être regardés comme fondés de procuration tacite pour le société toute entière (5 November 1792).

On fighting the counter-revolution

– *the need to be on one's guard, at least when in opposition*
Brissot La défiance est la base éternelle d'un régime libre (4 May 1791).
Donner un facile accès aux soupçons, c'est vouloir perdre tout par la défiance (3 April 1792).
Robespierre La défiance est un état affreux! Est-ce lá la langage d'un homme libre? (2 January 1792).
Le peuple ne doit pas écouter ceux qui veulent lui inspirer une défiance universelle (14 June 1793).

– *only the guilty need fear*
Brissot Pour trembler sous le nouveau régime il faut être bien mauvais citoyen (6 February 1790).
Robespierre Quiconque tremble en ce moment est coupable (31 March 1793).

– *all opponents are part of the same plot*
Brissot Les factieux royalistes et les agitateurs démagogues ont constamment marché au même but (4 May 1792).
Robespierre Les bonnets rouges sont plus voisins des talons rouges qu'on ne pourrait le penser (25 December 1793).

– *the need for denunciation*
Brissot Autrefois, on abhorrait le personnage du *délateur* ... Aujourd'hui tout est changé (9 December 1789).
Robespierre Il fallait, enfin, encourager les dénonciations civiques (March 1793).

– *moderation the enemy*
Brissot Les modérés sont les aristocrates du nouveau régime (16 December 1791).
Robespierre Ce sont ces personnages cruellement modérés dont il faut vous défier le plus (19 June 1791).

– the cruelty of kindness

Brissot L'indulgence peut compromettre le sort de 25 millions d'hommes (10 March 1793).

Robespierre La clémence qui leur [the tyrants] pardonne est barbare; c'est un crime contre l'humanité (*c*.20 August 1792).

– freedom of the press – for the right newspapers

Brissot Quelle est donc l'espèce d'hommes qui redoutent l'accusation publique? (2 February 1790).

Robespierre C'est en effet aux hommes que je viens de peindre, qu'il appartient d'envisager avec effroi la liberté de la presse (11 May 1791).

Brissot La libre circulation des écrits ne prouve rien en faveur de la libre circulation de ces journaux ouvertement vendus aux ennemis de la révolution (1 August 1792).

Robespierre J'ai demandé ... que les journalistes qui pervertissent l'opinion publique furent reduits au silence (8 May 1793).

On ideological crusading

Brissot La philosophie ne s'inspire ni par la violence, ni par la séduction et ce n'est pas avec des sabres qu'on fait naître l'amour de la liberté (May 1793).

Robespierre La plus extravagante idée qui puisse naître dans la tête d'un politique est de croire qu'il suffise à un peuple d'entrer à main armée chez un peuple étranger, pour lui faire adopter ses lois et sa constitution. Personne n'aime les missionnaires armés (2 January 1792).

On the wickedness of the world

Brissot Les fripons seront toujours les gens comme il faut, le peuple sera toujours dupe et malheureux (26 July 1791)

Robespierre La vertu est toujours minoritaire sur la terre (28 December 1792).

Bibliography

Primary Sources

Brissot

Testament politique de l'Angleterre. n.p. 1780

Recherches philosophiques sur le droit de propriété. n.p. 1780

De la vérité. Neuchâtel, 1782

Correspondence universelle sur ce qui intéresse le bonheur de l'homme et de la société. Neuchâtel, 1783

Lettres sur la liberté politique. Liége, 1783

Le Philadelphien à Genève. Dublin, 1783

Un défenseur du peuple à l'empereur Joseph II. Dublin, 1785

Dénonciation au public d'un nouveau projet d'agiotage. London, 1786

Seconde lettre contre la Compagnie des Assurances pour les Incendies, à Paris, et sur l'agiotage en général. London, 1786

De la France et des Etats-Unis (with Clavière). London, 1787. 3v.

Lettre à l'auteur du Mercure Politique. Bouillon, 1787

Observations d'un républicain sur les différents systèmes d'administrations provinciales. Lausanne, 1787

Point de banqueroute, ou lettre à un créancier de l'état. London, 1787

Mémoire sur les noirs d'amérique septentrionale. Paris, 1789

Discours prononcé à l'élection du District de la rue des Filles-Saint-Thomas. Paris, 1789

Mémoire aux Etats-généraux sur la nécessité de rendre dès ce moment la presse libre. Paris, 1789

Discours prononcé au District des Filles-Saint-Thomas le 21 juillet 1789, sur la constitution municipale à former dans la ville de Paris. Paris, 1789

Motifs des commissions pour adopter le plan de municipalité. Paris, 1789

Lettre de Jacques-Pierre Brissot à tous les libellistes qui ont attaqué et qui attaquent sa vie passée. Paris, 1791

Réplique de J-P Brissot à Charles Théveneau de Morande. Paris 1791

Discours sur l'utilité des sociétés patriotiques et populaires. Paris, 1791

A tous les républicains de France, sur la Société des Jacobins. Paris, 1792

J-P Brissot, député du Département d'Eure-et-Loir, à ses commettans. Paris, 1793

Le Patriote Français, 1789-93

Mémoires (ed. C. Perroud). Paris, n.d. 3v.

Speeches in the *Moniteur*.

Marat

Un roman du coeur: les aventures du jeune comte Potowski. Paris, 1848

The chains of slavery. London, 1774

De l'homme. Amsterdam, 1775-76. 3v.

Plan de législation criminelle. n.p. 1780

Eloge de Montesquieu. Libourne, 1883

La constitution, ou projet de déclaration des droits de l'homme et du citoyen, suivi d'un plan de constitution. Paris, 1789

Ami du Peuple, 1789-93

Le Junius Français, June 1790

Correspondence (ed. C. Vellay) Paris, 1908

Les pamphlets de Marat (ed. C. Vellay) Paris, 1911

Supplément à la correspondence de Marat (C. Vellay). *Revue historique de la révolution française*, 1910

Deux lettres inédites de Marat, *id*. 1919

Lettres inédites de Marat à Benjamin Franklin. *id*. 1912

Du Marat inédit (L.R. Gottschalk). *Annales historiques de la révolution française*, 1926

Speeches in the *Moniteur*

Mercier

La bonheur des gens de lettres. London, 1766

Des malheurs de la guerre et des avantages de la paix. Paris, 1767

Contes moraux, ou les hommes comme il y en a peu. Paris, 1768

L'an 2440. London, 1772

Histoire des hommes, ou histoire nouvelle de tous les peuples du
   monde. Paris, 1779-81. 6v.
Le philosophe de Port-au-Bled. Paris, 1782
Tableau de Paris. Amsterdam, 1779-89. 12v.
Mon bonnet de nuit. Neuchâtel, 1784. 2v.
L'observateur de Paris et du royaume. London, 1785
Les entretiens du Palais-Royal. Paris, 1786
Notions claires sur les gouvernements. Amsterdam, 1787. 2v.
Adieux à l'année 1789. Paris, 1789
De J-J Rousseau, considéré comme l'un des premiers auteurs de
   la révolution. Paris, 1791. 2v.
Le nouveau Paris. Paris, 1798. 6v.

Robespierre
Discours couronné par la société royale des arts et des sciences de
   Metz. Paris and Amsterdam, 1785
Eloge de Gresset. London, 1786
Les droits et l'état des bâtards. (ed. L-N Berthe). Arras, 1971
A la nation artésienne. n.p. 1789
Les ennemis de la patrie démasqués, n.p. 1789
Lettre de M. de Robespierre à M. de Beaumetz. n.p., n.d.
Adresse au peuple Belgique. n.p., n.d.
Aux fédérés. n.p., n.d.
Oeuvres complètes (various editors). Paris, 1910-67. 10v.
Speeches in the *Moniteur*

Saint-Just
De la nature (in A. Liénard, Saint-Just, théorie politique. Paris,
   1976)
Oeuvres complètes (ed. C. Vellay). Paris, 1908. 2v.
Speeches in the *Moniteur*

Index